African
English
Literature

(Northqrare)

EDITED BY ANNE TIBBLE

OCTOBER HOUSE INC
New York

TO EZEKIEL MPHAHLELE

with respect

First published in the United States of America 1965
by October House Inc
55 West Thirteenth Street, New York 10011
Reprinted 1969
Copyright © 1965 by Anne Tibble
All rights reserved
Library of Congress catalog card number 65–22929

Acknowledgments

We wish to thank the following publishers, agents and authors for their kind permission to reprint from the undermentioned books and periodicals :

The American Folklore Society, for 'The Englishman and his Pet Animals', translated by Rev. A. N. Krug; Messrs Collins Ltd and Editions Plon, for *The Radiance of the King* (1956) and *The Dark Child* (1959) by Camara Laye and translated by James Kirkup; Messrs André Deutsch Ltd, for *Danda* (1964) by Nkem Nwankwo, and *The Voice* (1964) by Gabriel Okara; The Vanguard Press Inc., for 'The Devil at Yolahun Bridge' by Abioseh Nicol; Grove Press Inc., for *The Palm Wine Drinkard* (1952) by Amos Tutuola; John Day Co. Inc., for *Road to Ghana* (1960) by Alfred Hutchinson; Little, Brown & Co., for *The African* (1960) by William Conton; Ivan Obolensky Inc., for *Things Fall Apart* (1958) by Chinua Achebe; Messrs David Higham Ltd and Hutchinson Ltd, for *Jagua Nana* (1960) by Cyprian Ekwensi; Messrs Curtis Brown Ltd, for *Blade Among the Boys* (1962) by Onuora Nzekwu, *Down Second Avenue* (1959) by Ezekial Mphahlele, and *Tell Freedom* (1954) by Peter Abrahams; The Lovedale Press, for *Mhudi* (1930) by Solomon Plaatje; James Ngugi, for his story, 'The Wind'; Mbari Publications, for *The Song of a Goat* (1961) by John Pepper Clark, *A Walk in the Night* (1962) by Alex la Guma, 'We Have Found a New Land' from *Rediscovery* (1964) by George Awoonor-Williams, 'Sirens, Knuckles, Boots' and 'Somehow We Survive' from *Sirens, Knuckles, Boots* (1964) by Dennis Brutus, 'We the Amazons' and 'Dead-Born Love' from *African Songs of Love, War, Grief & Abuse* (1961) by Léon Damas, 'Prelude to The Limits' (1964) by Christopher Okigbo, 'We Have come Home' and 'If I was Asked' from *Poems* (1964) by Lenrie Peters, 'The White Bull' and 'Birth of Day II & III' from *24 Poems* (1962) by Jean-Joseph Rabéarivelo; Harcourt, Brace & World Inc., for *I Was A Savage* (1958) by Prince Modupe; Oxford University Press, for *Chaka the Zulu* (1949) by Thomas Mofolo, and *The Lion and the Jewel* (1963) by Wole Soyinka; Mrs Efua Theodora Sutherland, for 'New Life at Kyerefaso'; M. Pierre-Jean Oswald, for 'Appeal' by Noemia de Sousa; St Martin's Press Inc., for *The Ochre People* (1963) by Noni Jabavu; *Black Orpheus*, for 'The Change' by Ellis Ayitey Komey, 'Telephone Conversation' and 'Death in the Dawn' by Wole Soyinka, 'Melting Pot' by Michael Echeruo, 'To the Anxious Mother' by Valente Malangatana, 'Our Frame' by Shaaban Robert, 'Were I to Choose' and 'Piano and Drums', by Gabriel Okara; Gabriel Okara, for 'The Snowflakes Sail Gently Down' and 'One Night at Victoria Beach'; *Okyeame*, for

v

'The Sea Eats the Land at Home' by George Awoonor-Williams, and 'The Search' by Kwesi Brew; *Transition*, for 'The Ceremonial Mugumo' by Joseph Mutiga, and 'Sabotage, 1962' by Dennis Brutus; Presses Universitaires de France, for 'Song of a Young Girl' and 'Love Song' by Flavien Ranaivo and also 'In What Tempestuous Night' and 'New York' (Section 1) by Léopold Senghor, from *Anthologie de la Nouvelle Poésie Nègre et Malgache; Présence Africaine*, for 'Diptych' by Birago Diop, and 'Africa' by David Diop.

Whilst we have made every possible effort to trace all persons having any rights or interests in material used in the anthology, and to clear reprint permissions, in some instances, we have been unable to do so. We therefore apologize if any required acknowledgments have been unintentionally omitted or rights overlooked.

Contents

A*

'No person of one race and culture can truly interpret from the angle of individuals belonging to a totally different race and culture.'

ELSPETH HUXLEY : *Red Strangers*

'If the men inaugurating the new ways have the sense and the patience to preserve the finer qualities of the old ways and fuse these with the new, then we can expect something magnificently new out of Africa.'

PETER ABRAHAMS : *'The Blacks'*

Preface

The aim of this book must be two-fold because the book is in two parts. The first half offers a short account of the more important written prose and poetry of Africa, south of the Sahara. This survey relates to the upsurge that began in South Africa and was heard outside the African continent early this century; and it discusses African writing up to 1964. The second part of the book offers a selection of African-English prose and poetry – with a bibliography : bibliographies of African writing, not only of literature but of all books relating to Africa are scarce and are much needed. These – the selection and bibliography – may help to persuade readers in sixth form, college, and university, as well as the rapidly increasing numbers of general readers of African books both inside and outside Africa, to seek the whole books or other books of authors representative of this flow of literature emerging from Africa in increasing flood.

Following from this double aim, the immediate limitations of the book will be obvious. Both halves must be necessarily incomplete. Dealing only with Africa south of the Sahara meant leaving out the Arabic-speaking northern fringe – Egypt, Libya, Tunisia, Algeria, Morocco, Mauretania. Little of the literatures of Mali, Niger, and Chad is known – or this author is ignorant about them – so these new republics are undiscussed and unrepresented. The one-time Egyptian Minister of Education, the blind Taha Hussein, and his autobiography *The Stream of Days*, are given in the bibliography only because there is a useful English translation of a book it would be a pity to ignore. Equally, African-French writing will be found or be discussed here only if there is a well-known English translation, as James Kirkup's of Camara Laye's *The African Child*, of 1955, or Peter Green's rendering of Mongo Beti's *Le Roi Miraculé* as *King Lazarus* in 1960; or *Négritude* poems by Léopold Senghor, David Diop, and Birago Diop, translated by Ulli Beier and Gerald Moore. For studies by French scholars and the fruits of these, interested readers will seek elsewhere.

The survey is taken in four sections or chronological units, after two general chapters on African history and African languages. The first section (Chapter 3) is about African-English literature's beginnings in South Africa. The second (Chapter 4) is about African-French writing. The third (Chapter 5) concerns some oral literature of East Africa, with the most important of the written literature of that part of the continent. The fourth section (Chapter 6) describes the late burst of written poetry and prose of West Africa. Chapter 7, concluding, and again general, attempts a very brief assessment of African writing, at present and for the future.

xii

Background references, beliefs, customs, are seen as those of fellow human beings rather than as 'alien', 'quaint', 'different', 'ancient', 'exotic', certainly not as 'social-anthropological', most certainly not as 'primitive', 'savage', or 'inferior'. They are the content of a vast literature that is taking its place in world literature.

Fortunately, Elspeth Huxley's cautionary words printed at the front of this book do not preclude tentative insights by which alone, with incredible slowness, human understanding can grow. If there are one of two in this book, it will not have failed entirely in a further aim.

Henceforward, canons of literary excellence cannot be tied entirely, by authoritative European critics and centuries of their unified agreement, to European masterpieces such as, in novels for instance, George Eliot's *Middlemarch*, Tolstoi's *Anna Karenina*, or Flaubert's *Madame Bovary*. Undoubted masterpieces these are and undoubted the measure of the scholars' assent upon them. But in poetry, too, sights cannot much longer be quite so wholly set by Shakespeare, Dante's *The Divine Comedy* or T. S. Eliot's *The Waste Land*. Widening of the literary canon is inevitable : it will include the best in African poetry and prose, later perhaps, the best in Chinese, Japanese, and other world-reaching poetry and prose. Some may think such a sweeping view too vast, too long, hence too vague. But it is preferable now to insularity or parochialism. For what, after all, is 'good' or the 'best' – both words from the vocabulary of ethics? The good and the best are what, as inclusively and with as little prejudice as possible, stands the test of time and by the consent of a continuing majority are deemed worthwhile. Obviously, as economics, travel, communications of all kinds, and cultural information, become world-wide, so will a more comprehensive grasp of literature's best from young countries widen the scope of literary judgement. Clearly there will be a great sifting among African writing, as among all new literature : the present African output is a torrent after drought.

Of course, in this book there will be a large part of the enormous amount of African poetry in the many African languages not discussed, not even touched upon. Much of this indigenous poetry waits to be written down, let alone translated. Yet the importance of Africa's oral literature is incalculable.

Here is not the place to discuss what literature *is*; whether there can be literature before there is writing down. The finely representative two volumes of *African Prose* (1964), with their introduction by W. H. Whiteley, show the close connection between oratory, story-telling, and written literature, and between spoken poetry and written poetry. Some African literature of the present is seeking to stress these connections. Scholars are trying to preserve the links. Literacy breaks them and then obscures the oral. After the break, links between oral and written verse and prose rapidly disappear. African literature of the last fifty years has been in a state of transition from oral to written. It is still in transition.

In spite of the valuable Mbari Publications of Longmans of Nigeria, and in spite of the work of Oxford University Press, certain important African books are hard to find. One of the earliest – if not the earliest – Olaudah Equiano's story, of 1790, is now to be reprinted. Among South African literature A. C. Jordan's Xhosa novel, translated into English as *The Wrath of the Ancestors* in 1937, seems to have no place in print and cannot be traced in the British Museum's Catalogue of Printed Books. Thomas Mofolo's *Chaka* is not in print in English except in a school-book abridgement. Solomon T. Plaatje's historical novel *Mhudi* is procurable only with difficulty and needs to be much more readily available. D. O. Fagunwa's four novels in Yoruba are not yet translated except in extract. H. I. E. Dhlomo's long, 1941 poem, *The Valley of a Thousand Hills*, is difficult to come by. Too little of the poetry of the Malagasy Rabéarivelo is in print. Only tantalizing glimpses of the exciting prose of Abioseh Nicol of Sierra Leone are available. I failed to find any writing of Babatunde Jones or Yetuosa Esam. And even Camara Laye's important *The Radiance of the King* (Collins, 1956), is at the time of writing 'out of print' and had to be chased a long way through weeks.

Thus one is aware of many gaps, gaps not only in one's own African reading but which need to be filled for the growing numbers of people interested in African literature. Such gaps may seem to make the following survey something of a presumption. The fact that the poetry coming out of Africa at the present time is, as Gerald Moore and Ulli Beier say in their introduction to *Modern Poetry from Africa* (1963), 'among the most original and exciting now being written anywhere in the world' is offered in extenuation. That African novels and short stories are of the quality of African poetry described by Mr Moore and Mr Beier gives this survey of both prose and poetry at least temporary value, incomplete as it of necessity must be.

White African writing of lasting adult value is listed in the bibliography. None of it could be discussed in detail in the text. Ezekiel Mphahlele, the South African writer and critic, in his book *The African Image* (1962), has a chapter 'White Man's Image of the Non-White'. This gives from the African point of view a far better account of white African writing, from Rider Haggard (1884-1911), through the laughable, lovable absurdity of *Mister Johnson* (1939), to Dan

Jacobson's *The Evidence of Love*, of 1959, than I can attempt. Readers are referred to Mr Mphahlele for an African impression of White African writing. And to Mr Mphahlele this book is tentatively offered.

There was difficulty in deciding whether autobiography should be included in the Survey and the Anthology. If there were reasons why political autobiographies could be kept out, Albert ·Luthuli's *Let My People Go* and even Kenneth Kaunda's *Zambia Shall be Free* were hard to pronounce against. Confessedly factual life-stories of such grace and relevance as Prince Modupe's *I Was a Savage*, Mugo Gatheru's *Child of Two Worlds*, and Josiah Kariuki's *Mau Mau Detainee*, so begged for admission that no proposed text on African books could deny account of them. William Conton's *The African*, though written in the first person, is plainly writing of such high fictional standard that it is both offered in extract and discussed.

Africans assessing African writing and African problems have been quoted whenever possible. But – happily from more than one point of view – there is African creative work in plenty compared with the amount of African criticism yet. Chary of European approaches to African work, African critics as well as writers are still groping for their own terms and perspectives. Some people might say that African literature itself is still searching for its own definitions. And so, of course, it is; and it will continue to search.

The poems of the Anthology have all been printed before. Only the Shukria *dobeit* from the Sudan in the text of Chapter 5 are printed for the first time. The prose extracts are from books already published, though in some cases out of print. The Anthology's intention is not only to present new African writers, but to make the best – that is, the already significantly individual – African writers more widely known.

Dates of birth of African authors and the spellings of their names will have to be taken as only reasonably correct. Registration of births and deaths has but recently come into force; and few Africans are interested in their dates of birth. In Shaaban Robert's autobiography, *Maisha ya Shaaban Robert*, for instance, the author makes no reference at all to when he was born.

Its indirect aim, too, is to illustrate, by the extracts and poems, points made in discussion of the authors in the Survey.

My thanks are due to the librarians of the Leicester Reference and Lending Libraries, particularly to Miss C. L. Wright, for unfailing help and advice over books that, to say the least, have sometimes been more than a little elusive. For the map of Africa, 1965,

I am indebted to my son. I am grateful to my publisher, and to Miss Elfreda Powell who read the manuscript. To Mr Gerald Moore who read the proofs I owe much, too.

1964   ANNE TIBBLE
                                        School of Education
                                        University of Leicester

PART ONE

A Survey

Chapter 1

A BRIEF HISTORICAL OUTLINE

Between Africa and Europe there has been a steady exchange in inventions and culture since the Stone Age. This human give-and-take grows more exciting as our knowledge of Africa and of our own past increases. Mutual influence between Europe and Africa was carried on by land long before the land-route between Asia and Africa was interrupted in 1870 by the opening of the Suez Canal. Communication between Africa and Europe may have been in existence even before the drying of the Sahara some 10,000 to 15,000 years ago.

Yet only in the past fifty years have we become conscious that Africa is, as Charles Darwin forecast in the nineteenth century she might be, a continent possessing the most ancient of civilizations. Today she vies for the first place as a possible cradle of the human race. She is also a region where modern culture is being nurtured at top speed.

The first half of Darwin's surmise was emphasized by the realization that the Oldowan Stone-Age culture was the oldest known to the world. This knowledge became certain when 'pebble tools' were found in South Africa in 1931 – 'pebble tools' are thought to be older by 500,000 years than the 'hand-axe' of palaeolithic man. In 1959 the proto-human form now called Zinjanthropus was discovered in Olduvai Gorge in Tanganyika. In 1964 L. S. B. Leakey found, in the same part of East Africa, the fossil he called *Homo habilis*. This he described as 'the world's earliest yet known man'. Whether this was man or man-ape, scholars are still disputing. Much pre-history is yet to be known. But evidence is also mounting, as Melville Herskovits writes in *The Human Factor in Changing Africa*, 'that the present Negroid form of *Homo sapiens* may have been differentiated in the general area of the bend of the west coast [of Africa].[1]

Zinjanthropus, *Homo habilis*, and the fact that the earliest *Homo sapiens* form found in Africa resembled European Cro-Magnon man, and again, the rock and cave paintings scattered over the African continent, are all evidence of the important part played by Africa in prehistoric man's evolution.

[1] P. 29.

19

We may trace the development of African civilization through its neolithic stage comparable with the Middle East's and with Europe's beginnings in settled agriculture : gold, silver, and copper were worked, in the area that changed its name in 1964 from Northern Rhodesia to Zambia, during what we call the Bronze Age; the domestication of animals was also carried out : thus the humped cattle that comprise most African herds are now thought to have been indigenous rather than imported from India.

Glimpses afforded by facts such as the foregoing give a little help towards understanding the complexities of human form, language, and culture which Africa contains. The rich confusion of these three has come from centuries of migration and conquest both from outside the continent and within it, and from the miscegenation that inevitably follows conquest and migration of peoples.

About 600 B.C. Phoenician sailors, at the behest of Necho, ruler of Egypt, first rounded the African continent. Centuries before that, Arabs and other merchants from the Orient had been trading with the East African coast. Since the Portuguese under Vasco da Gama again rounded the Cape of Good Hope and opened the European passage to India in 1497, Africa's South and West coasts have been in constant contact with Europeans as well as with the Far East.

It was the hinterland, the whole of the centre of the 'dark' continent, that remained largely unknown to Europeans until the nineteenth century. Slavery seems to have been a practice of many cultures of developing man, including many of the African cultures. But Africa has certainly endured her share of enslavement by foreigners. During the past nine or ten decades, since the days of intrepid missionary-explorers like David Livingstone and Bishop Hannington, and of explorers no less intrepid but of less obvious humanity – men like Burton, Speke, Stanley, Rhodes – Africa has been under European domination. Since the legal prohibitions of slavery in the 1870s and 1880s, up to the 1940s, Africa has remained under 'protection' and exploitation. Though far from slavery, these dominating foreign influences have been intensive, irksome, often economically unfair, and sometimes, by any human standards, ruthlessly cruel. Yet they are what has helped to make Africa modern.

The term 'race' cannot any longer be accurate. But, allowing it wide limits of meaning, we may still make use of it. The term 'race' is used here to mean a group of people with likenesses such as blood-grouping, head-shape, texture and colour of hair, and colour of skin. According to Seligman in his *Races of Africa* there are five of these groups in the continent. They have marked differences in physical form. In his much fuller book *The Human Factor in Changing Africa*, Herskovits divides the continent into six 'culture areas' and thus avoids the word 'race'. Herskovits's divisions of sub-Saharan Africa, however, roughly follow Seligman's; but Herskovits uses names such as the East African Cattle area, the Eastern Sudan, the Congo, the Guinea Coast, and the Western Sudan. These may be confused with political names, and political names, in Africa as elsewhere, often define very artificial entities. Herskovits also groups his 'culture areas' into two parts – the food-gathering and herding economies and the agricultural economies. This wide division has excellent clarity. But, of course, Africa's exuberent variety cannot wholly be contained in any such scientific formula. Nuba agriculturists are in Herskovits's culture areas found in the midst of 'Eastern Sudan' cattle people such as Kababish and Baggara; the 'East African Cattle area' stretches across the agriculture of a tsetsi-fly domain; Negro Muslim Hausas of West Africa speak an Hamitic language; and so on and so on.

With deep respect to these well-known scholars, Seligman and Herskovits, in such a cursory survey as this, one may perhaps be allowed to combine their grouping. The picture thus presented will be grossly over-simplified. But it may be clear for the general reader; and it may not be altogether false.

Let us include for the moment the whole continent. Most scholars still divide Africa's race-stocks thus :

1 Hamites, Semites, and Nilotes	2 'True' Negroes, Sudanic-speaking Negroes, and Bantu-speaking Negroes	3 Negrillos	4 Bushmen and Hottentots

1 Hamites, Semites, and Nilotes

The Hamites and Semites are of 'Caucasian', 'Mediterranean', or 'European' origin. Both occupy the northern coastal fringe of Africa, and parts of the desert belt; peoples with Hamitic blood mixture or language reach as far south along the east coast as Zanzibar. Nile-valley people may be said to belong to this group. These Nilotes, or Nilo-Hamites, are of Negro stock mingled with Hamitic or Semitic stock, but with much Negro culture character.

Hamites and Semites may speak Arabic, as along the whole of the north African coast, in Egypt, or in the northern part of the Sudan Republic; they may speak the Hamitic To Bedawi as do the Beja (Hadendoa), or the Semitic Tigré and Arabic as do the Beja (Beni Amer): both of these are sections of the proud, aloof Red Sea hillmen. Hamites and Semites may speak Amharic languages as in Ethiopia; or they may speak Sudanic tongues as do some of the Pagan Nilotes. Most peoples along the northern African coast follow the Islamic religion. Ezekiel Mphahlele says that Islamic links with sub-Saharan Africa are slender. The Islamic Arabs still live much in tribes, but tribalism is slowly breaking under urbanization. Semitic peoples have been in North Africa for some two thousand years. Hamitic peoples have been there much longer.

In desert and semi-desert, Hamitic, Semitic, or Nilotic peoples may be seasonal nomads. Some of the Nilotes such as Nuer and Masai, are among the tallest people on Earth. Long legged, slender, and fine-featured, these people often possess great beauty. Like Beja – Nuer and Masai and a few other tribes are proud and reticent. They do not take easily to interference, change, and enforced civilization. Shilluk, another Nilotic tribe, have a kingship that has elements in common with some of the early Greek city-state kingships. Nuer have a democratic clan-and-kinship system by which social powers are balanced among individuals to prevent too much accruing to one person. Like Muslims and Christians Nilotic Pagans have their own explanations of life's mysteries and their own systems of ethic; and like Muslims, some Pagan tribes practise personal mutilation as a means of demonstrating the individual's growth from childhood to pain-bearing adulthood.

2 *'True' Negroes, Sudanic-speaking Negroes, and Bantu-speaking Negroes*

This group is intended here to include all African peoples who can be called Negro in physical form, language, or culture. It is by far the biggest group. First, it includes those called 'true' Negroes. These peoples live along the Guinea coast in the west (see map), and inward and northward to the Niger. In this second of the four large sections, too, are peoples living along the Congo basin and north of the Congo into the centre of the continent; Bantu extend east and south-east into Bechuanaland, Swaziland, and Basutoland. They comprise the hundred or more tribes which, living then in a social system similar to the Scottish clan structure – family, sub-tribe, and tribe – were, in the early nineteenth century, conquered by the military leader Chaka to form the Zulu nation. Most, but not all (e.g. the Hausa-speaking language-group), speak Bantu tongues. Their cultures, however, are extremely varied. Most of them are settled cultivators. Their social unit is the village. But towns like Lagos, Freetown, Accra, Ibadan, Kampala, Nairobi, Kumasi, Salisbury, Leopoldville, and others, have grown greatly and become very modern. Yet before the European impact they already had a developed market system which supplied the necessities of life.

Because of their previous knowledge of barter, money, and trading, 'true' Negroes as well as many Bantu-speaking Negroes accepted with alacrity what the white man had to offer of profit and 'progress'. Rapidly the Negro, having dallied for centuries in an environment that was at once too hostile and too kind to provide sufficient challenge, set themselves, once they had received its impact, to 'catch up with the advanced races'. 'Catching up' is what Nelson Mandela called the process in his moving speech from Pretoria dock in May 1964.

The Fulani-Hausa, the Yoruba, the Ibo, the Sierra Leonian, and the Liberian – these and scores of other richly variant divisions in West Africa are skilful artisans. They have well-developed institutions. Most religions include belief in a Creator their lesser deities personifying powers like thunder, wind, rain, or famine. Common, as in many cultures, is a belief in 'supernatural' possibilities. This personal 'magic' often stems from knowing each other's feelings intuitively and from an immense network of secrecy, common interests, and gossip; these are linked with a concentrated power in certain individuals of going into trance. This kind of intensity of awareness of others' thoughts and feelings, the strange capacity for self-induced unconsciousness, much of the exploration of extra-sensory perception, have, in what are called 'advanced' civilizations, been left unexplored in favour of intellectual-rational development and individual responsibility; and they are relatively undeveloped in the West. Among Bantu there is general reverence for elders and for ancestors. The dead are thought to have power to help or harm the living.

Connected with the religions and with their craftsmanship go West Africans' plastic arts both 'classic' and 'modern'. To this part of the continent belong the Nok figures, the Bronzes of Benin, and the Ife Heads, the Dahomey Brasses, and Yoruba Wood-carvings. All these have been influencing European sculpture and painting since the first years of the twentieth century. In the last ten or fifteen years, by way of the West Indies and America, West African and South African Negro music, with its many musical instruments, its micro-tonic scale, and its hypnotic rhythms, together with Negro dance, have made immense impact. The rich outburst of literature in English that the next chapters of this book will deal with, valuable in itself, is also proof of the splendid personal traditions in story, song, poetry, and drama.

In spite of the aptitude with which the West and South African Bantu Negro took to European culture, West African literature was late in developing compared with South African Bantu literature : Sotho, Xhosa, and Zulu writing began early this century, earliest of all the writing in sub-Saharan Africa. West African literature came into its own later, during the 1940s.

3 Negrillos

Negrillos are Pygmies. These, together with the fourth and last division of African race stocks, Bushmen and Hottentots, are found in far fewer numbers than the Hamite-Semite-Nilotes, or than the 'true'-Negro and Bantu-speaking Negro group. But to suppose hastily that these numerically smaller groups, so often declared with 'convincing' statistics to be dying out, are of so much less importance, might be both short-sighted and unimaginative. In an 'atomic' world basic variations can produce amazingly unforeseen futures.

Pygmies are scattered in small pockets over most of the northern and east-central forest parts of the Bantu-speaking areas. They are also found further north. Their numbers are perhaps more than we think, especially in areas like the Nile Sudd where 'Thoony' exist for years without being discovered. Pygmies have remained hunters and food-gatherers without knowledge of the wheel or the boat over the millennia. Some are as dark as the Negro; some are more coppery, or some yellower in skin-colouring. Some have a certain lightness like that of north African 'Arabs'. Negrillos average four foot six to four foot eight inches in height. Like some of their neighbours the tallest of men, in the Nile swamps these smallest of men do not take kindly to change and interference, though they have borrowed many words and customs through their barter with neighbouring Bantu. Their languages are not well known. One authority regards Efé as the tongue of the Ituri forest Pygmies only.

The position of the Pygmy in the story of Man is still uncertain. Pygmies have been known to be dancers and expert mimics since 'dwarfs' mocked and mimed in Pharaoh's court. If they have dance and drama and children's stories, as is known they have, then almost certainly they have adult, though oral, literature. The collecting and preserving of Pygmy verse and prose should be fascinating work for some African scholars of the future.

4 Bushmen and Hottentots

Fourth of these African race-stocks or culture groups are the Bushmen and Hottentots. These are sometimes grouped under the name Khoisan because both peoples speak what is called a 'click' language. Both Hottentots and Bushmen inhabit South Africa. Bushmen are found from the south coast northward to the Kalahari desert. Hottentots live along the west coast northward as far as Angola. Both have resisted – and though much diminished have survived – relatively severe attemps at extermination by Boer and Bantu. Their numbers are now said, together, to be about 55,000. Bushmen are small as Pygmies, but distinct in form. They are about five foot two in height with well-shaped heads, hands and feet. They live in family groups, on a food-gathering pattern. The women collect fruit and berries and roots. The men hunt with poisoned arrows. They are a happy, gentle people, with a High-God, Mantis, and a well-defined culture and ethos. Their rock- and cave-paintings and other remains, scattered all over the continent, prove them to have been widely distributed at one time; but no evidence shows them to be related to the Pygmies of the forests.

Hottentots are herders. They keep long-horned cattle and flocks of fat-tailed sheep. They are slightly taller than Bushmen, and their culture, both material and otherwise, is a little more elaborate. Like many peoples badly named 'primitive' they are ethically conscious of and respectful towards others' feelings and observe certain cautions in personal relations. They have ceremonies for birth, marriage, and death, and ceremonies to help the transitions for the individual from childhood to puberty to adulthood. Each person knows his place in the group and his social duties. Neither Bushmen nor Hottentots practise self-mutilation. Nor have either ever been warlike or aggressive. Hottentots have not developed the arts of sculpture or painting. But should not both Bushmen's and Hottentots' myths and ethos be written down and preserved before so much of them is lost perhaps for good?

By the 1960s the whole African continent was emerging into freedom again from its servitude under colonialism. Suffering and intense misery in certain areas like South Africa, Southern Rhodesia, the Congo, and Angola, were not yet over. But to say that in one sense Africa has emerged may be more accurate. The aim of most Africans, literate and non-literate is to be in charge of their own destinies in trade and politics; and perhaps, in poetry, art, or purely in human living, to seek to 'add a fresh colour to the rainbow'. Understandably, those ready for change want to retain the best in their traditions whilst taking advantage of modern methods. They also would like to avoid some of the blunders they consider Europe has made. Such aims have been said not to be in touch with realistic thinking and 'hard' facts; 'hard' often refers only to politics and economics. But if African 'simplicity' means vital directness and adequacy of response, then these aims are to be reckoned with as well as the 'harder' economic and political ones.

Chapter 2

LANGUAGES AND LANGUAGE IN AFRICA

James Baldwin, the Negro-American, in the course of an article 'Why I stopped hating Shakespeare', wrote :

> I felt it so bitterly anomalous that a black man should be forced to deal with the English language at all – should be forced to assault the English language in order to speak . . . when . . . the language reflected none of my experience.[1]

Baldwin writes English with persuasive passion; and it is his mother-tongue. We recall, however, Joseph Conrad, whose style may owe at least some of its elusive beauty to the fact that English was only his adopted language. The pages that follow will give evidence of African writers using English as a second language with expert creativity and many talents.

Perhaps English holds what place it has among the languages of the twentieth-century world because of two traits, developed over a thousand years. It was driven to strategy under at least two periods of bitter subjection to foreign conquest; twice the English tongue was nearly annihilated. It is first known to have been in use – a rigid language with fixed and strict case-endings by the Anglo-Saxons when those invaders took possession of the continental approaches to this storm-rid, North-Atlantic island.

Yet the first thing anyone may note about English now is its lack of strictness, its flexibility, even its fluidity. It has become incredibly supple. Thus it has adapted itself to keep pace with change and with the incessant danger of extinction.

The second modern trait to notice is the shamelessness with which English borrows from many other languages. These two traits, gained at some cost, may ensure that English has still a tolerable life-span before it.

In this mid-twentieth century English is again under pressures from outside. One present straining of its make-up and resources comes from the U.S.A. The living tongue of two hundred million Americans should perhaps be thought of as a language in its own

---

[1] *The Observer*, 19 April 1964.

right. Yet it is English, its poets, Whitman, Frost, Wilbur, and Creeley, astonishingly so. The infusion of American into English comprises fresh and vivid idiom, graphic new slang, esoteric and technical terms, new pronunciations, confusing re-naming in geography, natural history, social science, and a species of Press diction that can be far more bloodless than, as unconsciously villainous, and just as devilishly abstract, as some English Press diction can be.

Other pressures on the language come from Canadian, Australian, New Zealand, Indian, and West Indian, English. These off-shoots are in process of their own vital growth. Their influence on English will be stronger and more felt in the future.

Perhaps the most complex yet single influence on the English tongue at the present day is coming from Africa. This is so important that it is like a blood-transfusion. One of the foremost African writers, the South African Ezekiel Mphahlele, has shown up one or two of the paradoxes in language and culture changes that are rapidly taking place before our eyes :

> I personally cannot think of the future of my people in South Africa as something in which the white man does not feature. Whether he likes it or not, our destinies are inseparable. I have seen too much that is good in Western culture – for example, its music, literature and theatre – to want to repudiate it. If the white man shuts his eyes to the good that is in my culture, he is the poorer for it and I am one up on him. There is nothing I can do to cure his malady. He has used the labour of my people for three centuries. To this extent he is deeply committed to a co-habitation with us – and that is reducing the relationship to its barest terms. He has no just reason to deny me the political rights many other workers in the world enjoy, and the other good things education creates an awareness of and a desire for. The white man has de-tribalized me. He had better go the whole hog. He must know that I'm the personification of the African paradox, detribalized, Westernized, but still African.[1]

In a paper not yet published on African Writers, Mr Mphahlele emphasizes how

> The African for whom English is a second language is always translating thoughts that originally operate in his mother tongue; and because he is writing in a rich medium like English, he can even do violence to it when he records dialogue he can 'hear' only in the language spoken by his characters.

The following instances out of thousands may serve to indicate the kind of violence that can be done by youthful African writers of English. A schoolgirl writes :

[1] *The African Image*, Faber, 1962, p. 66.

'I am eager to see you in good healthy pleasure's way, have no grieve because the life abhors the grieve.' A student tells his former master : 'I prepared myself to the English examination and by the Queen's helping passed my exam in splendid way'; in both these instances the grammar and syntax may be tenuous; but in neither case is there obscurity, though there may be need to understand the point of view. The same can be said of most African English, literary or other than literary. It has a capacity to confront the new that makes its scarcely ever less than fresh and clear. Most often, even when naïve, it is vividly alive and expressive.

Europeans in Africa over the past four centuries left behind them many disparate things. They left scattered medical help that was nearly always sceptical of traditional African herbalists. This contempt, seen also for European herbalists, of course, may be noted in the word for the African medicine-man – 'witch doctor'. Often enough the 'witch doctor' developed into an astute, rich, perhaps evil, autocrat and tyrant. But quite frequently he remained, as Ezekiel Mphahlele, as Chinua Achebe, and as others, have revealed, 'not a mere dealer in charms and potions, but . . . the moral conscience of his people.[1]

Europeans also introduced changes, not in every aspect and instance improvement unqualified, in agriculture, engineering, building, and industry. It is a fine illusion, hard to combat, to suppose that new ways, new inventions, new products, are always a 100 per cent better than old methods and simpler techniques.

Americans and Europeans also left the Christian religion. Bringers of that faith did not always practise what they preached. Who does? Some Christians narrowly thought all other religions 'heathen', even 'evil', 'savage', 'wicked', 'untrue', 'low'. 'Heathen' is another word that denigrates and so misunderstands. It has to be confessed that the supremely difficult passing on of Christ's message about bearing one another's burdens and not judging lest we ourselves be judged, as often separates people as it unites them.

In those parts of Africa where Britain sought to influence, Britons left an educational pattern as well as a religion. Most Africans who came in contact with this educational pattern only too eagerly accepted it. The pattern gave unquestioned superiority to literacy and academicism. Too quickly it assumed that the wisdom accumulated by pre-literate societies was out-dated and therefore of little account.

At first many Africans eagerly accepted these two changes, Christianity and school literacy, as 'progress'. Their initial welcome is part

[1] Discussion paper on 'The Language of African Literature', Fourah Bay College, Sierra Leone, 1963.

of Africa's recent story. But by the 1950s a few scholars in most of the new African nations were becoming aware of their need to work out both an ideology and its practice for themselves.

The British also left in some parts of Africa the English language. The first book written by an African in English, printed over a hundred and seventy years ago, a little before 1790, was by a freed slave of Sierra Leone, Gustavus Vassa. Since 1870 black South Africans have been political journalists, poets and novelists. But only during the last twenty years has there been the great upsurge of black African writing.

Where the French dominated, such writing was, and still is, in French. Spanish Guinea has, as far as I know, no writers; yet Mozambique has a number of good writers in Portuguese. Where the chief language was Africaans, African writing was first in vernaculars such as Sotho or Xhosa, and later translated into English. For African writers using any language other than their vernacular, conflict was bound to be acute. In African writing in French this conflict produced the movement called '*Négritude*'.

Négritude flourished in the 1930s and 1940s. Its protest is not over yet, but its impact is in decline, as also, perhaps, its usefulness. Its definition is usually attributed to Léopold Sédar Senghor, the poet-president of Senegal; its outlook is defined in verse rather than in prose, in the poetry of Senghor, David Diop, Birago Diop, and others.

Senegal has known French influence since the seventeenth century. It has known French domination, with its policy of *assimilation* since 1865. This policy supposes, according to Senghor, the only civilized Senegalese to be a French-speaking Catholic. Its purpose, as Senghor has put it, must be to produce Black Frenchmen. Senghor was the first African to receive a French Doctorate. His sense of isolation in Paris was so overwhelming that he felt himself driven back to rediscover his identity as an African. Yet he, Guillon, Alioune Diop and Thomas Diop, both connected with *Présence Africaine*, Birago Diop, David Diop, and others, have created a far bigger body of African French poetry than poets writing in English have produced in African English poetry.

In the 1950s the *Négritude* movement took fresh strength from Kwame Nkrumah's stress on 'the African Personality'. I cannot do better than quote at length and without apology the words of one who sees from the African point of view the need to outlive *Négritude*.[1]

[1] 'Remarks on *Négritude*', read at a conference on *African Literature in French, and the University Curriculum*; Faculté des Lettres, University of Dakar, March 1963, by Ezekiel Mphahlele.

Who is so stupid as to deny the historical fact of *Négritude* as both a protest and a positive assertion of African cultural values? All this is valid. What I do not accept is the way in which too much of the poetry inspired by it romanticizes Africa – as a symbol of innocence, purity, and artless primitiveness. I feel insulted when some people imply that Africa is not also a violent continent. I am a violent person, and proud of it because it is often a healthy human state of mind; someday I'm going to plunder, rape, set things on fire; I'm going to cut someone's throat; I'm going to subvert a government; I'm going to organize a *coup d'état*; yes, I'm going to oppress my own people; I'm going to hunt down the rich fat black men who bully the small, weak black men and destroy them; I'm going to become a capitalist. . . . The image of Africa consists of all these and others. And *Négritude* poetry pretends that they do not constitute the image and leaves them out. So we are told only half – often even a falsified half – of the story of Africa. Sheer romanticism that fails to see the large landscape of the African makes bad poetry. . . .

Mr Mphahlele continues astringently :

Several of us, as a result of the physical and mental agony we have been going through in South Africa, have rejected Christianity or any other religion as a cure for human ills. But if I wrote a poem or novel expressly to preach against religion without my seeing the irony of Christians and educated Africans who still revere ancestral spirits, and several other ironies and paradoxes, then it would not be a lasting work of art. I think that a writer who is too sure about his rejection of the use of a god can be as overbearing as the one who is too sure about his need of the existence of a god, like Browning. I say, then, that *Négritude* can go on as a socio-political slogan, but that it has no right to set itself up as a standard of literary performance; there I refuse to go along. I refuse to be put in a Negro file – for sociologists to come and examine me. Art unifies even while it distinguishes men. . . .

. . . literature springs from an individual's experience, and in its effort to take in the whole man, it also tries to see far ahead, to project a prophetic vision, such as the writer is capable of, based on contemporary experience. It must at least set in motion vibrations in use that will contiue even after we have read it, prompting us to continue inquiring into its meaning. If African culture is worth anything at all, it should not require myths to prop it up. These thoughts are not new at all. I have come to them after mental and physical agony. And this is, of course, not my monopoly either. It is the price Africa has to pay. And if you thought that the end of colonialism was the end of the agony, then it is time to wake up.

So, far beyond the protest of *Négritude* is the question of what language African literature *as* African should be written in. French will continue to be used for a long time. For those writers using English, their conflict may lessen or it may become more acute than it is at present. Their second language happens to be fluid rather than, as French is, formal; and what they combat is not *assimilation* but the example in front of them of a great literature already created to which is added a critical parentalism always well-meant but occasionally heavily patronizing.

However much the South African government may think Africaans the *lingua franca* of that part of Africa, there is little present evidence that Africaans is or can be.

Again, Africans writing in some of the continent's five hundred local languages will be sure only of smaller audiences than they may deserve.

What of Arabic as an African language? An ancient tongue, with a classical tradition and a modern colloquial virility, Arabic is the language of modern Egypt, north Sudan, and the north African coastal peoples. So far as I know Arabic has not been proposed as the language of the African continent.

Discussing the problem of an African language in the magazine *Transition*,[1] Dr Jan Knappert proposed Swahili, which, he wrote,

> is a Bantu language, predominantly African. It is *not*, as many people still think, a mixture of Arabic. It is true that Swahili has thousands of words of Arabic origin, but do we call English French because it contains tens of thousands of French words?
>
> Swahili has been at home on the East-Coast of Africa for as long as human records go. There is no indication at all that it has come from outside. There is no reason to suppose that ever any other language was spoken on Africa's East Coast. We do not know that any other people ever lived on the Coast, and there is no shadow of proof that the Azanians of ancient times were not Swahili speaking . . .

Dr Knappert's second paragraph contains negative statements that are unconvincing. Yet it should be remembered that Swahili, written five centuries ago in Arabic characters and now in Roman, has a strong poetic tradition that has been influenced by Persian epic poetry and by classical Arabic poetry of the first thousand years A.D. Dr Knappert goes on to write of Swahili's claims more persuasively when he notes its 'flexibility' and its capacity for incorporating words from other tongues. He then categorically adds :

> Since Swahili literature is more than a century older than any other African literature, including Xhosa, Zulu, Hausa and Amharic, there can be no better language for Africans to write their literature in than Swahili.

[1] *Transition*, No. 13, March-April 1964, p. 5.

African writers will decide for themselves. Krio, the tongue of a part of West Africa, for those who do not speak English traditionally, is a language in its own right; and there is a handful of poets writing in Krio. Again, this may be no more than a transient groping towards something new. All literatures, oral and written, and all languages, deserve written exploration by their own speakers. I cannot quite agree when Dr Knappert writes that African literature in Swahili would 'not feel isolated because very few foreigners read what they publish'. They very well might in time feel isolated. Ezekiel Mphahlele writes with more insight when he envisages African literature as part of all human experience. The give-and-take that has been between Africa and Europe and Asia for at least three thousand years bears him out. If Swahili or any other African language should be decided upon, we shall need scores of devoted translators from Swahili, English, and other languages, that will be all.

There is naturally a mental 'block' over writing in a second language. The same kind of 'block', though smaller, is there between oral and written literature. Folk stories, legends, idiom, customs, 'won't translate' even in the writing down; some of their essence escapes. They become something different. This is true, inevitably, of translation into another language. It is true when Shakespeare and Chaucer are put into present-day English. The three sets of Pasternak's poems by different translators are three sets of almost completely distinct poems.

For an African writer using any second language this most immediate of the problems he faces is huge, both directly and indirectly. Directly, the problem is how to translate local customs, the vitality and rhythms of vernacular speech, and the habits and traditions of his own social life and thought into a written dimension. And the problem is doubled and made indirect when the written dimension is a second language. Should he, in order to present his characters, his background, and his African heart and mind to his readers proceed as the Nigerian poet, Gabriel Okara, suggests :[1]

> In order to capture the vivid images of African speech, I had to eschew the habit of expressing my thoughts first in English. It was difficult at first, but I had to learn. I had to study each Ijaw expression I used and to discover the probable situation in which it was used in order to bring out the nearest meaning in English.

Instead of 'Goodnight', which no Ijaw would say, Okara continues, should he not give the expressive Ijaw idiom for parting with a

---

[1] 'African Speech . . . English Words', *Transition*, No. 10, p. 15.

B

friend? 'May we live to see ourselves tomorrow!' Describing 'a too timid man' an Ijaw might say : 'he who has no shadow'. This phrase is richly expressive; its obvious meaning is 'a man who isn't strong enough, either physically or in personality, for the sun to cast his shadow on the ground'. The man's two kinds of strength are identified with the sun's. As well as brightness the sun casts shadows. If a man has the brightness of physical bravery or of strength, or personality, he will probably also have the shadow of ruthlessness. All this is implied in 'he who has no shadow'. On a modern level of meaning, by a man's 'shadow' or 'dark' side, a psychologist means the crude instincts of brutality however self-preserving these are. Such a phrase as 'he who has no shadow', found in other African languages, such as Sotho, for instance, and echoing in English, should certainly not be lost. But striving to keep speech and writing 'live' is part of the task of all writers in all languages.

Indirectly, therefore, use of special idiom must always hold pitfalls. Thoughts or emotions shared or capable of being shared by human beings from whatever culture must somehow shine through constantly changing meanings. Most African writers of any seriousness are sensitive to the balance to be presented and preserved between known and unknown experience. Such balance is perilously held, but it *is* held, in Nkem Nwankwo's story 'Rain' and in the extract from his *Danda* in this Anthology.

A method poised between that of Nwankwo and an over-sedulous acceptance of speech infiltration (particularly that of American commercial films) is the method used by the South African Alex La Guma in his novella *A Walk in the Night*. A similar method David Owoyele employs in his short story *The Will of Allah*. (This method can also be observed in Wole Soyinka's play *The Lion and the Jewel*, and in John Pepper Clark's plays, particularly *Song of a Goat*.) The method may be described as that of avoiding very obscure ritual or tradition-referenced conversation that might be felt to belong to impenetrably different people, or (often falsely) to particular social classes. As Okot p'Bitek points out, human societies are now seen by ethnologists as 'functional'; African society and people are not 'simple'. European society has not evolved from the 'simple' to the 'civilized'. Both African and European are complex. Terms such as 'primitive', 'savage', and 'simple', p'Bitek observes, are therefore now used only by 'die-hard, intellectual conservatives'.[1]

In La Guma's *A Walk in the Night*, the activities, scene, and dialogue might be those of almost any city at midnight; the talk in this book approaches film argot but remains just sufficiently distinct.

---

[1] 'Fr Tempels's *Bantu Philosophy*', *Transition*, No. 13.

In *The Will of Allah* the happenings might be those of any village on Earth. The effect of this method of writing is tellingly to lift characters that remain highly individual on to a universal level. In Owoyele's story the two chief characters startlingly become two faces of Everyman peering from unknown, surrounding dark. In La Guma's novel inter-racial prejudice is seen all through as a sporadic character-weakness that, so long as it is common among human beings, can 'get by' as realism and strength. Constable Raalt's clinging to his prejudice is brought from latency into action by Raalt's continued incapacity to deal with his own unhappiness. This is what La Guma beautifully shows.

One or two South African writers chronically imitate American film talk. Surely this is a high price to pay in order to reach readers. Such a take-over of a foreign, transient speech-idiom is obviously 'fake' because however much Africa, particularly South Africa, is a mixture of cultures, English like that is not heard except in American or Anglo-American commercial films.

In literary criticism, as well as in writing, by too wholly accepting European or American standards Africans invite aridity. Obiajunwa Wali fears such a 'dead end' for African literature. Wali writes :

The criticism being done today in African writing in English and French . . . is the same *clichés* over and over again – romantic and classic realism, sentimentality, Victorianism, *surréalism*, and so on. There is no need for creative thinking in order to become a 'leading critic or authority' in African literature. Fraser, Freud, Darwin, and Marx, are, as in European literature, the necessary reading for the acquisition of fundamental critical tools.

What I am advocating here is not easy, for it entails a good deal of hard work and hard thinking, and what is more, a necessary casting overboard of hardened débris of the overblown ego. It would force some 'leading' critics to go in for the hard school of African linguistic studies, a knowledge of some of the important African languages, before generalizing and formulating all kinds of philosophical and literary theories. Literature in Africa would then become the serious business that all literature truly is, reaching out to the people for whom it is meant, and creating a true culture of the African peoples that would not rely on slogans and propaganda, nor on patronage of doubtful intentions.[1]

Onlookers will see throughout the discussion the one wide issue both direct and indirect that concerns African writers deeply but also concerns writers everywhere. Mr Mphahlele refers to this issue

[1] *Transition*, No. 10, pp. 13-14.

in yet another of his papers. He says that before Africa was 'invaded by a money economy . . . Culture was not separate . . . Culture was life.' In these words he is stating what happens in all cultures that become urbanized; and he is suggesting what overtakes all societies that enter the 'civilization process'. The separation of culture from life did not happen only in Africa.

Most of the five hundred or more culture groups speaking their different languages in the present Africa of 280 million people, have for a long time had both oral prose and verse. Most pre-literate peoples use social leisure and freedom practising the social arts, reciting verse, singing songs, dancing, and playing musical instruments. Gifted tale-tellers tell stories round their hearths or in the moonlight. Thus they shorten the long African night before the boon of electricity reaches them. Traditional poems and songs may be sung or recited only on special occasions such as births, marriages, deaths and festivals. Among some peoples it would be sacrilege to arouse feelings at inappropriate moments.

Most early poetry of any society is popular poetry in the sense that it was usually chanted or sung to many listeners. The listeners often joined in a chorus; individuals or groups added to the original verses. Sometimes that original form and substance, again either by individuals or by groups, could be changed beyond recognition.

After the writing down of a people's language, or after a culture group becomes literate, a cleavage sets in. This is not only between oral and written literature, but between 'popular' poetry and prose and what comes to be called scholarly, educated, or 'literary' poetry and prose. Such a division between popular and literary verse is observable in Greek poetry in the sophisticated cult, by Theocritus and others; this was an attempt to join again to the 'simple' or 'pastoral', or 'popular'. Cleavage is observable between English popular and literary poetry since Caedmon the swineherd's lyrics of the seventh century. Robert Graves has noted such cleavage between 'popular' and 'academic' in Celtic literature. Exactly when cleavage begins in each society obviously we have no means of knowing. That the separation eventually produces academic Arts of all kinds which are esoteric, and popular Arts of all kinds which, commercially exploited, become debased in most 'civilized' cultures, would seem to be obvious. We are watching such a process of cleavage at work in African prose and poetry at the present time.

In his beautiful book, *Primitive Song*, Sir Maurice Bowra maintains that poetry could not advance beyond a single impassioned utterance or a closely-seen description except through academic schools and rules. No doubt this is true. But the intricacy and discipline of traditional African poetry is a revelation. Such poetry may have strictly formal rhythm. Often, but by no means always, it may have rhyme. Some verbal poetry is based on syllabic values. Other oral verse has what seems best called by the poet Gerard Hopkins's term 'sprung rhythm'. The oral poetry of the Ewe people in Ghana,[1] for example, appears to have strict syllabic units of one, two, or three, beats to a line; there is no unaccented beat. Akan (Ghanaian) poetry, on the other hand, seems to have no 'syllabic foot' : it has 'tonal' patterning and its repeated sound-arrangements are similar to, but cannot be said precisely to be, rhyme.[2] English poetry, since it freed itself from Greek and Latin syllables, may have rhyme, half-rhyme, off-rhyme, mid-line or end-line rhyme, or no rhyme at all; it may have rhythm formal or non-formal, and/or unaccented sounds in precise or imprecise numbers. The fluidity of the language may give poetry written in English its strongest asset – possibilities of an almost infinite variety. But adaptation of traditional African verse methods obviously has great relevance for African poetry of the present and the future. The toughest problem facing young, academically-trained writers such as Wole Soyinka, John Pepper Clark, and Christopher Okigbo, all of Nigeria, must surely be the making of verse-forms that will undoubtedly be influenced by British classics, but which pay attention to African traditions, and yet remain individually each author's own.

This point need not be laboured any longer here : already African legacies of prose and poetry have at least two levels of awareness, the popular and the literary. These two levels are by no means wholly due to the fact that African writers and scholars are using a second language. The two awarenesses belong to the slow, inevitable divergence between literate and oral verse and prose. Once faced squarely and accepted, these two levels of awareness are sure to have fruitful consequences on the contribution of African literature to a wider literature. The tests they impose are those that all serious writing undergoes. For African literature of the present they are part of what Ezekiel Mphahlele quotes Raymond Williams as calling the 'driven impetus of a new kind of society'. For African writers they involve, too, all the possibilities of a more universal 'court of human appeal'.[3]

---

[1] Geormbeeyi Adali-Mortti : 'Ewe Poetry', *Black Orpheus*, No. 4, p. 36.
[2] Kwabena Nketia : 'Akan Poetry', *Black Orpheus*, No. 3, pp. 5, 8.
[3] Quoted by Ezekiel Mphahlele in the First International Congress of Africanists in his paper 'African Literature', University of Accra, 1962.

Chapter 3

SOUTH AFRICA

The First African Prose Writer – Early South African Writers – Present-Day South African Prose and Poetry

The First African Writer

Probably the very first book of an African was *The Interesting Narrative of the Life of Olaudah Equiano or Gustavus Vassa, the African. Written by himself*, 1790 (?). By 1793 this had reached its seventh edition : it was 'Printed for and sold by the Author', at a price of four shillings.

The story is that of a West African Elder's son, kidnapped at eleven from up-country, Sierra Leone or East Nigeria. The slavers shipped him to America; from there he later reshipped, a sailor, to free Britain. For years his base was London, but being of a 'roving disposition' he saw much of the world as a deck-hand on ocean-going British vessels. He became a Christian through the friendliness of a group of London Christians.

Vassa's book owed its first appearance partly to those British people who were collecting evidence of the sufferings of slaves, with intent to do their utmost to put an end to the traffic of buying and selling our own kind. Vassa's preface offered the book 'to the friends of humanity, hoping it may still be the means, in its measure, of showing the enormous cruelties practised on my sable brethren'. A second foreword offered it 'To the Lords Spiritual and Temporal, and the Commons of the Parliament of Great Britain' . . . 'Permit me,' the author went on, 'with the greatest deference to lay at your feet the following genuine narrative, the chief design of which is to excite in your august assemblies a sense of compassion. . . . I am sensible I ought to entreat your pardon for addressing to you a work so wholly devoid of literary merit as the production of an unlettered African. . . .' But whoever Olaudah Equiano was, so carefully following the obsequious form of eighteenth-century England's address to literary patrons, and whoever may have helped the writing of such an unlettered man as he claims to be, Gustavas Vassa's narrative is by no means so devoid of merit – if transparent genuineness be taken as part of such merit – as he protests it is.

Vassa had acted as 'commissary for government', 1786-7, on

38

board 'The Vernon'. This vessel was taking a load of five or six hundred Africans who had been freed by British slave-owning householders back to Freetown, Sierra Leone. Vassa made enemies during this voyage, presumably because of his outcry against the treatment of the freed-men during the voyage; he was dismissed from his post. But this did not stop him from agitating and lecturing against the cruelty to slaves by British planters in Jamaica; and presumably he continued to work for the freeing of his countrymen by the writing and publication of the *Life of Olaudah Equiano*. His chief argument towards the end of the volume is down-to-earth : it is that with an Africa of vast mineral and vegetable wealth a basis of equalized trade would be far more profitable to Europeans than slaving.

Vassa married an East Anglian girl. Perhaps his book made some contribution towards the legislation against slavery by Britain. The book is certainly worthy of a reprint.

Early South African Writers

THOMAS MOFOLO By the 1870s the South African negro had wakened to his present world and was writing creatively as well as politically. Thomas Mofolo of Basutoland is generally accounted the first African novelist of repute in the twentieth century. He was born in 1873 (or 5), educated at Mission school, became a Christian, and died in 1948.

Mofolo's earliest novel was in his indigenous tongue, Sotho, the language of the Mosotho. The title of this novel, *Moeti oa Bochabela*, is sometimes given in English as *The Pilgrim of the East*, at other times as *The Wanderer to the East*, and at other times, incorrectly, as *The Traveller from the East*. Published in English in 1920, *The Pilgrim of the East* is about a boy who sets off to seek 'the unknown Creator'. The story can be seen as a Christian parable about an earnest child's search for a God who disapproves of hatred, brutality and false speaking in any created beings. But from another angle, on another level – two or more levels often being necessary in African as in any imaginative writing – it may also be seen as a fable indicating a troubled inquiry into the new Christian ideas even before 1920.

Mofolo's second novel, *Pitseng*, also in Sotho and not yet translated, recounts the childhood, education, and courtship of a twentieth-century South African.

His third novel is the Sotho classic, *Chaka the Zulu*. Finished by 1920, this was translated into English by F. H. Dutton but it was not published in England until 1931. It is in print at the moment in a very abridged version useful chiefly for children.

Thomas Mofolo's sources were memories, legends, hearsay. Yet he believed himself, Sir Henry Newbolt says in his introduction to the 1931 edition, to be making a serious contribution to history. Mofolo does not idealize Chaka's ruthlessness – as does A. E. Ritter in his detailed and 'thrilling' *Shaka Zulu* (1955). Nor does Mofolo make of Chaka an unredeemed and unredeemable barbarian, as some earlier writers in English made of him. Mofolo gives him his stature : Caesar, Titus, Napoleon – Chaka was of the company of these – as E. A. Ritter also testifies.

But besides having a historical aim, Mofolo also seeks to show how the boy Chaka came to be the blood-thirsty, homicidal maniac that undoubtedly he became. According to Mofolo the child Chaka was what Europeans call illegitimate. Zulu warriors were allowed 'purification', after they had killed someone in battle and before they could be received back into daily life, by sexual intercourse. The 'self-restraint' of both warrior and girl was supposed to prevent pregnancy. Chaka was got by the petty chief, Senzangakona, from such a 'purification'; but the girl Nandi, was actually 'forced' by him. Chaka became the chief's first son.

Before the child was born, Nandi's people told Senzangakona of her plight, and she was received into the chief's household. A strong personality, Nandi became passionately devoted to her son, but both she and he were subjected to the jealousies of Senzangakona's other wives. A few years later, as herdboy with the younger sons of the chief, Chaka, growing tall, strong, brave, headstrong and hand-some, was isolated because of the inevitable gossip about his origin. Yet soon he won the envy of his companions and the love and admiration of the girls by rescuing, single-handed, a girl from a hyena.

Nandi's position did not improve in the royal house. Such were the Zulu rigours about pre-marital discretion that Senzangakona would have lost his life had it become known that he had made Nandi pregnant against her will. At length the other wives' threats to disclose the situation forced him to order her and her son from the royal house. They went back to Nandi's people.

According to Mofolo, this unhappiness of Chaka's early child-hood was primarily what hardened him. Slowly he grew into the most resolute young Zulu. Contemporary witnesses have seen the Zulu tribes of that time as an orderly, cleanly people, without knowledge of the boat or the wheel, with hideous burial rites, fero-cious 'smelling-out of witches', and indulging in human sacrifice. Zulu children were disciplined through submission to authority and self-sacrifice for the community, by self-restraint, fearlessness, and hard work – all, by Victorian standards, the finest virtues.

Stronger, more intelligent, and more energetic than his peers, physically Chaka seemed tireless; that, too, made him different. As early as his training in the chief's military cattle-kraal, which all Zulu youths underwent, he showed signs of the military genius that was to revolutionize Zulu fighting methods. He discarded his sandals to make himself swifter. Secretly he made a long journey to get a short stabbing spear made, with all the cunning and magic of the greatest iron-smith in the land. Successful in single combat from then on, he became applauded, admired – loved. But like many children who are early despised and rejected, even had he been less than outstanding physically and mentally, he could not have found satisfaction in normal directions. Ceaselessly hungering for revenge for himself and his mother, he resolved, Mofolo writes :

> that from that time he would do as he liked : whether a man was guilty or not he would kill him if he wished. . . . Until now his purposes had been good. Henceforth he had put one purpose – to do as he liked, even if it was wrong, and to take the most complete vengeance.

After this point in his novel Mofolo attempts a complex analysis of the conflict between soaring, ambitious, restless energy and human compassion. Mofolo wrote with a deeply moral outlook. What centrally concerns him is the African proverb : 'Wisdom is better than force.' The conflict between wisdom and force, like the very idea of the antithesis between good and evil, is probably as old as Man. The conflict is as far from being solved as ever it was. Most serious novelists take it into account.

Nineteenth-century travellers, such as Henry Francis Fynn, have described the adult Chaka as noble, genial, with 'Western powers of reason and Western wiles', of extraordinary brutality, yet with feelings of delicacy and loyal affection for those near to him. An admirer of bravery, he was generous to those he conquered. According to Mofolo, Chaka's boast that he slew only cowards was true.

He was a dancer, a singer, in his young manhood, popular. But unbeaten strength and his mother's devotion may both have helped to develop the belief that he was destined to weld the feudally organized Zulu people into a powerful nation. Superstitiously, or 'religiously', but with growing monomania, he believed that Isanusi the great witch-doctor, intercessor with the ancestors, would help him to this end.

Isanusi appears. Isanusi outlines to Chaka the moral choice : he shall obtain the empire and the dominion he covets only with the blood of Noliwe, the girl he loves, who loves him, and who already is pregnant by him. Again we are shown the conflict between

B*

hardihood and human tenderness that by the very nature of life
is deep in all human ethic and therefore in the Zulu.

Two servants of Isanusi serve Chaka. These are Ndlebe the spy,
and Malunga the procurer of people's subservience. The repulsive
Ndlebe personifies the Secret Service that political ambition in
most dominant cultures is forced to take for granted as part of
'civilized' politics. Malunga stands for that little-understood but also
prevalently accepted quality by which a strong and determined
personality always finds thousands who will sedulously obey his
will and thousands more who will give their lives or follow him
to death.

Finally Chaka, though only after great mental torment, decides
to sacrifice Noliwe for what he thinks is the reward for his own
struggle and for his mother's suffering – empire and autocracy for
himself, pomp and riches for Nandi. With his own hand Chaka
kills Noliwe.

He builds an unbeatable army. As Robert Bruce united the
Scottish clans, so Chaka unifies the Zulu clans. He clips the atrocious,
hypnotic power of some of the worst of the witch-doctors. But he
cannot forgo entirely their brutal help in 'smelling-out' supposed
enemies. And furiously these enemies grow in numbers once Chaka
becomes 'king' of the Zulus.

But what, conquests made, can idle warriors do to keep fit and
hard? Nandi dies. Did Chaka kill her or not? Mofolo says he
did. . . .

Retribution sets in. The alternative to dying in battle Chaka sees
as pining away in decrepit old age. He has refused to have children,
lest some turn on him. By his early forties he who was once loved
is friendless : in spite of his Regiment of Girls, his harem of 12,000
'sisters', he is unmarried with one non-legitimate son.

After Nandi – she who had always backed him but always coun-
selled mercy – is no more, Chaka's sanctions and moral equilibrium
are lost. His aim crumbles. Black melancholy overtakes him. For
hours he sits brooding. Nightmares haunt his sleep. He who has
committed foul deeds without number is now confronted by the
spirits of the most innocent among his victims.

Better than anyone Chaka knew his star had set. His vile attendants, Ndlebe and Malunga, disappear without a word. Isanusi claims
his reward. Chaka's half-brothers murder him.

Much will still be written about the contradictions and strange
quirks in Chaka's character. We do not know whether Mofolo had
read Marlowe. It is not very likely that he had. But he writes, as do
Abrahams, Achebe, Mphahlele, Nicol, and Ngugi, after him, as if
certain age-old ethics are common to most of mankind, almost as

eternal as time. It is not too high praise to call Mofolo's *Chaka* a novel of sufficient depth to remind readers here and there of Marlowe's *Dr Faustus*. A full and modern translation by an African of this romance of psychological subtlety is important to African literature.

SOLOMON T. PLAATJE   Like Thomas Mofolo, Solomon Plaatje was South African, was born towards the turn of this century, and is no longer alive. Plaatje's native tongue was Tswana, the chief language of Bechuanaland. He translated *Julius Caesar, A Comedy of Errors, The Merchant of Venice, Othello,* and *Much Ado About Nothing* into Tswana, and he published a political work, *Native Life in South Africa,* in 1916. Later he published a novel and *Sechuana Proverbs and their European Equivalents,* and *Bantu Folk-Tales and Poems.*

Plaatje was among the first South Africans to become aware of the need to rescue traditional stories and poetry before oblivion overtook them; he was also an early defender of the rights of the black South African against the rule of the Boer. Of his booklet, *The Mote and the Beam,* the sale of 18,000 copies of which financed Plaatje's trip to the U.S.A., the author wrote : 'It was a disquisition on a delicate social problem, known to Europeans in South Africa as the *Black Peril* and to the Bantu as the *White Peril.*'

Mhudi, of which three extracts are given in this Selection, was written before 1920; but it was not, for some reason, printed until 1930. Plaatje's preface to *Mhudi* begins : 'South African literature has hitherto been almost exclusively European, so that a foreword seems necessary to give reasons for a Native venture. . . . This book has been written with two objects in view, viz., (a) to interpret to the reading public one phase of "the back of the Native mind"; and (b) with the readers' money, to collect and print (for Bantu schools) Sechuana folk-tales, which, with the spread of European ideas, are fast being forgotten.'

If by 'interpreting' 'one phase of "the back of the Native mind" ' Plaatje meant that he would show his African characters as individuals with moral conflicts as complex as those of European characters, then he succeeds in his first aim. The back of the minds of his Barolongs, Matabeles, and Zulus, on life's principle of almost infinite variety within essential likeness, are curiously similar to the backs of European minds.

Mhudi is a story of love and battle, battle between Barolong and Zulu, and between Zulu and Boer helped by Barolong. Its scene is the Vaal river in the Orange Free State and the Southern Transvaal in the nineteenth century. Mhudi herself is a harvester girl, a

daughter of the Barolong people of Kunana. Chaka's general, the
Matabele Mzilikazi, who crossed the Drakensberg to found a kingdom for himself, sacked Kunana in retaliation for the killing of two
of his tax-gatherers. Gubuzu, capable, cunning lieutenant of
Mzilikazi's fierce Matabele, openly denounces the sack and burning
of Kunana as a cheap victory over defenceless people. Fleeing home-
less and far from her murdered people, Mhudi meets Ra-Thaga,
who has also escaped from Kunana. Though they did not previously
know each other, they love and marry in the peaceful country of
Chief Moroka. But Moroka agrees to help the Boer, Sarel Cilliers,
most of whose family group has been exterminated by the warlike
Zulu-Matabele, against the common enemy. Ra-Thaga is caught
up in the need to avenge his people and Mhudi's killed at Kunana.
He escapes death. He and his faithful Mhudi live to rear their
family.

As in Mofolo's *Chaka*, and later in Abrahams's *Wild Conquest*,
African characters, portrayed so often by European writers as savage
rulers, credulous idiots, faithful slaves, or rebel servants, are people.
They have free characteristics such as loyalty and good faith. Some
have mature minds. They also possess cowardice, vengefulness, lusti-
ness, cruelty, necessary – perhaps – to our human stock. Boer, representative of European civilization, is seen to be the owner, though
not the inventor, of a superior, deadly war-machine which re-
duces some Africans to temporary submission through terror.
Yet the 'back' of the Boer mind is no more brave, though it is
certainly more competently brutal, than the 'back of the Native
mind'.

Plaatje, Mr Mphahlele thinks, writes as politician and historian
rather than as novelist. True, Plaatje is less of a moralist than
Thomas Mofolo. Certainly, too, he writes as one of a people whose
inherited land was ravaged by both Zulu and Boer; and he who had
cause to be bitter writes without bitterness. Since his story is of
days 'one hundred years ago', days before money 'and without silver
watches', when 'abject poverty was practically unknown' among the
Barolong, his qualities as a historian come out. Like Mofolo, Plaatje
writes as a traditional tale-teller might have spoken : he intersperses
songs with his prose. His historical characters, Mzilikazi and Gubuzu,
may be less than life-size. But his chief fictional characters, because,
as Mr Mphahlele says, of Plaatje's compassion, live vividly. Plaatje's
heroines, Mhudi and Queen Umandi, may be more impressive than
his hero Ra-Thaga; certainly they are more impressive than
Mzilikazi. Like the mention of Chaka, the memory of Mzilikazi
excites feelings of heroic patriotism in the breast of every South
African Negro. But the figures of womanly gentleness, in Mofolo's

Nandi, mother of Chaka, and in the girl Noliwe whom Chaka is believed to have murdered, as well as in Plaatje's Mhudi and Umnandi the Queen, are all symbols with whom most readers out of any culture might discover sympathy.

Present-Day South African Writers

PETER ABRAHAMS Born in 1919, he was the first South African Negro to publish a novel after Plaatje's Mhudi of 1930. Abrahams began with a collection of short stories entitled Dark Testament. Then came his novels, Song of a City, Mine Boy, The Path of Thunder (1948), and Wild Conquest (1951). But by the later 1940s he had left South Africa for good. His novels were written in England, though all make use of the Africa of his early experiences. In 1954, he wrote an autobiography. This, Tell Freedom, reveals the physical urban poverty offset by love, thrift, and care, amid the racial oppression and intolerable injustice of a childhood in Johannesburg : Abrahams now lives in Jamaica.

His novel Wild Conquest takes up Plaatje's story of the empire-seeking Mzilikazi, his generals Gubuzu and Dabula, and his witch-doctor, Mkomozi. It continues at a point where Boer trekkers clash with Matabele who have fled disrupted to the north. Some African criticism suggests that Abrahams has 'bent history to his will' : he has blown historical characters out of their time-setting by giving them impulses and attributes that are acceptable to Western sophisticates rather than to African readers : he has tried – fair enough – to correct the Rider Haggard tradition of the blood-thirsty Gagool. (Gagool is a quite incredible creation to adult readers, incidentally.) Maybe, Abrahams does fail to control the character of his Mkomozi : he makes Mkomozi too knowing of all the moral answers, too good to be true. Yet Wild Conquest was acclaimed by English critics. C. P. Snow found it 'movingly full of restraint', possibly the 'forerunner of an entire school of African literary art'.

Thus Abrahams's autobiographical Tell Freedom was well received in Britain in 1954. It deserves to be. Abrahams is anglicized. But in this book he 'pulls no punches'; his Johannesburg working people, some industrious, some slatternly, show social snobberies similar to those of the working-class in Britain. They have the same warm, neighbourly kindness. Desire to go one better than the next man, 'status-seeking' in the American term, cannot be laid at the door of any Boerish herrenvolk theory, as Ezekiel Mphahlele implies it can in The African Image : desire to improve and a sharp need to compare ourselves with others or to contrast neighbour with neighbour, is deep in us all for good and ill. Abrahams accepts this. His overall concept of human nature in *Tell Freedom* is generously wide. His article 'The Blacks' in *African Treasury* is the most perceptive I know on those contradiction-riddled characters, Kenyatta and Nkrumah.

Abrahams's latest novel *A Wreath for Udomo*, 1956, has importance for African readers in that it is concerned with political conflict in a state called 'Panafrica'. The dictator Udomo's logic, when he betrays a friend for political motives, may alienate some readers' sympathy : such logic does seem to be overmuch condoned by the author; and Abrahams will certainly make African readers think about what forces in their land are embroiled in politics, economics, and in progress.

But Abrahams's use of English in his best work, *Tell Freedom*, has that simplicity that is like a blood transfusion to an old English language tired, but only occasionally dulled, by time.

EZEKIEL MPHAHLELE   Creative writer, Africanist, and critic, for some years Ezekiel Mphahlele was a tutor in the Extra-Mural Department of one of the University Colleges of Nigeria. At the present time he runs a Writers' Club in Nairobi. As did Abrahams and others, Mphahlele fled from his native South Africa when a second awakening among Bantu and South African writers began to be shackled by more and more deadly government restrictions. After years vainly seeking to adjust to exile in Nigeria he left for East Africa.

In 1957 Ezekiel Mphahlele published *Down Second Avenue*. This is the story of his mother's move from a bad husband, the village, and the tribe, to the crowded black ghetto in the back streets of Pretoria. His childhood's impressionable years and his young manhood were spent there, and his education was obtained with great sacrifice on his mother's part and with difficulty on his own.

Mphahlele's method with English in his story is to mix a stark and candid realism that now and then drops deliberately into the squalid or the startlingly banal with passages of idealism and involuntary beauty. This exquisite perception of the two poles of life is Mr Mphahlele's contribution to African prose.

As a critic of Black African literature he holds perhaps the first place. As a critic of White African literature he offers a much needed balance to white criticism. His book *The African Image* is important because of these two aspects. Particularly useful are the chapters in which the author is concerned with the white man's image of the non-white and the black man's literary image of himself. 'English fiction in South Africa,' Mr Mphahlele writes, is obsessed with race-relations . . . so character counts for little or nothing . . . in broader human perspective. . . . Deep under these layers of emotive interpretation and colour distinctions you will realize that human beings are basically the same. This is a platitude, but I must risk raising a yawn in order to drive this point home.

The African Image is not entirely a book of literary criticism; it contains affectionately astringent impressions, such as the following, of his visit to Britain in 1959 :

During that drive I was trying to organize every part of me so as to recognize the thrill of being in a place that had for years been a distant dream, a thought that was written with smoke across the sky and was swallowed up by the blue. Dickensian images that had piled up in my mind began to make sense.

Jenny, Sylvester's wife, stood at the gate to welcome me. Suddenly she drew her husband to one side. Something was wrong. I was apprehensive for them. Sylvester disappeared, with a tragic look on his face. Another tense moment. . . .

'What's wrong?' I asked lightheartedly.

'Felicity's dog's lost,' said Jenny, and I saw part of the profile of despair in her slightly drooping attitude.

'I don't know how to tell her. . . . She'll break down. . . . It'll just kill the poor thing.'

I couldn't work myself up into a state over the dog, not even on behalf of friends. Funny these people are, I thought, not without a feeling of ungrateful impatience. If it isn't dogs, it's cats, it's parrots, or canaries, it's monkeys, it's rabbits, and then it's . . . dogs.

I thought of South African pets on which whites lavish heaps of love, but I refused to believe that dogs were treated better than human beings here too.

Recently – in 1964 – and jointly with Ellis Ayitey Komey of Ghana – Ezekiel Mphahlele edited *Modern African Stories*. This is a valuable collection, its value lying in its variety and representativeness. To mention some of its authors here will therefore be worthwhile, though their work will be further discussed in Chapters 5 and 6, where some belong. There are stories by Can Themba and Alex La Guma of South Africa, by William Conton and Abioseh Nicol of Sierra Leone, by James Ngugi of Kenya, and by Cyprian Ekwensi, Gabriel Okara, Chinua Achebe, and Amos Tutuola all of Nigeria. There is work by writers not yet so well known as these – by Christiana Aidoo and Ado Bedwei, both of Ghana, Sarif Easmon of Sierra Leone, James Matthews of South Africa, Grace Ogot of Kenya, and others.

Four characteristics stand out from amongst this rich variety of writers and styles. The first of these characteristics we may call, for want of a better term, 'Africanness'. Ezekiel Mphahlele has suggested that African written literature came as a response to the white man's intervention. Thus, by Africanness is meant a centrality, an assurance in each writer that he or she has something new and therefore interesting or important to convey. There is nothing marginal or peripheral about any of the writing collected here by Ezekiel Mphahlele and Ellis Komey.

A second characteristic is the lighthearted laughter, or humour, that has come to be associated with African writing. In most of his creative writing, as we have seen, Mphahlele unites down-to-earth laughter with delicacy. These become the tender mockery seen in this collection in his 'Grieg on a Stolen Piano'. Ellis Komey's story, 'I can Face You', has a detached derision that is very effective. Peter Buahin, in 'This is Experience Speaking', decorates his English with apparent ease into an amazingly individual, almost exotically humorous, prose style. But Ato Bedwei's humour was not explanatory enough in interpreting tribal superstitions – or at least so it seemed to one white reader – in his 'Me and the Fish God'.

Delicacy, the third characteristic observable in this collection, is also seen in the women writers, Christiana Aidoo and Grace Ogot, in their stories 'Cut Me a Drink' and 'The Rain Came'. Sarif Easmon's 'Koya' has this quality too.

The fourth most noticeable element in these stories is delineation of violence. It would be too facile for white readers and white critics to praise humour, or delicacy, above this depicting of violence or savagery. Most preferences in literary criticism have their roots in cultural evolution and individual experience. Knowledge of the influence of both these on his own mind often escapes the critic. Scholarliness, that is, can never ensure complete detachment. Ezekiel Mphahlele, aware of the violence both in tribalism and in those of us who must for ever be responsible for the savagery of Hiroshima and Nagasaki, has no use for what he calls 'romanticizing' the African. In this collection William Conton's 'The Blood in the Washbasin', James Ngugi's 'A Meeting in the Dark', James Matthew's 'The Second Coming', Alex La Guma's 'Coffee for the Road', and Can Themba's 'The Dube Train', are all concerned with that portrayal of savagery that is so necessary to art because savagery is part of life.

But dealing with any character's tendency to violence or cruelty means that some preparation for his capacity for unrestraint must be there to precede any climax of action. There is no such previous preparation of the reader in William Conton's story of a black skipper whose overwrought nerves made him drive his passenger-laden vessel full speed against Freetown quay. As a result the story's end does not 'ring true'. Readers are left, horrified, bewildered, but disbelieving. A similar discrepancy in character portrayal leaves us sceptical and unmoved when an educated young man kills his pregnant girl at the close of Ngugi's story.

Furthermore, the most telling way of depicting violence is always by the barest words that are almost always understatement. Here Mr Mphahlele's countrymen, the South African writers, score in this collection. As if the undercurrents of human cruelty in their actual situations could ensure unforced treatment of such bleakness, Can Themba, Alex La Guma, and James Matthews have all contributed movingly successful stories to this volume. All who are interested in African writing should not miss *Modern African Stories*.

It is to be hoped Ezekiel Mphahlele's voice from East Africa, where writing is not a cry choked from throats by immediate tyranny, will be frequently heard for the next decade or two.

A. C. JORDAN   The two earlier writers, both South Africans, both twentieth century, Thomas Mofolo and Solomon Plaatje, were provoked to creative protest by the 1913 Land Act which made all black South African farmers tenants of white farmers. Dr A. C. Jordan belongs to the second group of writers, all Bantu South Africans, of which Peter Abrahams and Ezekiel Mphahlele are the best known. Of these three Dr A. C. Jordan stayed longest in South Africa. He lectured (1964) in African studies in the University of Cape Town, but is now in Wisconsin.

So far I have been unable to glimpse a copy of Dr Jordan's novel *The Wrath of the Ancestors*. It was written as *Ingqumbo Yeminyanya* originally in Xhosa, one of the Bantu languages; but it was also translated into English. The British Museum can find no trace of the English version.

The Wrath of the Ancestors has as its theme the marriage of two Mission schoolmates and their return to the tribe of which the young man was the hereditary chief. The wife is driven mad because her Christianized ways seem to flout the sacred traditions of the tribe and the tribe persecute her. Ezekiel Mphahlele comments that now there is no hereditary chiefdom left in South Africa and, therefore, Jordan's plot may have little present relevance. But there are inherited chiefdoms in other parts of Africa, and the inherited situation is one that has occurred in the past and will continue to occur, though in changed environments. Jordan's plot may be compared, as Mr Mphahlele does compare it, with the young Nigerian Chinua Achebe's plot of conflict between old and new ways and customs

in *Things Fall Apart* (1958). *The Wrath of the Ancestors* may also
be compared and contrasted with the white South African Dan
Jacobson's *The Evidence of Love*. Jacobson, who also fled the vicious
political climate of South Africa, outlines with a modern, unemo-
tional percipience that is very convincing, the union of a coloured
South African and a white woman. These two return to their home-
land, and they are left at the end of the book 'guilty', facing prison for
their law-breaking love. The fact that books such as Jacobson's
(1959), and Chinua Achebe's, were written twenty years after
Jordan's, and that Achebe has written no less than three on the
same subject of individual and social conflict, goes a little way to
make the point that such plots are dateless. They may always have
relevance because such conflict will not depart from us. Certainly
they will be part of Africa's substance for novels for some time to
come.

And A. C. Jordan's 'Xhosa classic' needs a place among free England's printed books.

Present-Day South African Prose and Poetry

There are other South African writings that should be made available : such are R. R. R. Dhlomo's Zulu novel, *An African Tragedy*,
and Samuel Yosia Ntara's *Headman's Enterprise*. Both belong to the
1930s.

H. I. E. DHLOMO   Of poetry of the 'thirties and 'forties, the Zulu
poet, H. I. E. Dhlomo, published a long poem 'The Valley of a
Thousand Hills' in 1941, but it is now unobtainable. The valley in
question contains some of the most magnificent scenery in Natal
province. Dhlomo's poem, inspired by Keats, Byron, and Shelley, is a
struggle to understand himself as an individual. It wrestles with the
mysteries of the self, of joy, beauty, power, greed, and wrong done
to a proud people :

> . . . Our God or Devil is the feeling Self,
> Catastrophe or life the self-same Self. . . .
>
> Where joys of life drip hot with pain;
> Where but to live is sacrifice. . . .
>
> A fog of tribulation spreads,
> Engulfs and robes the wrong-torn land. . . .
>
> Midst these sweet hills and dales, under these stars,
> To live and to be free, my fathers fought.
> Must I still fight and bear anew the scars? . . .

B. W. VILAKAZI[1] Poet and scholar of Natal, Vilakazi wrote 'In the Gold Mines' which was translated by Dr A. C. Jordan in *Africa South*. Vilakazi's poem is a forcible reminder of how much South Africa's present travail has in common with the sufferings of British poor under industrial landlordism in the early nineteenth century. Vilakazi's language is reminiscent, though perhaps only coincidentally, of Tom Hood's 'Song of a Shirt'.

The twenty years since Dhlomo published 'The Valley of a Thousand Hills' have seen the climate for writers in South Africa grow more and more harsh. Since the appearance of *Drum* magazine in 1950 there has arisen a number of young writers who have created a modern, urban, journalistic style that leans a little hard on what can only be called commercial-formulae emotions and American export-film language. Since the estrangement of the Mission presses, many Black South African writers have had to depend on being printed in weeklies that have a large, exclusively non-white readership. Is it stark, cold necessity, one hardly dares to wonder, that drives some of them to borrow so from American writing in which the depicting of violence and use of slang and cynicism lose what impact they may have by being overdone? Yet some short stories by other members of what we must call this virile culture that will not be silenced often show a cryptic economy that may be a weapon of self-defence. This is also a far more effective yard-stick in any artistic medium than commercial borrowing.

Among this group of younger, Black South African writers are Can Themba, Richard Rive, Dyke Sentso, Casey Motsisi, Alex La Guma, Bloke Modisane, Tod Matshikiza, Arthur Maimane, Alfred Hutchinson, and Lewis Nkosi. Only the first five of these have remained in South Africa.

ALEX LA GUMA His short story, 'Out of Darkness', like his novel, *A Walk in the Night,* is excellent in its economy of style and balance of perceptive outlook. La Guma was one of the 156 South Africans charged with high treason. La Guma's second novel, *And a Threefold Cord* (1965), was written when he was under house-arrest in 1963 in Cape Town. It is an account of the degradation of human life under Apartheid in that town; it cannot be read without provocation of a reader's respect for the novelist's protest against such conditions. It has not been possible to find out even the dates of birth of those writers who are still in South Africa.

BLOKE MODISANE His *Blame Me On History* was published in England in 1964. This bears marks of that 'corrosion of fibre' among

---

[1] As spelt in *The African Image.*

those who endure in South Africa, that Ezekiel Mphahlele talks about. Modisane's satirical story 'The Dignity of Begging' free of this corrosion, is therefore better work. But Modisane has written : 'I knew I had to run, or lose . . . even my sanity. . . . I felt the relentless inevitability of the clash, the direct immediacy of blood'. He reached England in 1959.

ARTHUR MAIMANE   fled in 1958 and is a journalist in Accra.

TOD MATSHIKIZA   composer of the music of the jazz opera, *King Kong,* lives now in Britain. He left South Africa in 1960.

ALFRED HUTCHINSON   Also in the first treason trial, his situation was made worse by the fact that he was in love with a white woman and therefore no life for them was possible in South Africa. He jumped bail and managed to escape by way of Zambia (then Northern Rhodesia), Malawi (then Nyasaland), Tanganyika, and Ghana – to Britain, where he now is. Hutchinson related his experiences and his meeting with friends, enemies, and political leaders, in *Road to Ghana.* Doris Lessing has described this book as 'a record of brutality and stupidity' and 'also one of the most exciting and moving adventure stories'. It is Alfred Hutchinson's almost lyrical gaiety that is so misleading. You would not think he was running for his life. He made an eventual escape from Dar-es-Salaam jail because a telegram arrived telling him that Christian Action would pay his fare 'to country of choice'. *Road to Ghana* is an inspiring book because it is valiant and happy and entirely without rancour.

LEWIS NKOSI   The last mentioned in the above list, Lewis Nkosi, is a young South African journalist and critic who also now lives in London. Recently he has put out a play, *The Rhythm of Violence* (1964). The modern currency in treatment of theme may invite comparison with plays such as John Arden's *Sergeant Musgrove's Dance.* The scene of Nkosi's play is Johannesburg by night. The first of the three acts gives an exhibition of the coarse brutality of Boer police. This kind of scene will be familiar to those who have read Alex La Guma's *A Walk in the Night.* This time the crudities are towards a seventeen-year-old student, Tula Zulu, who is naïvely trying to deliver tracts against Apartheid at the police station. Nkosi's second act depicts an inter-racial, rather drunken, students' party. The party is held in the basement room of an English student, Mary, whilst they all, nerves on edge, wait for the bomb they have arranged to blow up the City Hall full of Africaaners, to go off at midnight. Among the students is the elder brother of Tula, Gama.

One day Gama will become the Bantu leader. He has all the typical qualities of a soldier or a politican whose aim, to the exclusion of all other considerations, is the destruction of his enemy.

There is also an Africaans girl, Sarie, at the party. Tula and Sarie talk. They like each other. Sarie discloses that her kind and gentle father has gone to the City Hall to give in his resignation to the Apartheid party. Tula slips secretly out to warn him. He is blown up, along with Sarie's father and the other Africaaners at the meeting.

The final scene is of Sarie mourning over the body of Tula – a little hurriedly forgetting her father, it might seem – under the cruelly gloating eyes of the two Boer police. But the play's dictum is clear : the more innocent and young among men and women nearly always suffer first.

Most British readers of Lewis Nkosi's play will not fail in a certain sympathy. They cannot withhold this because in the depths of our minds lives the centuries-old memory of Britain's having been conquered again and again by the superior weapons of foreigners – Roman, Saxon, Dane, and Norman. Human memories are as long as this, however fleeting they may sometimes appear to be.

Nkosi's play contains some effective and thoughtful dialogue. It sacrifices its lastingness as a play by making use of modern stereotypes instead of characters. It bows to box-office dictates rather than gives itself to the patient, original exploring of individual human minds. It might almost have been written by an American or an Englishman. I hope the above criticisms do not convey an impression of frothy theorizing on the delineation of a situation of agony. Out of the deep urgency of Nkosi's theme his play will no doubt be played frequently in the next few years; and it will do its work, not letting us forget – if there were the least danger of our forgetting – how South Africa still suffers.

NONI JABAVU   Noni Jabavu is the only woman writing among the Xhosa people of the East Cape Province of South Africa. Of a well-to-do, intellectual family, she was educated in England and is married to one of the Cadburys. Her two books are *Drawn in Colour* (1960) and *The Ochre People* (1963). What is remarkable about both these is the author's command of an English that conveys with such exactitude those nuances of emotion that lie below actions and words. Training in personal relationships among members of tribal families still forms part of many Africans' education. Noni Jabavu's first book is about a visit to her sister in Uganda. Her second book is about a return home to her Xhosa people. No doubt Noni

Jabavu is much anglicized; but that is not why her exploring of
personal and family loves, preferences, dislikes, and tragic alien-
ations, is at once so illuminating and so familiar to English readers.
The reason for the familiarity of the psychological penetration lies
in a correspondence (within great differences, of course) between
Xhosa family patterns and British family individualisms. Mrs
Cadbury writes an admirably supple, though not at all simple,
English. It is an English that relegates psychological jargon to the
unnecessary element it is.

DENNIS BRUTUS   There are not many South African poets. Dennis
Brutus is the best known. He is still young – born in the 'thirties :
but he has published one book. This is *Sirens, Knuckles, Boots*
(Mbari, Ibadan, 1963). The thirty-three poems of *Sirens, Knuckles,
Boots* have a directness and an urgent intensity joined with a resilience that cannot but command admiration. Such a combination
is partly the result of suffering known to be shared by many, not
isolated. The poems come, in fact, straight out of war :

> The sounds begin again;
> the siren in the night
> the thunder at the door
> the shriek of nerves in pain.
>
> Then the keening crescendo
> of faces split by pain
> the wordless endless wail
> none but the unfree know.
>
> Importunate as rain
> the wraiths exhale their woe
> over the sirens, knuckles, boots;
> my sounds begin again.

In this 5s. volume Dennis Brutus tells what he feels may need to
be known of his wartime condition :

> . . . Banned from all gatherings for five years in October 1961, and
> also dismissed from a Government High School in Port Elizabeth
> where I taught English (and some Afrikaans) for the past ten
> years. Banned this year from teaching in a private school. Banned
> and gagged by the Minister of Justice, so that no words of mine
> can be quoted or printed. This is maybe why I have now thought
> of getting my work published. . . .
> A coloured myself – mixed descent – with a family from whom
> I am separated, as they are in Port Elizabeth. . . . I must warn
> you that on practical details you will probably find me as dithery

as poets are traditionally supposed to be. The business side of this thing [*Sirens, Knuckles, Boots*] is not my business (money must in any case go to my wife, May), but I would like to say that my preference would be for a cheap thing which people could easily buy if they wished. . . . Time may be running out at this end : house arrest looms, and it is never sure how much rope (!) one has. It may be more difficult for me to keep in touch in future. . . .

The critic Ulli Beier has described Dennis Brutus's poetry as 'transfigured by a quiet fortitude'. His situation seems scarcely tolerable. The two of Dennis Brutus's poems given in the Anthology, 'Sabotage, 1962', and 'Somehow we survive', illustrate his fortitude. They are also poems that can stand apart from their author and his circumstances as good poems in their own right : and, we hope, as heralds of more.

Chapter 4

AFRICAN–FRENCH WRITING

African-French Prose and Poetry and English Translation of their work – The Négritude Poets in English Translation

African-French Prose

CAMARA LAYE   M. Laye has been an internationally known writer since the publication of his autobiographical *L'Enfant Noir*, in 1955, and its translation the next year into English as *The Dark Child* by the English poet James Kirkup.

Camara Laye was born in ancient Kouroussa at the head of the Niger in Upper Guinea about 1924. Guinea was then under French influence; but in spite of the French having *assimilation* as a direct aim, African country life away from towns was then little touched. Laye's father, as metal worker, was a smith who made ornaments in precious gold. *The Dark Child* tells of Laye's childhood, of his going to school at Konakry, Guinea's Atlantic port and capital, and then of inevitable separation from devoted parents for practical apprenticeship in a Paris car-factory. He lived in Paris many years and is now at the Institut des Recherches, Conatry.

What is at once apparent about *The Dark Child* is the limpid transparence of its style closely bound with a candid simplicity of content. Utterly different is Kirkup-Laye English from that of Noni Jabavu. Perhaps the two elements, transparency of style and simplicity of content are one and the same; in Laye both enclose a compassionate respect for the most ordinary people and the simplest objects in a daily life whose kind is now said – with what accuracy remains to be seen – to be passing for good. This evocative immediacy of *The Dark Child* will remind those readers who know John Clare of that English lyric poet's autobiography in which Clare evoked a way of early nineteenth-century English village life that under a period of agricultural revolution did vanish. In *The Dark Child* there is not the least hint of resentment at what Russians call 'imperialist interference' and Americans call 'colonialism'. No foreign power might have been hovering over Laye's Kouroussa childhood for all the direct reference he gives to it. His people, particularly his father, mother, and the girl Marie with whom he had his first love-affair, are of any culture, almost of any time

56

and place. The essence of their common humanity is what fills the book.

Perhaps any translator of *L'Enfant Noir* might have had a more straightforward task rendering Laye's delicate prose with its clear yet obviously conscious artistry than – say – a translator of Mongo Beti – whom we shall consider next. But whatever the difficulties and risks of translation, *The Dark Child* in James Kirkup's sensitive gloss must be one of the beautiful books of the 1950s.

An artist such as Laye is does not repeat himself. Laye's second book is a symbolic story. This is in English translation as *The Radiance of the King*. It appeared only a year after *The Dark Child*, in 1956, and it is also rendered by James Kirkup. The same lucent language is there. But this time it recounts the search of the fictitious Clarence – a white man newly come to Africa but turned out of his white hotel when he has gambled all his money away – for the King he believes can give him peaceful work. Such self-lost serenity is what Clarence, harried by time, money, and his own weaknesses, craves.

Camara Laye's candid immediacy has, in *The Radiance of the King*, been put to symbolic service. But symbolic of what? The cover-description of the book suggests that the story is an allegory of man's search for God. This may be true; but if so, the search of the white man for God is seen by an African interpreter of book and author as 'through a self-abasement . . . out of a misplaced European sense of sin and shame.'[1]

Certainly Clarence is humbled and shamed continually by his series of adventures. Sometimes these experiences are mysteriously dream-like, sometimes harrowing, sometimes lunatic. They are accompanied by nightmare changes of scene. These scene-changes bring to mind a comparison of the book with Franz Kafka's *The Trial*; but only in the matter of scenic atmosphere. *The Radiance of the King* is in no way sombre as Kafka's book is sombre. On the contrary, Laye lights his book with typically African humour, so that it resounds with uproarious African laughter. Yet through both these Laye conveys a sense of deeply serious intention.

Clarence falls foul of a black judge but escapes from him; he sleeps, without really being aware of his lust, with innumerable black women; he has a faithful black mistress; he is befriended by a black eunuch; he is helped – and tricked – by a black beggar, and he is loyally aided – in their fashion – by two irrepressible black boys. But when finally he meets the King – a brown boy-king who folds him in his radiant arms and whose great mantle 'enveloped

[1] Ezekiel Mphahlele in a paper read at the First International Conference of Africanists, 'African Literature', December 1962.

him for ever' – is Clarence meant to be seen as safe for good? Or is
he only beyond help of any human kind through his over-eating,
over-drinking, and his sensuality among white and black companions?

The author of *Muntu. An Outline of Neo-African Culture*,
Janheinz Jahn, has commented[1] of *The Radiance of the King* that
surely Laye is putting forward the concept that the white man must
eventually be able to allow himself to learn from as well as to teach
the black man. Gerald Moore suggests more broadly that the interpretation of Laye's symbolism 'occupies the mind in such a
way that new perceptions keep rising to its surface when the reading
is over'.[2]

Confining the whole of any creative writer's symbolism in plainer
words is probably neither possible nor would it be very fruitful
could it be done. Perhaps Laye is wrestling to present one aspect
of the huge problem that is at present occupying so many African
writers – Mphahlele himself, Abrahams, Okara, Abioseh Nicol – the
problem the young Nigerian novelist, Chinua Achebe, seeks to present realistically : this problem concerns us all. It has to do with a
vision of wisdom both white men and black men have been fumbling
towards separately for centuries in their vastly different approaches;
but both so far are hardly more than aware of the vision. In this
modern age, when wider meanings are vainly sought for by so
many, Laye may be implying that peace, in so far as it means a
serenity of knowledge, is not realizable on earth.

Eight years have passed since the publication of *The Radiance of
the King*. Incapable of repeating himself, what else will Camara
Laye produce? So far he has published only the short story, 'The
Eyes of the Statue'.[3] This is about human loneliness. It tells of a
woman who comes to a crumbled city where, in the ruins, an aged
caretaker unearths for her among the weeds a statue of a once-
glorious monarch. 'The Eyes of the Statue' reads like a first sketch
for a novel rather than a short story. It is translated by Una Mac-
Lean :

> – . . . Don't imagine that others are any less alone. But who wants
> to admit that? All the same, it is not an unendurable state of
> affairs; it is quite bearable in fact. Solitude. . . . Listen, solitude
> isn't what you imagine. I don't want to run away from my soli-
> tude; it is the last desirable thing left me, it is my only wealth, a
> great treasure, of ultimate value.

[1] *Black Orpheus*, No. 6, p. 35.
[2] *Seven African Writers*, p. 38.
[3] *Black Orpheus*, No. 5, pp. 19-27.

'Is he just saying that to comfort me,' she wondered. 'But it is no consolation, a shared solitude can be no consolation. The sharing only makes the solitude doubly lonely.'

Aloud she said, That doesn't console me in the least.

– I didn't think it would, he replied. They had by now reached the foot of the staircase and the old man showed her the little corridor leading to his room.

– My lodge is here.

– Yes, I know, she said. You told me already.

– But I haven't told you everything : I didn't say that my room is right beneath the staircase. When visitors used to climb up there in throngs they were walking over my lodge. Do you understand?

– Yes.

– No, you don't understand at all, you don't realize that they were marching on my head, wiping their feet on my hair. I had plenty of hair in those days.

– But they weren't really wiping their feet, she said; they. . . .

– Don't you think it was humiliating enough anyway?

She did not know how to reply. The old man seemed slightly crazed : some of what he said was very sensible but a lot of it was sheer nonsense. 'The solitude has gone to his head,' she told herself, and she looked at him afresh. He was certainly very old. There must be times when age and loneliness together. . . . Aloud she remarked

– I don't know. And then, all of a sudden,

– What made you say that solitude is an ultimate good?

– How very young you are, was his only reply, you should never have come here. . . .

MONGO BETI   Paris-educated Mongo Beti of the Cameroun Republic changed his pen-name from Eza Bote when he wanted to repudiate the faults he saw in his first novel *Ville Cruelle*, of 1954. Though Beti is now only thirty-three, he has written three other novels. Two of these, *Mission Terminée* (1957), is translated into English as *Mission to Kala* and *Le Roi Miraculé* (1958), as *King Lazarus*, both by Peter Green.

Beti's brilliant irony and his exuberant yet corrosive humour flood the most solemn problems but leave Beti's penetrating criticism of human self-ignorance more devastating than that of any other African writer. This is the characteristic which sets Beti apart. His laughter-provoking skill is used entirely in showing up all his characters' self-deceptions. He satirizes such monumental matters as white missions, modern sociology, colonial rule, the Catholic Church, white administration, but not less does he ridicule tribal ways, village morality, reverence for elders, and reverence for the past. Satire like Beti's may not be always palatable, either to Africans or to Europeans. But we must take it if only because flight before the sensitive swing of its balance would be useless even if possible.

The lapse of Beti's first novel, *Ville Cruelle*, was into cheap over-writing – a mistake due to an over-energetic talent in a young writer. Beti's second novel, *Le Pauvre Christ de Bomba* 'adds up', Gerald Moore writes in his account of Beti's work in *Seven African Writers*: 'to a radical and final rejection of White missionary activity in Africa, at least as practised within a White colonial order.' This point of view, Mr Moore adds, 'is driven home with great force, ironic skill, and insight.' But the novel is long and repetitive.

Mission to Kala shows a complete change in Beti's writing in respect of economy. It is a story of hilarious comedy, speed, and sensuous relish. It has probably an auto-biographical basis, as Beti seems to imply at the book's close.

King Lazarus is much the best constructed of Beti's novels so far. His writing is still dazzlingly funny and his light-hearted perceptions of character are full of brilliant strokes of wit and irony. This third book is about the break-up of a Catholic mission in the Bantu clan of Essazam in 1948. The well-loved Chief, pagan husband of twenty-three wives, is mysteriously and slowly dying. Bush relatives of all the wives have swelled the village's population and are now patiently waiting the inevitable. But the Chief's aged aunt, with a convert's fervour, suddenly rushes into the death-chamber and pours jug after jug of cold water over the helpless invalid; from which moment the ageing Chief begins miraculously to recover.

Le Guen the missionary seizes on the wonder of the Chief's return from death to persuade him – successfully – to become Christian. He re-names him Lazarus. And at once the Chief sends out messages that he will keep only one wife, the youngest and most attractive of his twenty-three women; she shall be his 'lawful' Christian wife.

Quite naturally his action causes tremendous confusion, plots, and finally uproar, among the relatives of the rejected wives and among the women themselves whose whole lives have been centred in the village. Fighting breaks out between the clans of the cast-offs and the relatives of the chosen. Trying to make peace, the missionary Le Guen gets trounced by both parties. He retires to bed insisting that they hurt him only because they didn't recognize him. The French Military are called in by his fellow priest; but by the time Monsieur le Chef de la région and his soldiery arrive, the Chief himself has restored order. 'King Lazarus' returns to his old ways with all his wives happily reinstated; the missionary, accused by the political administrator of having been the cause of all the trouble, is sent away by the foreign government. Difficult Essazam, backward or decadent already, is once more left to itself.

Mongo Beti's piercing, individualistic candour about both African and European character and equally bizarre ways and habits is no doubt one of his strengths. Possibly this may verge on cynicism in some readers' estimation. Beti's way of writing is what can only be called very 'French' from an English point of view. Peter Green's translation of *King Lazarus* successfully reproduces the swift narrative and translates the French slang into an English counterpart. Whether the French faithfully reproduces Cameroun or Bantu slang the average British reader could not know. This doubt occupies the mind throughout enjoyment of a rumbustious novel. Such doubt brings back, of course, the whole problem of translating the language of one culture into the language of another.

No extracts from Beti are given in the Anthology. But here follow three short passages to give the tone or 'flavour' of *King Lazarus*. The first passage is a clash of words between Chris, who belongs to the new generation of school-educated Cameroun boys, and Raphael who got 'glory' as the 'hero of Kufra' by fighting for the Europeans in the 1939-45 War. As so often in Beti's writing, the satire is on at least two levels : the first passage, besides being a quarrel, is a probe into 'civilized' estimates of war-valour and into civilized estimates of prowess with machines. Counterpointing these is the probe into an educated generation's concept of 'natural' man's bravery, and the advance of that generation beyond superstition. Middle-aged Raphael stands for the civilized estimate of war-valour and of prowess with machines. Chris in his talk and his dealings with the snake stands for the outlook of the educated, younger generation :

'What the hell? Can't you hear me?' roared Raphael. 'If I hadn't come out yesterday and repaired your stinking truck, you wouldn't be sitting there like a toffee-nose now! The ingratitude of it! You fancy yourself, don't you? Think you're quite something. Well, you're wrong. Want to know what you really are? I'll tell you. You're just shit, brother.'

On this climax he hawked horribly and spat contempt. This achieved no reaction from Chris. The other was now nearly bursting with anger, under the cold and watchful eye of the snake. It had no intention of being off-guard during so crude a diversion.

Sitting slumped against the wall, Chris looked remote. Lots of locals were watching the Hero of Kufra, his contest no longer heroic but grotesque, attempting a two-fronted fight. Rubbernecks and no-good boys collected. They positioned themselves behind Raphael, not anywhere near the snake.

He rattled an incredible string of insults at Chris. Bored with the whole comedy, Chris consented to speak.

'Really, what a pathetic creature you are, Raphael! It's fantastic, really it is! Where on earth did you get the idea that it takes two to finish off a poor bloody little earthworm? You know, old man, it was hardly worth your while to go off and play the big shot at Kufra, if this is all the guts you've got when you come back!'

Chris abruptly rose, took up a large lump of hardened clay he had found outside and lobbed it accurately on to the snake's tiny head. The creature thrashed its tail two or three times and expired. This done, Chris gazed at Raphael with languishing appraisal, as though the Hero of Kufra were a pretty girl. Then he said : 'Oh, you poor little kid! Run home to Mummy and tell her to wash that horrible gob of yours. It *stinks*!'

A burst of jeering laughter broke from the spectators. . . .

Here is another passage between two educated boys, Chris and Bitama. Their conversation casts light – and shadow – on modern money-values and religious sincerity no less than on traditional integrity and African 'innocence' :

'Good God,' Bitama said, eyes widening. He had understood at last. 'Do you mean to say you're *distilling alcohol*?'

'Well, why shouldn't I ?'

With that they plunged into argument about drunkenness. Bitama claimed that Chris, by distilling strong liquor, was playing straight into the hands of the colonialists. Chris roared with laughter at this. He said he couldn't care less about the colonialists : all that interested him was making a little spot cash for Grigri and himself.

'Look, Bitama, you get dough from your father, right? Well, then, I suppose you wouldn't shell out a bit of it for me?'

'We haven't got all that much money,' Bitama said hastily. I mean, Dad drinks a hell of a lot, and – and – well, he's got three wives and ten kids : it does mount up rather.'

Chris whistled. 'What a family! There's three of us, with one girl and a half-wit Mum on the side. Come on, I've got to get cracking right away. Look, you know so bloody much about everything – tell me, what do you think of our bloody Pharaoh at the moment?'

'It appears,' said Bitama, his voice sceptical yet questioning, 'that he's been converted to Catholicism.'

'Conversion's a strong word in the circumstances. My aunt told me what really happened. They caught him at a moment when he was no longer capable of telling them what his opinions actually were.'

Bitama gave a sharp laugh. 'Nowadays Catholicism is nothing but a kind of baited nigger-trap.'

They began discussing the various elders. Bitama spoke endlessly in their praise, lauding their wisdom, courage and tradi-

tional skills, not to mention their tribal solidarity – all character-
istically Negro qualities, it appeared.

'It's not hard to see that *you* grew up in the city,' Chris remarked chaffingly. 'Do you really think all that much of the old
shags? You're a bit like Mama in some ways—'

'Oh yes? Half-witted, am I?'

'No, old chap. You know I didn't mean that. What I'm after
is this. Mama says one moment that we've to honour and venerate our eldest brother. This is what our ancestors have always
done. It worked very well for them. An instant later she's talking
about the Chief. Refers to him as a poligamous old swine. As
though poligamy weren't just as much a legacy from our ancestors! Can you honestly say there's any consistency of thought
in that kind of thing? Well, you're much the same yourself. You
call yourself a revolutionary. At the same time you're lost in
admiration for those crapulous old dotards representing the most
shameful, disgusting elements surviving from our history. Always
supposing we had a history. I don't know, myself. Anyway, I
don't give a damn.'

'You despise them, don't you?'

'Who, the old shags? No! I've never despised anyone in my
life. That doesn't stop me thinking sometimes they're lazy, greedy,
senile morons, nattering away aimlessly. They make a miserable
mess of anything they attempt. Take all these elders who've rolled
up lately. What are they here for? The Chief's ill. All right – and
then what? Must the whole world stand still because of that? . . .'

A third quotation shows some difference of opinion between the
political administrator and the missionary, Le Guen:

'I very much hope,' Lequeux said softly, 'I very much hope
you will be able to recognize and identify those insolent creatures
who had the unheard-of audacity to raise their filthy paws against
a Frenchman.'

'Listen to me,' Le Guen said, half-sitting up in bed and speaking quite calmly. 'Do not take that line, if you please, *Monsieur
le Chef de la région*. Here in Essazam, among provincials such
as myself, there are no such things as 'Frenchmen' or 'insolent
creatures'. There are only ourselves – that is, the Essazam—'

'Ah! Just so. The Essazam! And what then, pray? I've heard
a great deal about you, Father Le Guen. Even more of your beliefs and ideas, which seem to me – how shall I put it—'

'*Extravagant*, perhaps?' Le Guen suggested.

'With all due respect to your cloth, Father, yes. Extravagant
is exactly the word I had in mind. I have been working among
the Blacks even longer than you have. Do you catch *me* calling
myself an Essazam, or any nonsense of that sort?'

'That, *Monsieur le Chef de la région*, is your affair.'

'You are wrong, Father. I understand that in your profession

it is necessary to place oneself as far as possible on the same level as the natives. That's reasonable enough, I suppose. But to go on from there quite seriously to want to pass for a native yourself – that's extravagant, really extravagant. Listen, Father, the real truth of the matter is that you are a Frenchman above all else—'
    'If I might give you one piece of advice, *Monsieur le Chef de la région*, it would be this. Since you hold these opinions, leave us – and by us, I mean the Essazam – severely alone. . . .'

But it is when Mongo Beti introduces the taunting song of the favourite wife's sister, the girl Medzo, against King Lazarus's repudiated wives that the author of the present book felt the greatest discrepancy between the atmosphere of Medzo's chant and the whole of the rest of the translation of the book :

Medzo began to improvise. She was blissfully happy, floating in a haze, fresh from the discovery of her full womanhood. Fluently she threaded verse after verse together : her facility and relaxed grace aroused the admiration and astonishment of the whole circle. Medzo was attacking her sister's rivals. . . .

'O you who hear my words, sisters of mine.
Tell me sisters, what names can our tongue command
For women such as these, lizards with crooked claws,
Women who, though dishonoured, rejected and disowned,
Still hang around, still cling and grovel and beg?

. . .

O you who hear my words, dear sisters of mine,
To think how they cling and grovel, though they
                                have been disowned!
Ah weep for this miserable soul, most simple and
                                innocent!
Weep for him, worthy man, poor bird limed in the snare,
What plight is his, struggling, weeping, crying,
Calling on God, his mother, the ghosts of his
                                ancestors :
O you who hear my words, dear sisters, weep with him.
How will he ever free his limbs from the snare?
Weep and lament for him—'

The Ekameyong girls applauded wildly.

On the whole question of whether Mongo Beti intended whatever discrepancy there may be in atmosphere between Medzo's song and the rest of the novel, or whether Peter Green, perhaps deliberately, has not harmonized the atmosphere of the girl's chant with the rest of the modern slang, only an African reader, maybe only a reader from the Cameroun, can answer. It is an important question.

PRINCE MODUPE   This author of the autobiography *I Was a Savage* (1958), though born in French-dominated Guinea just before the turn of this century, needed no translator, since he writes in English. He is married to an American, and he has lived in the States for almost the past forty years.

He is the son of a Nigerian Yoruba trader and a daughter of the royal house of a Guinea tribe, the Sousou. He was brought up in the same region as that which Camara Laye so lovingly described in *L'Enfant Noir*; but Modupe's upbringing was twenty years earlier. Both writers left their native West Africa in search of education. At twenty Modupe fled secretly from his own people who would have kept their royal heir at all costs. He abandoned the chief-stool. Inspired by a black African missionary and helped by an American missionary, he escaped from 'bush' life for good. He tells of hair-raising adventures on the slopes of the Fouta Djalon, waiting for an elephant to die in order to cut out the tusks to pay his passage to the U.S.A.; he describes losing the brave girl who was his Sousou wife in the rapids of the Niger. He writes with an individual voice, romantic with nostalgia, of events remembered after a long time. If his story is true, and there seems no reason why it should not be true, Prince Modupe has added a chapter to a new adventure literature of the new Africa.

His most noteworthy chapters are the early ones on his childhood. In these he gives himself to recapturing the way of life, harmonious with nature, of a people who had seen no European. He describes for us the birth ceremony of 'tying' a child to the earth, the stern teaching of morals to the young; he recounts fascinating details of what Sousou boys were taught at puberty in the initiation rites known as the 'Bondo Bush'; he recalls the terrors of killing his first beast alone at thirteen.

His title, *I Was a Savage*, as Elspeth Huxley explains in a Foreword, is humorously ironic. Modupe does not really think his childhood was lived among 'savages'. He conveys to us what he is sure his upbringing was – dignified, decent, austere. As Mrs Huxley points out, tribalism did satisfy most of the basic instincts of men. That was its strength. Our own urbanized society often frustrates rather than satisfies. But all its strength could not annul the weakness of tribalism : as Mrs Huxley adds, its very harmony 'closed the circle to change'. And change may be as deeply necessary to man as stability.

c

The Négritude Poets

Any book about African literature, however short, would be almost valueless without illustration of the work of the movement of Négritude which concerns, chiefly, a group of poets writing in French. Léopold Sédar Senghor, poet-president of the Senegal Republic, born in 1906 of Christian parents at the coast town of Joal where his father was a dealer in groundnuts, is the leader of the movement.

Senghor's childhood was lived among farmers and fishermen, listening to the tales of ancient Africa. His intellect soon took him up the French-educational, and then the French-political ladder. He was made first president of the Independent Republic of Senegal in 1960. Senghor has produced the biggest body of poetry of any African poet so far. He has written five books of verse in French. *Chants d'Ombre* (1945), *Hosties Noires* (1948, 1956), *Chants pour Naett* (1949), and *Ethiopiques* (1956). He has also written critical works on the *Négritude* movement.

Senghor's poem 'The Dead', for 'Senegalese prisoners darkly stretched on the soil of France', breathes a deep parental protectiveness for the sons of Africa whose lives have been lost and personalities buried beneath 'foreign domination'. The music of his well-known 'Prayer to Masks' also shows this almost obsessive tenderness that encloses an equally extravagant ambition for black people : they will 'teach rhythm to the world that has died of machine and canons'. Neither of these two poems has been given in this Anthology. They can be tracked in the Bibliography. I have preferred to offer the less didactic, more beautiful, hardly less well known, 'In What Tempestuous Night' and the first section of 'New York'. These are translated into English by Gerald Moore and Ulli Beier; and the best account in English of Senghor and his work is by Gerald Moore in his study, *Seven African Writers*.

Chief among Senghor's fellow *Négritude* poets – other than Aimé Césaire and Léon Damas from the Caribbean – are Birago Diop and David Diop. Birago Diop, also born in 1906, at Dakar, the Senegal capital, has published both stories and poems in French, and has spent most of his life as a veterinary surgeon in Upper Volta. His publications include the prose *Les Contes d'Amadou Koumba* (1947), *Les Nouveaux Contes d'Amadou Koumba* (1958), and poems *Leurres et lueurs* (1960). From his small poetical output Birago Diop's delicately wrought poem 'Diptych' is given in the Anthology rather than his better known 'Viaticum'.

David Diop, born in 1927 at Bordeaux and killed in an air crash

in 1960, was of Senegal-Cameroun blood. He moved between West
Africa and France and was a voice of importance among *Négritude*
poets before his tragically earl ydeath. He published poems, *Coups
de pilon*, in 1956.

The critic and writer on African literature, Ulli Beier, has translated David Diop's 'The Renegate', 'Africa', 'The Vultures', and
'Your Presence' in *Black Orpheus*, No. 5. In this Anthology 'Africa'
has been chosen as most representative. Mr Beier writes truly, that
David Diop did not live to become a mature poet. His poems are
mystic, passionate utterances, full of youthful bitterness and hate
against both the White dominator and the African traitors who sub-
mit. David Diop's stridency may fail to persuade some readers.
Others may accept it and sympathize deeply with him, as in 'The
Vultures', against

> The bitter memories of extorted kisses
> Of promise broken at the point of a gun
> Of foreigners who did not seem human
> Who knew all the books but did not know love. . . .

Where quite opposing responses are possible, it is well that readers
decide for themselves.

Chapter 5

EAST AFRICA

Oral Poetry of an East African Tribe – Dobeit of the Shukria – Modern East African Prose and Poetry

Oral Poetry of an East African Tribe

Let us pass for a while from sophisticated literature of South Africa and French-speaking Guinea, Cameroun and Senegal, to one of the East African remote oral verse-traditions – that of the Shukria nomads of the Sudan to the east of the Blue Nile. That an oral literary tradition is in no strict sense primary, has already been explained : often such a tradition is the product of centuries of artistic usage in prose and verse.

Today, scattered over much of Africa, there are many rural tribes almost entirely cut off from town literacy and academic learning. Many a tribe's unwritten verse or prose may be little known beyond their pasture range or land boundary – though more and more is being explored and translated.

In expanse the Sudan Republic is the largest political unit of Africa. It is as big as Europe and it was the first to become independent. It lies south of Egypt, north of Congo, Uganda, and Kenya, west of Eritrea and Ethiopia, and east of Chad and the Central African Republics.

Endless-seeming desert and savannah are interspersed with river-side cotton-pump-schemes and gardens of orange, lemon, mango, and pineapple. The desert and these paradisal gardens of the north Sudan are cut off by acre upon acre of *sudd* or swamp, from the rich, mountainous forests in the south of the Republic. Sudan is an empty land. Its one million square miles house only about thirteen million people. Its two apparent halves are a more advanced Muslim north and a Pagan-African south. Yet these halves are united by their common life-line the Nile, third river of the Earth, four thousand kilometres, well over two thousand miles, long. The people are also united, more than some of them care to think, by intermarriage and by other shared interests.

Miscegenetion, mingling in marriage, the anthropologists tell us, precedes and accompanies any considerable change anywhere in the total or communal heritage of our human adventure. More than two thousand years of the racial confusion indicated in Chapter 1, among Hamitic, Semitic and Negro stocks, have resulted, for the Sudan, as for other parts of Africa, in human beings of almost all shades between pale coffee and pitch-black. Like most Africans, Sudanese have that protective mental resilience that is best called strong 'identity'. At the present time Sudan contains, of Africa's five hundred and more languages, one hundred of these. It has, too, a rich variety of lovingly and fiercely guarded cultures.

Over the years between 1900 and 1956, Anglo-Egyptian rule introduced to the Sudan the successful, socio-economic experiment of the Gesira Cotton Scheme : and, as Europe left in part of the rest of Africa, so Britain left in the Sudan – the telegraph, a few railroads, some modern trade, a number of schools, and an outline of modern politics. The Sudan opted for independence from both Egypt and Britain in 1956. Yet in spite of the throes of nationhood, in spite of the attractions of technological culture, most Sudanese remember the tribe to which they belong; and many, feeling their links with the past threatened, and their present uncertain, cling to their tribe and their traditions the more.

Once outside the modern twin-capital of Khartoum-Omdurman at the joining of the White Nile and the Blue Nile, few townships have more than fifteen thousand people. Villages have square, sun-baked clay houses in agricultural areas, and round houses with conical thatch in nomad areas.

These round houses, earliest form of man's dwellings, are often beautifully constructed of wattle and *dom* palm. Villages may be scores of empty miles apart. They are joined by tracks impassable in the rains of May, June and July.

Electricity is advancing. But by night Sudanese hamlets, as hamlets over many parts of Africa, are unlighted by more than hurricane lanterns or wicks in oil.

Temporary Sudanese villages of the Butana house the Shukria; and many Shukria are still seasonal nomads. They move with flocks and herds to fresh pastures every six or eight weeks north-east or south-west across the flat Butana, with its volcanic *Gebels*. Shukria traverse land they consider their own.

Most villagers and nomads depend on themselves for pastimes. Leisure and work are often united. Shukria women dye and weave grass for tent or floor or basket. They cure skins. The men make tools. Some among them fashion by hand the beautiful urn-shaped *zeers* (English : *jar*) of Nile clay and animal dung and urine. Potters must have been making these artistic *zeers* for thousands of years – to keep water cool in a boiling sun.

A Shukria sheikh may reply, if asked, that his heart's desire is a transistor radio – so strong is the lure of knowledge of other men's endeavour. A sheikh may possess a transistor, though most of the tribe may not have seen a white man. But if you ask among Shukria, or among other Sudan tribes such as Beja (Red Sea hill-men), or Fur people of fertile Gebel Marra in the west, or Kababish – or indeed outside Sudan among pastoralists like Somali herdsmen, Bahima of Ankole in Uganda, or the Ewe of Togoland : 'Have you a poet?' a poet will appear in far less time than we might take to find a poet in Britain. The Shukria oral poet may be a ragged man. But he will recite from memory for half-an-hour narrative verse about his people's past, or lyric verse of personal feeling, that will hold his audience rapt.

African oral or folk heritage needs more and more to be saved. Some Sudan tribal songs can be heard on the radio in the capital; but much is still unrecorded. All Africa's vernacular languages and verbal literatures beg desperately for their own scholars' exploration.

The following poems or songs come from the mostly unrecorded verse of Shukria nomads. The division between song and poetry is not sharp or clear in the early history of the two arts. The chief poet, so far, of the Shukria was El Hardallo who died in 1919. A volume of El Hardallo's poems was published in 1960, in Arabic. There is, as far as I know, no translation into English.

The following four-line stanzas are *dobeit*, or shepherds' songs. These may be very roughly compared to English traditional ballad stanzas. Their authors are not known. Listeners do not join in adding and changing, though there are other Sudanese chants and tribal songs where listeners do join in. *Dobeit* have a set form. They are not comparable with ballads in stanza, rhyme, or rhythm. True, their stanzas are four-line; but they have heavy end-rhyme that is frequently mono-rhyme[1] in all four lines.

As Shakespeare said, 'Music and sweet poetry agree' : one or other of Africa's rich assortment of musical instruments is often used to accompany Shukria poems or songs. The *dobeit* below were chanted – or sung – these divisions merge – to a *zumbara*. A *zumbara* is a home-made, five-stop bamboo pipe. A *zithr*, also sometimes used, is the original form of guitar.

Dobeit do not follow on. They may be chanted or recited by a poet in any order. Most Shukria would know the following ones and scores of others by heart. So would today's Shukria' schoolboys.

[1] There was probably connection in the far past during the spread of poetic metres, between the Asian four-line *ōlong* and the Arabic *dobeit* stanza, and between both and the Provençal troubadour stanza; but I have not seen the relationships among earliest metres explored, and though exploration might reveal some startling comparisons, it must be too speculative to be of intellectual value.

The translations are by Sayed Ali Lutfi, a schoolmaster of the Reka-bieh tribe whose father was an educational pioneer at Rufaa.

At some time in the past Rekabieh gave land to the incoming Shukria and then tried to make themselves overlords. Quarrels ensued over pasture, so important in Africa, until Shukria threw off the Rekabieh yoke. Now Rekabieh and the much more numerous Shukria live side by side and intermarry.

The upbringing of Shukria children is based on the submission of the young to the older. Boys and girls are reared to obey and are beaten if they don't. The pattern is of strict obedience to parents, particularly the father, to seniors in age-groups, and to elders.

The social pattern may be observed by noting first the smallest unit, the family. This comprises husband, wife (or wives), and children (married sons or daughters and their children, later). The family lives in a 'compound' or ring of huts enclosed by a fence. Even permanent houses in the Butana are quickly and cheaply made of local materials and the whole family helps to build. The next division in the social pattern is the *fareig*: a *fareig* is that part of a village where descendants of a third or fourth generation ancestors live as neighbours. A sub-tribe may occupy a whole village. The largest unit is the tribe. A tribe lives, or moves across, a district it looks on as it own land.

DOBEIT 1

BRAVERY

Younger than any I crossed the ghosts' valley;
I scattered brave men; my shield refused flight.
I'm known for my manhood far, a long time.
Base law shall not bend me. I'll keep upright.

Translation of *dobeit* are bound to have a different tone or quality from the originals. The versions here are no more than most tentative attempts to hold transient mirrors to a few of the traditional ideas that are preserved in poetic form from the life of a highly individual, but strongly conservative, people. Shukria culture, as so many cultures of emergent Africa, may have temporarily retreated, to guard itself against encroaching new ways. The desire is understandable, from all parts of the continent, to save what is unique, while at the same time their people join in some modern advantages.

What, beyond the title, does the above *dobeit* say? The poet is extolling, but with a sense of conflict involved, his own valour. Shukria have great respect for elders and much fear of the dead. Many Africans, Muslim Shukria certainly, and even among the sophisticates, still believe that the dead have direct influence, baleful or benevolent, on the living.

As a child, then – the poet of the *dobeit* says – he dared pass alone the ghosts' valley of ancestral spirits. Graveyards in most parts of rural Africa are well outside most villages and towns. Even the much-visited saints' tombs in Sudan are not near dwellings of the living. Domes in shining aluminium, these can be seen for miles. Unimportant graves are simply enclosed with small pebbles. A white flag waves here and there to remind an ancestor of some promise kept by the living. Most people are careful to placate all ghosts of their dead. Certainly the young man in the *dobeit* would not pass heedlessly through the vale of ghosts, however valiant his errand.

In the second and third lines the poet's bravery is the kind most of us know about. It is man's deep need to challenge his fellows or circumstances to the point of death, and to seek renown by that hazard. But the manhood of the last line is again traditional conduct, this time in conflict with modern law. Such manhood is similar to the bravery extolled in our own older ballads. A limited comparison is possible with the manhood depicted in the Robin Hood ballad cycle. Like Robin Hood ballads some *dobeit* may be products of a period of change when primary morality comes to clash with changing social law. Robin Hood was a brave outlaw who did not mind robbing the new rich to give to the poor. The *dobeit* poet speaking for Shukria herdsmen is an individualist not averse to a daring camel theft to break the monotony of a hard life. By old standards which mankind finds hard to lose, might could equal right and valour be better than virtue. The last line suggests contempt for a new foreign rule of law.

DOBEIT 2

TRUSTWORTHINESS

Our hearts want no cowards to settle strange
among us;
Our steps follow the high road of the Elders :
steadfast as stones they. Can true rock crumble?
– Only he who spawns evil need have furtive thoughts.

This *dobeit* describes a character-attribute close in importance to physical bravery in the well-defined code of virtue in Shukria culture. A primary quality known to all of us is that of being forthright, brave and honest in speech. Shukria, like many Africans, speak their minds to the point of bluntness – provided, of course, they are speaking to somebody of equality, and whom they can trust. Nobody can put up a better performance of deviousness or of polite not-knowing before somebody not trusted or before somebody in authority. The Shukria is liable to quarrel : he sounds as if he is raging with a companion in a most bitter disagreement. But he is quick to laugh and forget – unless about some deep wrong he or his family have endured. This he may be pledged to avenge.

Blue Nile Shukria have lived this way for centuries. Once a person is accepted as a friend, loyalty becomes unquestionable. Life in the tribe may be curtailed by formidable hardships and frustrations. But as in most tribal life of the African continent – sun and darkness and desert and jungle teach patience and endurance; tribal life, close as it must be, is no more and no less hampered than sophisticated western life, by personal, meticulously-hidden jealousies that 'spawn' the 'evil' of 'furtive thoughts'.

Dobeit 3

GENEROSITY

From a child I've been wayward, have carried swords :
I feel big as the sea, year-round, east to west :
O God for some money to complete life's rewards !
To relieve begging people, lavish food on each guest.

This *dobeit* celebrates the poet's expansive sense of being as bountifully big as the sea he is almost sure not to have seen. He asks as reward from life only that he may have enough money to be charitable. Wealth in rural Africa, certainly among the Shukria, is often not prized in itself or for the power or grandeur it may confer : it is certainly prized; but to kill a sheep, enough to prepare a feast in a region without inns is the hospitality that gives a man friends and standing.

Dobeit 4

PRIDE

We ride pedigree camels, refusing the common blood;
We are patient, persistent, like the Prophet's friends.
In their hearts all know us for this kind of manhood :
– not for us girlish dancing with our bottom-ends.

Herdsmen of camels, humped cattle, sheep, and goats are proud of their animals, particularly of riding camels. They are strongly attached to them. If the Shukria owner of a camel goes away he had better leave a bit of his clothing for his beast to sniff or no one will sleep for the camel's roaring. The fourth *dobeit's* first line reveals pride in camel descent nearly as strong as in family descent.

Among many tribal Africans, as well as among all Sudanese, the

c*

family extends beyond father, mother, sons, daughters, grandchildren, grandparents, and perhaps uncles, aunts and cousins. An African family unbroken by industrial conditions – certainly a Shukria family – may include all the descendants of a twelfth grandfather and that grandfather's many brothers and sisters. Any of the scores of descendants of these may be spoken of and welcomed after walking perhaps a hundred miles to visit his relative as a brother or a sister. And all who believe in the Prophet Mohammed are friends, of one family.

In the Butana of the Shukria, as in much of Africa, men's and women's activities are very separate. Women are attached to the home and the rearing of children. They may be over-worked. They will probably be over-confined. All are thought to have mental power inferior to men. But the idea of general active mal-treatment of women is often, though not always, European misreading of divergent social attitudes.

Herdsmen are not usually dancers. In most parts of Africa a men's dance would be quite different from a women's dance. Shukria girls dance at weddings and feasts. Men move in the stupefying rhythm of those religious rituals called, in Arabic, *zikrs*. Shukria men and girls would not dance together as they do in urban South Africa where night-life dance-halls have helped jazz to become the rage; as it is of so much of the world's urbanized youth. The *dobeit's* fourth-line reference to dancing with the bottom infers suspicion of encroaching, emasculating, 'civilized' dancing as a further threat to Shukria strengths.

DOBEIT 5

MISFORTUNE

After riding free as the flight of the eagle,
O Malik I'm now tilling and cutting *lubia*.
The young girls who love me weep at my absence,
while with snake-tongue sickle low grass in shame I shear.

Allied to pride in physical prowess, in trustworthiness, and in material generosity, is getting away with a daring animal theft against somebody who is hostile or mean. Allied to pride of another kind is a deep contempt among Shukria herd-owners for agriculturalists. Nuer and Masai and Dinka herd-owners have this contempt too. It may have something to do with the fact that growing crops where agriculture is practised was originally women's work. In some cultures, not only in Africa but in south-east Asia for instance, it still is. Women may actually have begun the tending of seeds. But apart from such speculation, irrational contempt for other ways of living, a complacency born often of ignorance, is in many of us. Is not assuming that people who live in the country and toil with their hands are slower and therefore clumsy, less intelligent, or less sensitive than ourselves, inaccurate? Certainly it is as mistaken as the pastoralists' unreasoning contempt for the tiller of the soil. Undoubtedly it is superficial; yet it is heard on the lips of psychologists. But contempt for the ways of others must be as old as the myth of Cain and Abel. That such contempt is strong in people remote from modernity can be seen in this fifth *dobeit*: the poem speaks of the misfortune of being caught, probably for a venturesome camel-theft, and made to cut cattle-feed (*lubia*); to be made to labour at agriculture while serving a sentence at one of the abhorred prisons under a 'base' foreign law is punishment indeed.

DOBEIT 6

LOVE

Come El Wagel, my camel, to her who has our own nature;
her slender throat rises high between ear and shoulder;
her heavy-hung hair needs no false hair to lengthen.
In love she will have me, for no man is bolder.

Men's and women's lives, as well as their work, are very distinct in many parts of Africa and certainly among the Shukria. This separateness does not mean that the youthful interest of boys and girls in each other is not intense. Their mutual interest is certainly not decreased among Shurkia nomads by its formal secrecy. They would be horrified by Anglo-American young people's open display of feeling. They might also be fascinated. Marriages in the Butana are arranged between the fathers of the boy and girl. The boy may have caught sight of the girl, who is kept fairly secluded after the age of about seven. She may not even know of his interest in her. He may rely on a description by one of her brothers in his agegroup. *Sub rosa* plans among young men are frequent in tribal life. These may lead to the approach of the boy's father to the girl's father. But all must be carried out with formal good manners. These must be in keeping with both the modesty of the girl and the pride of the young man.

In some parts of Africa, and certainly among Shukria, a girl, even in 1965, may be circumcized either by the severer Pharaonic method or by the less severe clitoridectomy. The severe, Pharaonic form of sexual mutilation of girls is said to derive from ancient Egypt, to have come into use among some slave-keeping peoples when castration of boys and household slaves was found insufficient to keep palace wives or rich city wives faithful. Female circumcision is carried out by the women, with the child gagged to prevent her screams, when she is six or seven. It is said by some to afford the future husband more sexual pleasure. By depriving the girl of any joy in love-making it ensures her chastity both before and after marriage. She will not bring 'shame' on her family. Pharaonic circumcision also ensures difficult childbirth. The custom is in process of dying out. Educated Sudanese are wholeheartedly against the cruelty – just as they are earnestly for the education of girls. The rarity of divorce in the Sudan does not make companionship between marriage partners more frequent.

Older women fanatically try to preserve female circumcision. The British legislated against the practice. Towards the end of the 1930s they imprisoned a woman who had her daughter circumcized. But a score of tribesmen mobbed the small, new, British-built jail. They demanded the woman's release, proclaiming that the problem could be solved only by themselves. Physical mutilation and self-mutilation, like sense of guilt, and shame, seem to be necessary stages of human development.

If she is circumcized, the Shukria girl will probably also be scarred. This means that she may have one, two, three, or four deep incisions made with a knife or razor on her cheeks before circumcision. The practice of scarring too, is passing. It was thought to show that a girl was of good family, enduring courage, and impeccable virtue – no Ethiopian pleasure-girl. It was further thought to enhance her beauty. Both forms of mutilation help to make the girl shy before strangers. But she is gay enough with her own kind. Those Shukria girls who attend school in 1965 are all unscarred. Lively, questioning, warm-hearted but undemonstative, these, with the increasing number of schoolgirls all over the continent, are the African women of the future.

Among much of rural Africa marriage is still very early. Among Shukria the couple may be only fourteen or fifteen years old. They may not have spoken to each other before the ceremony. Divorce is almost unknown. Love is thought, and with some psychological truth, to come as easily after as before marriage. After the prolonged family festivity of seven days that is a Shukria wedding, the couple may live with the girl's parents first and some months or years later they may live with the man's. Nomad women build the curved, skin-and-mat-covered nomad tents with *sidr* wood frames. Men can tell a devoted wife by the tent she builds.

After marriage a bride must be approached tenderly. She is shy. She must not be alarmed or hurt more than is necessary. Because of his pride in his virility a middle-aged African sometimes marries a very young second wife. But an attitude to love akin in some ways to the European medieval attitude of romance and chivalry which lays stress on the man's protectiveness, and on strict formality, manners, and secrecy, is glimpsed in both this sixth *dobeit* and in the following seventh.

Now let us look at what the singer of the sixth *dobeit* has found in the girl of his choice : first of all she is like him; she thinks as he does; they will, therefore, agree; she will not thwart him secretly. Second, she has two beauties that are to him important – a high slender throat (we may recall how Annie Laurie's neck was 'like the swan's), and thick, rich hair. Thick, rich hair on a woman's head is a token, a symbol, of faithful womanhood and of passion. This *dobeit* may have been composed before the prevalence of female circumcision : his love's passion might triumphantly match the singer's boldness.

DOBEIT 7

LOVE (2)

I swam the White Nile, the *arak* savannah crossed :
sword ready, the saddle on my camel tossed.
What can death matter? Life is never lost :
have I not kissed her lips whose cheeks are scar-embossed?

Under present pressures, in this area as remote as any in Africa, ancient and valued standards are severely threatened. There is this question that torments men perpetually. Lack of hard riding, lack of danger and physical endeavour may make a man soft. The eternal tension between manly hardness and love's tenderness is stated in this seventh *dobeit*. This Shukria bride will know that her lover has swum the half-mile of crocodile-infested, hippo-crowded White Nile to get to her.

The next two verses offered below are by Wad Hasab Rabu. They were part of a recording during a camel-back journey through the roadless Butana in 1963. They were recited in an evening's entertainment to strangers under the dim light of oil lanterns. The audience was entirely masculine and the poem unaccompanied. The rest of the entertainment consisted of onomatopoeic renderings of animal-cries, bird-songs and funeral noise of weeping women, on *zumbara* pipes.

The tribal poet, though an entertainer, among African tribes who have not come into close contact with schools, universities, and 'academic' poetry, is an ordinary man with herds to look after. He passes on his art by word of mouth to a successor. A successor is invariably forthcoming. The successor is not necessarily the poet's son. The verses of Wad Hasab Rabu, and the two poems by Ahmed Awad

Karim immediately following, are all in Shukria Butana Arabic, a dialect of educated Arabic. Yet the poems contain words that belong to a poetic tradition that dates back to pre-Islamic times.

The translation into urban or educated Arabic was made by Sheikh Ahmed Khalid, of the Rekabieh. Sheikh Ahmed lived his early life among the Shukria in the Butana. The rendering of the poems into English is by Ali Lutfi. Sayed Ali did not find it possible to reproduce the sonorous end-rhyme and the heavy beat which, like a *dobeit*, the poems have in the originals. Nor, he maintained, was the stern, outdoor atmosphere of a long tribal tradition really translatable :

I BY WAD HASAB RABU

My love is a cream, Hisseiniya she-camel, a virgin whose neck's
a silk garland;
She makes me sleepless as the thorn-eyed *sugda*-bird.
The longing to touch her gazelle-like, smooth body
is a fire that will never go out in my heart.

My heart is the target of her best-of-all eye;
I will not keep my love secret though custom demand it.
Her beauty spills over, a full fowl of *durra*, unequalled by any;
Her large black eye needs no *kohl*; her cheek lights the dark.

The next two poems were recited by the author himself, the unknown Ahmed Awad Karim. An old man in 1963, Karim's voice, vibrant with nostalgia for a lost youth, had his audience obviously stirred :

2 BY AHMED AWAD KARIM

'Often, my camel, you have been tired : lately, tied untired :
today we are going to my love.'
                Scraping a place the camel knelt.
'We are going to the one whose veiled face is pale as dust.
Modesty is under her feet; beneath her *tobe* is the eternal
decency of manners.'

The camel heard the voice praising its fine neck with hair thick
as a gazelle's.
It listened, heard itself called proud and wilful; it grunted :
'Our destination is with the one whose breast is gay with jewels.
I will arise; we shall haste to the home of the girl.'

Tightening my camel's girth, I – the poet – thought :
Tonight my sleep will be with the incomparable one;
with her of the long neck, the slim waist, the round, wide hips.

Again, Karim recited a very recent poem of his :

3

I watched an unknown girl in a passing caravan adorn herself :
one shoulder was bare of the silk *tobe*; her feet were in new
   nylon shoes;
Her hair hung down her back.
                    The she-camel called to her young.
The rain fell.
          The caravan moved on . . .
If you see my friend, Wad Jawir, with whom are my secrets,
and you sit with others, tell him I *saw* and my eyes wept :
I saw the young girl shine on in the darkness.
In her graceful walk, hips and earrings played hide-and-seek.

These verse translations from Shukria oral poetry have been given
chiefly to point to the range between unwritten African literature
and sophisticated work, by South Africans, or by modern French-
speaking Africans such as Senghor, or by young Nigerians, Okara,
Okigbo, Soyinka, and John Pepper Clark, all of whose work will
be discussed in the next chapter. In a sense *dobeit* may be called
popular poetry : they are certainly the poetry of a whole community, not of the educated section of a people. As Shaaban Robert,
writing of Swahili poetry as a pillar of Swahili culture, has truly
said : 'human beings are alike in most respects'; . . . 'poetry is natural
to man.'[1] It would be a loss if African verse tradition such as that
of the Shukria were irretrievably forgotten.

Modern East African Prose

With its rich medieval past and its present three universities, East
Africa has a slowly growing prose and poetry of variety and
sophistication. The field is uneven, The awakening came to the
East of the continent in general later than to the South. There are
autobiographical works of important people such as Albert Luthuli
with his *Let My People Go*, and there are well written stories by
less well-known people – *Mau Mau Detainee* (1963) by Josiah
Kariuki, and *Child of Two Worlds* by Mugo Gatheru (1964).
Kariuki and Gatheru are both from Kenya.

Kariuki's book is valuable and well-written. 'It must have a
deeply disturbing effect upon those British readers who believe its
story. . . . For us who were shocked by the character of the Mau
Mau outbreak, to know all may not be to forgive all but it is still
important to *know*'. So wrote Margery Perham.[2] When Josiah

[1] See his article *Black Orpheus*, No. XI, p. 22.
[2] Foreword to *Mau Mau Detainee*, p. XI, XII

Kariuki was introduced to one 'Who had no predisposition to like a "hard-core" ex-Mau Mau detainee' he made an impression of 'modesty, friendliness, balance, and humour'.

The following extracts may help to give the tone and tenor of Kariuki's book :

> I am a Kikuyu who was detained in fourteen of Kenya's detention camps between 1953 and 1960. This book is largely the story of my years in those camps. It is written not in any spirit of bitterness or spite but because no one has yet told the truth about them and because they have become an important part of the history of my country. 'Manyani', the largest camp, capable of holding up to 30,000 of us, is now a word deeply entrenched in the language of every tribe in Kenya, and no one can hope to understand the present temper of Kenya African politics without some awareness of the life led by our 80,000 detainees during those Emergency years. Possibly too, some description of how we organized ourselves in difficult conditions will be of interest to those who may still be in danger of a similar fate in other parts of colonial Africa.[1]

And again

> The future historian of these times may well find it difficult to get our side of the story. Many documents vital to his task will be burnt before independence. But in my narrative of the camps and our strange life together inside them he may perhaps see some glimpses of the truth and justice of the movements of unity, and he may begin to understand why we do not regard the soldiers of the forest as 'hard-core', 'terrorists' or 'murderers', but as the noblest of our fighters for freedom. May this book and our new state be a small part of their memorial. Their torture and their pain were the hard travail of a nation.[1]

Here follows Kariuki's poetic translation of the first oath taken by Mau Mau adherents :

> I speak the truth and vow before God
> And before this movement,
> The movement of Unity,
> The Unity that is put to the test
> The Unity that is mocked with the name of 'Mau Mau',
> That I shall go forward to fight for the land,
> The lands of Kirinyaga that we cultivated,
> The lands that were taken by the Europeans

[1] *Mau Mau Detainee*, pp. 1, 182

And if I fail to do this
May this oath kill me
May this seven kill me,
May this meat kill me

I speak the truth that I shall be working together
With the forces of the movement of Unity
And I shall help it with any contribution for which I am asked,
I am going to pay sixty-two shillings and fifty cents
    and a ram for the movement
If I do not have them now I shall pay in the future.
    And if I fail to do this
    May this oath kill me
    May this seven kill me,
    May this meat kill me.[1]

Those readers who wish to know a little more from the Kikuyu side about the reported 'bestiality' of the further oaths should read Kariuki's book for themselves. Though truth as an absolute cannot be wholly known, there, for 'future historians of these times', in this book published in Britain, must be some of the facts.

Critics of Britain use her record in Kenya deservedly against her. Yet many British people, sluggishly and imperfectly and always late, try, in Margery Perham's words, to 'maintain a standard of humanity'. The death of eleven 'hard-core' prisoners in Hola camp at the hands of African warders in 1959 and the Lari massacre by Mau Mau of a whole village were what aroused British opinion to make itself felt. Then it expressed itself not so much against Mau Mau as against concentration camps (condemned in Germans and Russians) that could provoke such outrage. That the Lari atrocity was a planned Mau Mau operation Josiah Kariuki, though without conclusive evidence, denies. This is the kind of uncertainty on a surely ascertainable fact that in the cause of mutual human understanding could have been cleared up.

MUGO GATHERU *Child of Two Worlds* (1964), Mugo Gatheru's one book, is another Kikuyu's story. Like both Kariuki and the West African Prince Modupe, Gatheru is a broad-minded intellectual. He has an American degree and a British Law degree. This son of an African medicine-man or witch-doctor has also an American wife.

Child of Two Worlds is therefore in one sense irrevocably western. The chapters on its author's African childhood have a distant, rather sad, atmosphere of 'far away and long ago'. Unlike *I Was a Savage*

[1] ibid. p. 26.

the book's most interesting chapters are its later ones. In these Gatheru describes his loneliness and sense of being an alien in New York and his poverty in London, all whilst in search of the prized higher education. His chapter on the similarities of approach to patients between Kikuyu medicine-men (Mugos) and American witch-doctors (psycho-analysts) is intriguing. His chapter on Mau Mau and its oath-taking ratifies the truth of Kariuki's account, and as is his chapter on the rivalries and unfairnesses attaching to poligamy, it is written in cool, detached, almost legal prose.

JAMES T. NGUGI Still another Kenyan, a young Kikuyu, but one who writes fictional, or imaginative, prose, is James Ngugi. Aged about twenty-seven, Ngugi read English at Makerere University College, Uganda, went into journalism, and entered the University of Leeds in 1964. So far he has written only short stories and two novels. The second novel is to appear in 1965. The first to be published, *Weep Not, Child* (1964), should be looked at carefully.

Weep Not, Child is the story of a closely-knit Kikuyu family – father, two mothers, and four sons – which becomes tragically entangled and broken in the struggle for Kenya land. After the Second World War – a 'World' war, let us remember, chiefly from a Western point of view – the eldest son of Ngotho returned from the White man's war in which he had learned to shoot. He found the inheritance he should have had from his ancestors still in the hands of the foreigner. There was not a sign that the prophecy his father Ngotho trusted in could ever come true; fondly Ngotho had kept on believing that the white men would pack and go back to their own land, letting the black people have theirs again.

The Bible had paved the way for the sword. But the magician's prophecy about the departure of the whites had cheated Ngotho. Some black men turned traitor to their own people : they took sides with the whites, getting their favour and being raised as servile chiefs. Three of Ngotho's sons went to the forest to fight for their own freedom and for their father's rightful land.

But the white man and the white man's Bible also offered 'the key to the future'. They had offered this key through schools – however few schools were, and however much these places told scholars and children that the white man's ways and civilization were far superior to the black man's. The key had been offered through education – scanty, and with the best advice often not lived up to in the teachers themselves; but, all the same, knowledge couldn't in the long run be anything but thinking with a more enlightened mind. Njoroge the boy felt thus, for this knowledge had been offered him as the youngest son of the family. Njoroge was quick, sensitive, a dreamer. He watched his father lose his manhood and die from hideous torture; he saw his three elder brothers imprisoned for murder. Was the freeing of minds wasted? Are ideals false? Are further ideals found only to be lost again? These were the questions with which Njoroge tormented himself.

Here is the beginning of an assessment of the human dilemma at a fairly deep level. For what, after all, is a serious novel but one individual's examination of some of the subtleties of our human nature? Perhaps the most important point about young James Ngugi as a novelist is the concentrated comprehensiveness that his theme achieves. It contrives this breadth and depth only partly though a use of language that is pure and direct. He makes little compromise with modern, supposedly 'readable' slickness. His prose is simpler and less categorical than Kariuki's; it is warmer than Chinua Achebe's; yet its impact is as direct as Achebe's apparent detachment.

Ngugi's characters use no pidgin and speak no proverbs. The prose of *Weep Not, Child* approaches closest to Camara Laye's in James Kirkup's translations and to Peter Abrahams's in *Tell Freedom*. Besides Ngugi's prose, Mongo Beti's, Cyprian Ekwensi's, Kariuki's, even Alex La Guma's, sounds deliberately sophisticated, too bullied in one way or another, too derivative.

Occasionally Ngugi approaches a shade close to what, in English critical terms, is called Edwardian or Georgian sentiment. But his vigour puts much-needed sap into an English language that competent commercial fiction, as well as social anthropolgy, currently threaten with dehydration. Whether directness like Ngugi's or Laye's, or whether a harder, more brittle detachment, or whether scintillating intelligence, is to be most commended – any answers to such a question may be safely, for the time being at any rate, left with new African readers.

Ngugi's method of simplification is what crystallizes his theme into its essentials. While for Ngugi a plot is clearly important, there is no 'hero' as part of that importance. The characters in *Weep Not, Child* are all seen with equal clarity; no one of them, that is, is felt to stand in special relationship with their author. All are sketched sympathetically from the inside; yet the story swings along with a kind of elemental far-seeing that has as little bitterness as have Plaatje's, Mphahlele's, and Abrahams's writing; and yet Ngugi the man may have had as much to contend against as any writer in Africa.

It is of no use, Ngugi infers, for any of us to say that the white man taught the black man violence. Cruelty is in all of us, however long it lies dormant or is thought to be outgrown. In some it is stronger than in others, whatever culture they belong to. No good, either, for the black man to think the white man taught him about the colour-bar. With whatever grossnesses *some* whites in power for a time enforce this horror here and there, *some* black men know all about the colour-bar and about cruelty without being taught. To want to be superior to a rival is in all of us.

Ngugi's short story given in the Anthology has the same elementary keenness of plot, depth of feeling, and clarity of characterization as has *Weep Not Child*. It is far too early to attempt to assess the work of this young writer with anything but tentativeness. His second novel, *The River Between* (1965), is also a story concerning tensions among Love, Gikuyu tradition, and Christianity's impact. (Mr Ngugi states that 'Gikuyu' is the correct spelling.) *The River Between* conveys a similar, sensitized balance to that found in *Weep Not, Child*. African novelists are not yet interested in the subtleties of technique. Far more vital is the exploration of an English which reveals a scale of values such as sophisticated humanity may seem bent on jeopardizing. Such a use of English is, in all he has so far written, James Ngugi's strength.

Modern East African Poetry

JEAN-JOSEPH RABÉARIVELO　French-speaking Rabéarivelo, of what is now the Malagasy Republic, was born in 1901. He was therefore writing long before the first *Négritude* poets, Senghor or the Diops in West Africa. Rabéarivelo died by his own hand at thirty-six and left seven volumes of poems. His work is not very well known. Yet of its quality there can be no doubt at all. Two of his volumes, written first in *Hovo* and then rewritten in French, have been published, and a translation in English by Gerald Moore and Ulli Beier, *24 Poems*, was issued by Mbari, Ibadan, in 1962. The use of superlatives is precarious : but surely Rabéarivelo is among the greatest of African poets so far.

Ulli Beier, noting how Rabéarivelo's is a cosmic vision, quotes : 'All seasons have been abolished in those unexplored zones that occupy half the world.' Mr Beier emphasizes Rabéarivelo's sense of catastrophe, frustration, death. This is seen in such poems translated into English by Mr Beier himself as : 'What invisible rat . . . gnaws at the milky cake of the moon?' or : 'The hide of the black cow is stretched . . . in the sevenfold shadow', or : 'Slowly . . . a large black spider emerges from the earth . . . and stretches its web across the azure'.

Yet this poet, in whom Gerald Moore hears, correctly, echoes of

Laforgue and Rimbaud, owes little of his essence to either of these, and less to Baudelaire who was his proclaimed favourite. Rabéarivelo may live most lastingly in poems such as his 'The White Bull', 'Birth of Day, II', and 'Birth of Day, III', all of which will be found in the Anthology. He was undoubtedly lonely. He was strongly even magnificently sufficient to himself; and he was not-of-this-time-or-place.

His poem 'The worshipper ends her morning prayers' has a last stanza that is completely unconcerned with death, castration, or despair. Rather than the abolition of seasons in unexplored zones, Rabéarivelo's outlook there is on the contrary cosmic yet full of scenic life. The poem's last stanza is unmorbidly sane, immemorially far-seeing :

> . . . I step on a mound of earth
> smelling the crushed and flattened grass
> and I scatter the foliage that impedes my sight.
> A small finch cries in the tree top
> and I lift my eyes :
> but what I see is the stars
> Bulbous like garlic
> spotted like quails
> and they remind me of the prayers I have confused;
> and it seems to me
> that the flight from Pharaoh
> took place in this azure desert of Imerina
> here where all Religions meet –
> and poems too.

SHAABAN ROBERT was the most important poet writing in Swahili and he wrote also in English. I have failed to find enough of this Tanganyikan's work to speak about it with the detailed knowledge it merits. In the one poem, 'Our Frame', given in this Anthology in its English translation by Gerald Moore and Shaaban Robert himself, he sets down in grave, almost banal, words, shorn of myth and dogma, some essentials that our bodily impermanence entails. He died in 1962.

Shele Kibwana also writes in Swahili. There, is too, John Mbiti of Kenya who has published poems in Kikamba and also in English. There is David Rubardiri of the new Malawi Republic, once Nyasaland; and there are Rabemananjara and Flavien Ranaivo of the Malagasy Republic, that used to be Madagascar.

Writing in parts of Africa still under the sway of Portugal is often, Gerald Moore writes, a 'cry of sheer agony'. But the one poem of Valente Malangatana given in this Anthology, translated by Ulli Beier and Gerald Moore, is without agony, but is tender in its perception of the feeling of others. It is a good poem in that it also conveys so precisely what it sets out to convey.

FELIX TCHICAYA U TAM'SI   A native of Congo, U Tam'si must be regarded in some detail because between 1955 and 1964 he produced four books of poetry in French. Two of these, *Feu de Brousses* and *Epitome* are being printed in English by Mbari.

Writing of M. Senghor's claim for U Tam'si as an apostle of *Négritude*, Gerald Moore outlines U Tam'si as a poet of some importance who uses (without punctuating) a complexly consistent set of images. U Tam'si's imagery is of sex, crucifixion, and resurrection. Sometimes mocking, tortured, crude, violent, and all of these by unexpected turns of 'Une syntaxe qui déraisonne', U Tam'si's images are also symbols, as : tree-man-phallus; river-Congo-life; knife-tongue-penis; fire-emotions-buffaloes-ladybirds; some of these may remind readers a little of Dylan Thomas's symbols.

But they are said to have much in common with the crowded but 'free' associations of images in Aimé Césaire's *Négritude* work. Senghor interprets U Tam'si's placing side by side disparate symbols as descending from Bantu poetry. I do not know enough to speak about this. U Tam'si's terrible, frenzied, seemingly unfulfilled, sexuality that is so tangled with his religion needs to be accepted with complete understanding before his poetry can be appreciated in any way other than intellectually. Its perverse, shadowy brilliance may be seen in :

> . . . We were foolish among the vines
> and stroked the seas in order to weep
> between the pine needles
> her agony my agony our agony oh virgin
> but love not being a christian virtue
> I have given joy to none
> my face to the backs of men
> all christians tactically
> thrusting at me the cross of a god betrayed
> whom I betray to remain faithful
> to the shadow

Women beginning to write in East Africa are *Noemia de Sousa* of Mozambique, *Rebecca Njau* and *Grace Ogot* both of Kenya; but none of these has yet published enough for discussion of their work.

Chapter 6

WEST AFRICA

Late Flowering of West African Literature – Poets and Playwrights – Novelists up to 1965

Late Flowering of West African Literature

Thinking, briefly, of West Africa as a self-contained literary unit – which of course it is not, though cross-currents with East and South Africa are not strong – we may say that this section of the continent began its production of a written literature latest of the three. There was Gustavus Vassa of Guinea and London, in 1790. When as late as the 1940s, West Africa did awake, the number of its writers quickly grew. Especially so was this the case in Nigeria, in spite of the hundred or more indigenous languages there. The total of poets, novelists, and dramatists in West Africa as a whole quickly exceeded those in the South or East.

West Africa's outlook, horizon, literary scene and themes may all need less of the blast of protest, and be able to be more quietly written about than those of South Africa. West African poets are certainly very variously, less urgently perhaps, yet very individually themselves.

WOLE SOYINKA The most outstanding among Nigerian poet-dramatists is Wole Soyinka, at thirty, the author of five plays, as well as of well-known poems such as the humorous-satiric 'Telephone Conversation' and the gravely beautiful 'Death in the Dawn'. Soyinka's plays are *The Swamp Dwellers, Brother Jero, The Strong Breed*, all published in 1962; *The Lion and the Jewel*, published in 1963, and *A Dance of the Forests*, also 1963. *Brother Jero* is a farce, hilariously funny at nobody's expense. It is about a rascal of a prophet of the Victoria Beach 'prayer-churches', who lives by fooling his followers. But there can't be rascally prophets unless there are foolishly credulous believers. Wole Soyinka has devised a glorious satire that is bound to be a theatre success and is very funny to read.

The Strong Breed is set in an unlocated African community which had the practice of using stray lunatics or foreigners as sacrificial 'carriers' of all their sins. Here Soyinka is probing much more deeply into parallels among strange cultural habits and beliefs. The teacher-

87

hero in *The Strong Breed*, Eman, points out with undeniably enlightened truth, to the villagers, that a redeemer must be aware of what he is doing and must not be an idiot : otherwise those seeking redemption by his torture and death become themselves pitiless gulls without the vision that we must call humanity in the sense of human intelligence. Eman himself becomes the 'carrier' : thus, almost as important as Soyinka's searching analysis of humaneness is his handling of dramatic suspense in this play. This handling is superb.

Soyinka's *A Dance of the Forests* is a most puzzling play. Three or four careful readings can leave only glimmers of what it is about. It might be an exposure of traditional ancestor-reverence so successfully hidden among ant-leaders, a half-child, forest-spirits, tribal dance, mime, and ritual, that the play's dialogue, however scintillating, is rendered almost superfluous : except to those who wish to puzzle endlessly as to what such as the following may mean :

Physician : . . . Are you sure that no one else may waste your life except you?

or

Historian : . . . history has always revealed that the soldier who will not fight has the blood of slaves in him.

or

Soothsayer : . . . it is in the nature of men to seek power over the lives of others, and there is always something lower than a servant.

or

Madame Tortoise : . . . I am the one who outlasts you all, Madame Tortoise.

or

Murete (A tree-imp) : . . . limb for limb, the forest has always proved victor.

But quotations such as these out of context in a short account of the play are hardly fair. Soyinka's traditional Nigeria may be still so near to myth and ritual belief of the kinds he shows that *A Dance of the Forests* has a future on the African stage and in discussion.

His next play, *The Lion and the Jewel*, returns to a probably universal theme, certainly one that burrows deep, in multifarious disguises, into human nature – a man's potency. This play of Soyinka's is clever, funny, and dramatic. Its characters are modern-Everyman, symbols from the canon of Samuel Beckett or Brecht; yet they are people. And Soyinka laughs throughout in both words and character, as Ezekiel Mphahlele says. He also has the capacity of handling what might be serious themes with the finest, lightest fun.

JOHN PEPPER CLARK   Also Nigerian, and, like Soyinka, John Pepper Clark is both poet and playwright, as well as being a writer of critical prose and academically trained. Besides *Poems* (1962), Clark has written *Song of a Goat* (1962). Two other of his plays, *The Masquerade* and *The Raft*, were both published in England with *Song of a Goat* in *Three Plays*, in 1964. *Song of a Goat* (of which the Final Movement is given in this Anthology) has a theme similar to *The Lion and the Jewel*; but Clark handles the subject tragically; his play's structure, atmosphere, and sense of inescapable, malignant fate have affinities with those of classical Greek drama. Zifa loses his wife to his younger brother because he cannot give her a child; but with a kind of dumb submission to an overwhelming Oedipus-destiny he walks into the sea, after his young brother in his own guilt has hanged himself. This bald outline does little justice to a moving play on a theme which, despite all modern scientific preoccupations with an overcrowded world, seems to haunt mankind.

Clark's second play, *The Masquerade*, is also concerned with the curse of impotency, this time the curse working itself out in three generations of a family. Again there is the pervading motif of the possible purification of wrong through suffering the curse – suffering not necessarily by the one who did the wrong. There is probably a strong likeness between classical Greek society and Nigerian traditional society, and John Pepper Clark is exploring this.

But his third play, *The Raft*, also a tragedy, has a self-contained inevitability of event that makes no attempt to enlarge its own significance by comparisons. This play tells of four woodmen adrift in the Niger estuary. It is written in flat, staccato, conversational, irregular blank verse; and it is philosophical rather than dramatic.

Recently J. P. Clark has terminated a course in America. One outcome of his stay was a book of searching, astringent criticism, *America, their America*. Clark admits he might have been 'the Awkward Guest'. His courage in speaking his mind must be what wins our tolerance, even our forgiveness. He did not succumb to American verbiage demonstrating the justice of America's Supreme Court, to American self-praise of their generosity, without retorting about the depth to which American democracy has fallen in its treatment of its black minority since the days when Thomas Paine praised American ideal beginnings. Nor did Clark keep silent about those in America who undoubtedly stand to profit – as do armament-manufacturers anywhere – from limited war.

Had Clark met some American poets, he might have turned aside from fault-finding among the people whose generous scholarship-money he was using. Instead he lashed out against the shallowness, derided American ignorance about countries and people outside America, was appalled at the insensitiveness in their human approach, at the snobberies based on money, at the pretentiousness concerning culture. *America, their America* has not, so far as I know, been published in America; and its author's course was abruptly cut short as useless by his hosts.

Yet J. P. Clark is outstanding among Nigerian poets. 'River bird', 'For Granny', 'The year's first rain', and the pictorially beautiful 'Ibadan', all have a spontaneous warmth that is so much an antithesis of sceptic criticism that it cannot but point to a richness of capacity in J. P. Clark. Such potential range – in prose as well as poetry – would promise much for the future of any creative writer.

GABRIEL OKARA Outstanding among Nigerian poets, equally with Wole Soyinka and John Pepper Clark, is Gabriel Okara. Okara is original in that, a non-academic, he owes little of his essential quality to other poets. Now about forty-four, he is a poet with a well-stored mind who uses his learning with exceeding modesty and control. This control, as if it were strength in reverse, infers the haunting truth that much of all that there is to say is not tellable in words and so is beyond what Okara himself can ever hope to put down :

> I felt my knees touch living sands –
> but the rushing wind killed the budding words.
> > (One night at Victoria Beach)

and again :

> Then the massive dark
> descends, and flesh and bone
> are razed. And (O were I
> to choose) I'd cheat the worms
> and silence seek in stone.
> > (Were I to choose)

This suppressed, explosive strength of sadness runs through Okara's poetry. Yet all his poems are explorations of life's depths in which both sharing and the fruits of the experience shared enrich his reader.

In his most successful poems, as 'Were I to choose' above, Okara makes a reticent but masterly use of that most ancient adornment of verse – rhyme. Rhyme is probably the easiest of all embellishments of poetry to use blatently or badly. It is also probably the most difficult to use with supreme success. Okara, essentially an original poet as well as one of very considered technique, may have been sparing, up to the present, in his use of rhyme because of his Ijaw poetic tradition. He will also be cognizant of the present strong trend towards unrhymed verse in some poets both American and English. Most likely of all, he is aware of rhyme's hazard and is determined to transcend that hazard. Okara's future poetry will be watched with the liveliest interest.

Both poet and prose-writer, Okara has produced one novel so far, *The Voice* (1964). In an age when much that is trumpery is being published and when the novel itself as an art-form is at a dangerous cross-roads, *The Voice* is one of those contributions that a poet's novel usually is. It is also one of the very few novels so far by black Africans to concern itself solely with African characters and African values. The conflict in the central character, the young man Okolo, which leads to his tragedy, does not arise from European interference. It is a battle within the individual African mind itself, a fight between an other-worldly attempt at integrity, and materialistic workaday suspicions and distrusts.

The story is of the young Okolo leaving his village, with its jealous, power-loving chief, Izongo, to seek *it*. This *it* (though not clearly enough defined in the novel) is, presumably, the attempt at a more honest living of life. Soon Okolo is threatened with imprisonment for offering shelter to a betrothed girl under his raincoat in a thunderstorm. The girl's future mother-in-law at once accuses him of having tempted the girl under his coat and then of touching her sexually. None of the bystanders and townsmen believes Okolo's protestations of innocence, and neither does any official when he is detained. He is advised to return to his village before he is convicted of lunacy as well as of criminal indecency.

But when Okolo does return home, the prestige-loving, wary Izongo realizes at once that here is a trouble-maker, even a dangerous rival to whose words the weak may eventually give heed. The chief devises for Okolo and for a 'witch' who has befriended him the cruel death reserved traditionally among some tribes for any who dared to set themselves against the community by voicing strong emotional convictions.

In *The Voice* Gabriel Okara has fulfilled his determination to translate the idiom, word-order, and cadences of his native Ijaw into English. Thus he writes : 'It was the day's ending, and Okolo by a window stood'; or '. . . on the river canoes were crawling home with bent backs and tired hands paddling.'; or 'How can you on my head put a thing that happened not?' If we ask ourselves whether

Okara's experiment with Ijaw-English is successful, one answer is that English will stand up to any number of such attempts and will be in some basic way enriched and honoured by them.

Besides this, Okara's perception of his characters and of their surrounding, emerges in *The Voice* in prose that has an almost physical quality. On different levels, two of Okara's countrymen, Amos Tutuola and Cyprian Ekwensi, convey this physical quality in their prose. On a level nearer Okara's own, the American poet Robert Creeley, following William Carlos Williams, strives to explore the American search for historical identity in language using rhythms, cadences, and phrasings that echo physical hesitations of voice and mental refusals of superficial conviction.

The theme of *The Voice* suggests the motif treated at far greater length in Dostoevsky's *The Idiot*. Such a theme is, as far as I know, experimental in African writing. As an exploration into language the whole novel is new and of considerable importance. Its seriousness in theme makes it enormously worthwhile on a second count.

CHRISTOPHER OKIGBO   More than ten years younger than Okara, and a university graduate as are Soyinka and Clark, Okigbo is a difficult poet. One has the idea that Okigbo has chosen abstruse references as part of his luggage in his journey to being a poet, but also because he has been educated in the English 'moderns'. All poets must start somewhere; and, if there ever was, there now is no such thing as originality in any strictly primal sense. Ulli Beier's explanation of Okigbo's poetry in *Black Orpheus*, No. 12, is no doubt a correct one : that the poet wishes to throw a veil over his meaning which he does not want the reader totally to pierce. That in Okigbo's poems there is a collection of seemingly unconnected allusions and that this reminds us of Ezra Pound's method must be admitted. The poem 'Debtors' Lane' with its refrain 'watching the wall clock strike each hour in a dry cellar' may remind some readers too irresistibly of T. S. Eliot in 'Dry Salvages'; but this doesn't make 'Debtors' Lane' much less than a good poem. Non-African readers are sure to hear African poetry very differently from the way African readers hear it. That

> & the mortar is not yet dry
> & the mortar is not yet dry. . . .

also holds an Eliot echo, that 'Hurry on Down' may remind some of John Wain, and 'sun's dust sawdust of combat' hint to others of Hopkins or Dylan Thomas – all these in Okigbo show a genuine poet not yet beyond the influence of those who inspire him.

Like Okara and Soyinka, Okigbo most frequently uses modern unrhymed, uneven-lined stanzas, with a certain amount of the ancient poetic adornment of assonance.

Other Poets

FRANK AIG-IMOUKHUEDE is the first Nigerian to write verse in pidgin. It is impossible for a foreigner to judge the success of his 'One wife for one man' published in *Modern Poetry from Africa.*

JOHN EKWERE directs programmes in the Eastern Nigerian Television Service and has written plays, poems and short stories; 'Behind the counter', his poem in *Reflections* says something temporarily worth saying. So does his 'Rejoinder' – even if he is speaking with only a wry nostalgia that the hated 'colonialists' are gone for good :

> No more now the foreign hawks
> On alien chickens prey –
> But we on us !

Such clear-sighted hardness breeds a sympathetic response.

MABEL SEGUN confesses to 'half-digested alien thoughts'. These, with sad self-pity see African women as yet but

> infants overblown,
> poised between two civilizations.

MICHAEL ECHERUO'S nine poems, in *Black Orpheus*, No. 12, are not enough to give proof of how good a poet he may eventually be.

Poets in West Africa other than Nigeria include Lenrie Peters of Gambia, and the Ghanaians, George Awoonor-Williams, Efua Theodora Sutherland, Kwesi Brew, and Ellis Ayitey Komey:

LENRIE PETERS Born at Bathurst, Gambia, but of parents who came from Sierra Leone, Dr Peters read medicine at Trinity College, Cambridge, and trained as a surgeon in London. His first *Poems* were published in 1964 by Mbari, at Ibadan.

A sense of estrangement pervades some of these poems. This may be an effect that years of education in a land foreign to West Africa have produced. Still, such estrangement gives Lenrie Peters a cosmopolitan outlook that endows him with

> That spirit which asks no favour
> of the world
> But to have dignity.

And this wide and resounding reasonableness could win many readers.

If the fact that the fight for freedom in Gambia is over gave Lenrie Peters a temporary sense that there was less left to write about, later poems in his 1964 volume, such as

> If I was asked
> How would I face the task
> Of camping out in space

show new areas opening to his pen. Poems such as 'The Seagulls return', 'Fog strangles' and 'When winter is over' indicate avenues of accomplishment in technique that might give him a place among notable West African poets in the coming decade.

GEORGE AWOONOR WILLIAMS   In his only published volume so far, *Rediscovery and other Poems* (Mbari, 1964), George Awoonor Williams tells that he was born in 1935 at Keta in Ghana, 'the flood town, with the sea in my ears'. He was educated at Keta, at the college of Achimota, and he read English at his home university of Ghana, Legon.

Here, then, is a poet who, unlike Lenrie Peters and many of the Nigerian poets, has been educated entirely within his own Africa. Echoes of the Eliot-Pound poetic revolution of the twentieth-century can be heard from his university course. Yet his wholly African culture spares him the most acute sense of alienation. It also offers a wealth of indigenous ways, myths, beliefs, and flora and fauna, to write about. If non-African readers want to appreciate this poet better they will go to the trouble of finding out the meaning of 'sacraments' to the the 'sea-god', the beliefs surrounding the burying of a birth chord[1], the 'ceremony of oneness', and so on. George Awoonor Williams's poetry is an instance where explanatory notes would not be in any way superfluous. To say this is not to cast aspersion on the promise of this poet. A request for notes simply illustrates a problem attendant on the growth of an international poetry to which Africans are making a contribution which needs as full comment as possible.

EFUA THEODORA SUTHERLAND   Mrs Sutherland, a Ghanaian married to a Negro American, is both poet and prose-writer. Her poem 'The bitter thing' is an analysis of straightforward love made into a situation that is now the butt of common human prejudice. The poem

---

[1] The seventeenth-century spelling of this word may or may not have significance.

touches us sharply since the situation described may have to become even more common before it can shed the needless agony that
attaches to it :

> It happened
> And promptly I was aware
> Of the bitter thing. . . .
>
> What difference is there
> In us, he cried.
> What difference, my love? . . .
>
> But enough of this thrust pain.
> Our song lifts us up
> And lets our joys remain.
>
> Know you, races of earth,
> Two of your colours met
> And gave each other all
> As earth reeled blindly past
> In silence and in pain
> Our fountains did mingle
> Because of the bitter thing.
>
> It can be !
> How can it be ?
> No, it cannot be.
>
> O, you shall be free
> From the pain of me. . . .

A short story of Mrs Sutherland's is given in the Anthology. 'New
Life at Kyerefaso' also written unashamedly from a feminine point
of view, is doubly welcome. The African literary scene is still pre-
dominantly peopled by masculine writers.

West African Novelists up to 1965

AMOS TUTUOLA   A Nigerian Yoruba, Amos Tutuola sprang to fame
in 1952 with his book *The Palm-Wine Drinkard*. With this Tutuola
heralded in prose the West African torrent of literature that is still
in full spate. Almost immediately *The Palm-Wine Drinkard* was translated into three European languages. Since then Tutuola has published four other full-length stories, *My Life in the Bush of Ghosts*
(1954), *Simbi and the Satyr of the Dark Jungle* (1955), *The Brave
African Huntress* (1958), and *Feather Woman of the Jungle* (1962).
Tutuola was born in 1920 of Christian parents in the Yoruba

city of Abeokuta in Western Nigeria. He went to school until he was about fifteen, learnt his trade as a coppersmith, and moved to Lagos. Lately he has worked as store-keeper with Radio Nigeria at Ibadan. But he remains aloof from the travelled, academically trained, younger Nigerian writers of that university city.

Dylan Thomas rightly hailed *The Palm-Wine Drinkard* as 'thronged, grisly', a 'tall devilish story'. Other enthusiastic non-African critics likened it to *Pilgrim's Progress* and Tutuola to Bunyan, Blake, even to Dante. After such wide-of-the-mark praise of his first book, Tutuola has had to suffer as unfair a back-wash of dispraise of his later books : critics of *The Brave African Huntress* and *Feather Woman of the Jungle* assert that the 'magic' has 'leaked away'. Yet all Tutuola's books will be found in most British city libraries, though they are in the wrong place, among novels. Novels they are not. But one or other of them is usually out being read.

Neither the comparison with *Pilgrim's Progress* nor the statement about Tutuola's loss of 'magic' is justified. If there is a falling-off between his first book and his later books that is solely because there isn't a sufficient number of Afro-European myths to use effectively twice. In the first book, the Drinkard seeking his Palm-Wine Tapster through Unreturnable Heaven's Town to Deads' Town is certainly on one level a pilgrim who more invites comparison with Bunyan's : both men of little formal education, both know instinctively yet with supreme artistic and imaginative skill how to cram a basic adventure tale with significant happenings that will hold audience or readers spell-bound. Both *The Palm-Wine Drinkard* and *Pilgrim's Progress* are in the time-honoured art-form of a quest. There have been countless quests : Babylonian Gilgamesh set out, three thousand years B.C., to look for 'life', Greek Jason sought the Golden Fleece, Christian Galahad longed to see the Cup of the Holy Grael. There have been many, many more.

It is after general comparisons such as the quest theme of both books that likeness between *Pilgrim's Progress* and *The Palm-Wine Drinkard* falters. The quest Tutuola tells of incorporates fantasies that most of us as children encountered in dream and daydream or in legends. Legends would include Biblical myth, heroic myth, Greek, and north-European myth. Mingled with these are myths of a lurid Africa partly of Tutuola's fervent imagination, partly of his knowledge of Yoruba oral folk-tales. He tells of the African Bush of 'ancient days', before the coming of irksomely reasonable 'order'. None of these types of myth can properly be called universal, as sometimes Tutuola's myths are claimed to be. Present knowledge of world myths is not sufficient to pronounce universality for any. But many undoubtedly are common to a variety of cultures. African students of the future may delight themselves and us analysing origins within Tutuola's imaginative universe.

In the first category – myths of fantasy, that is, connected with our childish sense of helplessness – is the Drinkard's 'being able to do anything in the world' : his 'biggest *juju*' is to become 'Father of gods' who knows the 'secrets of all gods'.

Between fantasy and myth comes the Drinkard's 'further magic'. This power we humans must have longed for throughout ages : to change ourselves into birds, squirrels, creatures that airily leave the hard earth; or into mice that disappear into convenient small holes; into fish that swim into the deep far out of danger; into pebbles to be conveniently and easily lost sight of by enemies; or better still, to become quite invisible. All these mean a hero's escape when he gets into any of his inevitable tight corners as a result of adventurous daring. Between fantasy and myth proper, too, are Tutuola's monsters. These terrible reptiles live in haunted spots, in caverns, underground, in fearful forests, on bare mountains. His horrors have varying numbers of claws, eyes, tentacle-arms, legs, or horns. Between fantasy and myth are Tutuola's giants of imponderable size and incomprehensible terror. Perhaps to this category, too, belongs the 'complete' 'full-bodied gentleman' whom the strong-willed but beautiful lady follows into the dangerous forest : this gentleman has the parts of his body only on hire. At night he has to return his parts to the lenders before he becomes only a skull and retires to the skull family's house below ground.

The lady herself is the Beatrice of Dante or the Ariadne of European myth, the African Umnandi or Nandi of Plaatje and Mofolo. She becomes the Drinkard's wife and follows him loyally to the end of his journey and home again; she shares all his perils and never once fails to comfort or encourage. To myth – African but also with European parallel – belongs the Drinkard's encounter with 'Death in his yam garden'; and that terrible 'half-child' Zurrjir, who emerges from the Drinkard's wife's swollen left thumb; from the first this horror talks 'with a lower voice like a telephone'; he fights grown men; he eats so much he causes a famine. Clearly Zurrjir has affinity with the English Tom Thumb. His like is in folk-stories of many European nations. In Yoruba myth he is 'the child who knows more than his parents'; and in Tutuola's story he becomes so frightful his parents are forced to kill him. Killing him brings European readers up with a jolt. We are also jerked into dismay by those unchildlike children, symbolizing for psychology the helpless rebellion of all young human beings, African and non-African – the swarms of hostile, frightening 'dead babies' who infest with other deads the one road to and from Deads' Town. 'Drum,

Song and Dance, the three good creatures' are the wholesome three-in-one of music, poetry said or sung, and dance-mime. These three certainly belong together to the blessings of legendary time.

There is Tutuola's 'Faithful Mother who lived in the White Tree'. With Faithful Mother the Drinkard and his wife stay a customary 'one year and a few days'. They are then fortified with 'roast meat, cigarettes and drinks', told by Faithful Mother she can't hold them longer, and they must continue their journey. Faithful Mother, this time Asian, African, and European, is comparable with Graves's White Goddess, the earth-mother of Northern myth, the Mother Goddesses of Hindu villages, and of many another culture myth or religious myth. Her White Tree is comparable with the sacred Bo Tree, Igdrazil, The Druid's oak, the Tree of Knowledge, the Tree of Life. The swallowing of the Drinkard and his wife by the Hungry Creature, and the Drinkard's hacking his way out of Hungry Creature's stomach reminds us of Jonah and the Whale. There is the well-known golden egg : the dead Tapster, found at last after indomitable perseverence on the part of the Drinkard, sadly explains that deads can never again live with alives because they do everything backwards, even to walking. But the Tapster gives his master a miraculous egg. This boon will produce food for whoever asks for food.

'In good condition' the drinkard and his wife reach their home town again after crossing the river which the mountain-creatures with whom his wife had so dangerously danced cannot cross. But alas, at home there is Famine. The egg comes into use, gains the Drinkard standing and popularity until, recklessly enjoying themselves, his guests smash their source of beneficence.

But the Drinkard is wiser after his initiation by perilous travel to Deads' Town. Now he knows what life and people are like, what popularity is worth, and how gifts like the egg can be abused. He gums the egg together, produces whips instead of 'varieties of food' and 'kegs of palm-wine'; and the whips punish the irresponsible, merrymaking food-demanders. The whips kill many and scatter others into the bush. This reminds us a little of the money-changers whipped from the Temple.

The last chapter of *The Palm-Wine Drinkard* shows Tutuola using a final blend of African and European myth. Most African cultures have postulated, as part of their explanation of life's mysteries, a High God, a Creator, and a Great Mother. In some myths the High One is connected with the sun and is male, while Great Mother is connected with the female, fruitful earth. The Famine in the Drinkard's home town is found to be the result of a quarrel for seniority between a *male* Heaven and a *male* Land, once 'tight friends'. Wise from hard experiences, the Drinkard becomes the people's saviour, telling them how to stop the famine.

They are to send to Heaven a sacrifice of 'two fowls, 6 kolas, one bottle of palm oil, and 6 bitter kolas' by the only one who can be made to carry it – a slave. Heaven accepts the 'sacrifice' with gladness and *male* Land agrees to be junior to Heaven. Gerald Moore sees the slave as a human sacrifice sent to Heaven with the fowls and kolas : 'henceforth', Mr Moore writes, 'the supreme deity will be the male Sky God and not the old female Earth Goddess'.[1] If this is to be read into Tutuola's story, his variation on it must be accepted as either deliberate or unconscious. Mr Moore further sees the Drinkard as a hero,

> linked with the restoration of harmony between man and his gods, for it is the Drinkard's new understanding, won by the hard way of adventure, which enables him to settle the cosmic quarrel through which man is suffering.[1]

This may be so. Tutuola is certainly making visionary use of many ancient and almost infinitely mutable myths. Rain falls for three months after the Drinkard's plan has been carried out; in his home town 'there was no famine again'. There, after reminding us of the story of Gomorrah and of that of the Flood in reverse, Tutuola's tale ends.

Throughout *The Palm-Wine Drinkard*, Tutuola's style, so closely related to talk, and his content compounded of fantasy and variations on African-religious-Heroic myth, together hold his child-like lack of sophistication. This non-sophistication could not fail to captivate many European readers. They value Tutuola as lovable, often, unintentionally, funny; as when the Drinkard thanks God 'that He had created me without beauty'; as when he commands his wife to jump on his back with their loads (which evidently she had been carrying) while the Drinkard, thus encumbered with wife and loads, braves the bush where boa constrictors are 'uncountable as sand'; as when he is grateful to Faithful Mother for providing a special room in her White Tree for her guests to 'play gamble'; as when the Drinkard makes a good bargain – he has a nice eye for money all through his travels – he sells his own and his wife's deaths for 'the sum of £70 18s. 6d.' But through his gambling they have to keep their fears through all their hard experiences.

This amused appreciation of Tutuola by English readers has often baffled and needlessly offended African readers. They think it must be condescending. It is not at all condescending. It could not be, because however close to the wind of English eighteenth-century

[1] *Seven African Writers*, pp. 48, 49.

grammarians' rules Tutuola unwittingly sails, never once is he am-
biguous or obscure; and if he rapidly restores all his heroes and
heroines from broken limes, terrible beatings, hideous tortures rarely
is he anything but brilliantly graphic.

His mixing of modern wonders, radios, telephones, guns, and
bombers, with Crusoe-Andersen-Treasure-Island gnomes, imps, gob-
lins, cudgels, cutlasses, and jungles, openly states his debt to previous tale-tellers. Clearly he has read a great deal of non-African
folk- and fairy-tale. But his mixture of ancient and modern is an
added part of his fascination for the young.

Tutuola's second book *My Life in the Bush of Ghosts* (1954), is
longer than *The Palm-Wine Drinkard*, slightly less well packed, but
just as well constructed. It is about the initiation of a child, a boy
driven from his home by jealousy and hatred among his father's
wives; through his fabulous adventures for twenty-four years in the
Bush of Ghosts, he learns enough of life's necessary good and evil
to return home and finish his own life normally.

A third book, *Simbi and the Satyr of the Dark Jungle* (1955), has
a heroine, not a hero, to be initiated into the trouble and adventure
of living. Simbi is the most beautiful girl in her village, the only
child of the richest woman. But her father is dead. She is a singer
whose 'voice could wake deads'. But to be rich, Simbi feels, is cramp-
ing. She wishes to experience the 'Poverties and the Punishments'
on the 'Path of Death'. Without this how can anybody, even an
African girl, grow up? Simbi does suffer – an exhilarating, astonish-
ing series of hardships, in Sinners' Town, among the Multi-Coloured
People, with her girl companions, Rali, Sala, Kadara, and the cock-
lady. She becomes the wife of a woodcutter. Her children are sacri-
ficed so she leaves him. But before she can return to her home of
'wealths' which she now sensibly sees is the best place, she must
overcome the noxious, almost unkillable, Satyr of the Dark Jungle.
After all these feminine hardships she manages to exterminate the
Satyr by becoming an insect and 'entering into his nose unexpectedly'
– an equally feminine method of slaughter.

Tutuola's fourth book, *The Brave African Huntress* (1958), is
also for girls rather than boys. It is about a girl who feels she must
use her father's hunting skills in order to rescue her four 'senior
brothers' who have been imprisoned in the Jungle of the Pygmies.
On another level it is about the emancipation of African girls. And
on still another plane it is about the common human fear of the
unknown 'Little People', the Pygmies.

Tutuola's fifth book, *Feather Woman of the Jungle* (1962), returns to a masculine chief character. Here are the adventures of a
rich, seventy-eight-year-old Yoruba chief, told by himself each of

ten nights under the moonlight to his people, when he regales each with a keg of palm-wine.

'In eighteenth century', *Feather Woman of the Jungle* begins, 'the hunter who first came to Abeokuta', 'Oduduwa, was the hero father of Yorubas :'

> Hardly in the morning when the day's tasks began, the spinners would take up their spindles . . . the warriors would take up their weapons . . . the drummers would take up their drums and the hunters would take up their bows and arrows. . . .
>
> The women's dresses were aprons, head ties, veils for young ladies or newly married ladies and top covers for old and married women only. . . .
>
> Our plays and amusements were fables, folk-lores, proverbs, riddles, etc., etc., after day's work was over.
>
> Mighty trees round the town were reserved as they were the habitations of spirits and witches.

Such is the naïveté of Tutuola's inimitable style.

The motif or deeper level of *Feather Woman of the Jungle*, of these ten African Nights' Entertainments, is the ruthless, cool, perseverance men need to obtain any of the good things from life. Some of these good things Tutuola makes very clear : they are wisdom, wealth, and a 'stagnant' wife. The old chief who recounts his adventures only once failed to bring back from his dangerous travels plenty of 'gold blocks' or 'stores of diamonds'. Yet his amusing presence of mind in face of the most gruesome happenings is as endearing as his confident yet sufficiently humble opinion of himself. Sprinkled in the chief's stories is good advice for his listening people in decently small doses.

What Tutuola's first book is then, and what his four others are in only slightly less degree, is the most skilful, and frequently visionary, blend of psychological fantasy, myth, and fable. All five are fine fairy tales as well as contriving to be something more, for boys and girls and grown-ups. If Tutuola is to be likened to Bunyan, he may need also to be compared to Hans Andersen. He owes something, perhaps to the older D. O. Fagunwa, who writes in Yoruba.

Tutuola holds in his tales and in his person the most strongly descernable link for both African and non-African readers between spoken and written story-telling in his country. For a long time critics will contradict each other about his books and his meanings. But he will remain a weaver of tales that delight not only Africans but children and adults scattered over the world.

CHINUA ACHEBE A younger man than Tutuola, Achebe was born in Iboland, Eastern Nigeria, in 1930. He comes next to Tutuola in importance as a prose writer. Achebe as a novelist works not in imaginative fantasy but on the opposing basis of realism. With his three novels up to 1964, one of which is already translated into at least three European languages, he has built up a reputation. In each novel, in quiet, impartial-sounding prose that seems to be un-emotional but isn't, Achebe gives a detailed, traditional, Iboland-village background that is also richly African. All three novels light up the struggle between values that linger longest in rural areas and the values of modernity.

First, see Achebe's description of the African dark as background :

> The night was very quiet. It was always quiet except on moon-light nights. Darkness held a vague terror for these people, even the bravest among them. Children were warned not to whistle at night for fear of evil spirits. Dangerous animals became even more sinister and uncanny in the dark. A snake was never called by its name at night, because it would hear. It was called a string. And so on this particular night as the crier's voice was gradually swallowed up in the distance, silence returned to the world, a vibrant silence made more intense by the universal trill of a mil-lion million forest insects.

This background Achebe peoples with many characters, the chief of which have great weaknesses within great strengths. These weak-nesses by which Achebe's characters outrage perennially-known and universally-understood human ethics tear apart and crush the slow flowering of lives important in the villages to which they belong. With both his African characters and his African background Achebe interweaves as passionately impartial a description of the strengths and weaknesses, also very easily recognizable, of the white invaders bringing a new god, a new wealth, new ways. Over both traditional and modern values he throws a fitful humour, a mildly comic irony.

In his first novel, *Things Fall Apart*, his African characters in their Ibo village life follow a ceremonious ritual by no means simple. Their code of virtue is not unbecoming to human beings of the con-tinent from which some of our earliest ancestors may have set forth.

He describes the villagers of Umuofia. He tells about their feast of New Yam, about their communal rejoicing over a betrothal, about preparations of the *Ilo* wrestling ground for the Week of Peace that must precede the planting of the yams, about the village's fear of the pronouncements of the Oracle of the Hills and the Caves; he describes the mad Priestess of the Oracle (Is she the Oracle itself?) carrying off a loved only child; he tells of an Ozo dance when a man of worth takes one of the Clan titles, the procession of the nine Egwugwus or masked Ancestor Spirits and of their dispensing

of justice; he describes twin babies being put out to die, a superstitious practice that by no means all neighbouring tribes of the
Ibos followed; he gives the song for a woman who died.

> For whom is it well? For whom is it well?
> There is no one for whom it is well;

This brings to mind Euripides' 'Is there on God's earth one happy
man?'

Humour is in Achebe's account of the rain-maker. We are left
in no doubt at all that the rain-maker's magic claims come from
acute personal weather-lore and from far-reaching rain-rumour
in a dry land. The disguises of the *Egwugwu* 'spirits' is pierced.
Umuofia villagers' child-like, fear-thrilled acceptance of these Masks
is comparable to the fear-thrill that a horror film gives to a Western
audience. Deception and self-deception alike are seen through.

> Okonkwo's wives, and perhaps other women as well might have
> noticed that the second *egwugwu* had the springy walk of
> Okonkwo.
> . . . But if they thought these things they kept them within
> themselves. The *egwugwu* with the springy walk was one of the
> dead fathers of the clan. He looked terrible. . . .

Things Fall Apart is the tragedy of Obi Okonkwo of Umuofia,
the ambitious, energetic son reacting against a father scorned by
his fellows for being an idle 'loafer' who didn't 'get on'. Obi made
himself a person of substance, respected in eight of nine villages.
This was just before the time of the first missionaries. The missionaries were quickly followed by soldiers and officers of foreign law.

Here is an instance of Achebe's perception of how Obi's weakness
within strength, his lack of the integrity of real individuality, will bring
about his undoing :

> Okonkwo ruled his household with a heavy hand. His wives,
> especially the youngest, lived in pereptual fear of his fiery tem-
> per and so did his little children. Perhaps down in his heart
> Okonkwo was not a cruel man. But his whole life was dominated
> by fear, the fear of failure and weakness. It was deeper and more
> intimate than the fear of evil and capricious gods and of magic,
> the fear of the forest, and of the forces of nature, malevolent, red
> in tooth and claw. Okonkwo's fear was greater than these. It was
> not external but lay deep within himself. It was the fear of him-
> self, lest he should be found to resemble his father. Even as a
> little boy he had resented his father's failure and weakness . . .
> and so Okonkwo was ruled by one passion – to hate everything
> that his father Unoka had loved. One of these things was gentle-
> ness and another was idleness.

In keeping with his bullying, Okonkwo outrages true village tradition by beating one of his wives in the Week of Peace that should precede yam planting.

Threat of war comes to Umuofia. One of their girls is murdered by a villager of neighbouring Mbaino. Why or by whom she was murdered does not seem clear to at least one reader. But Achebe may have meant to imply that this kind of murder could happen in Iboland – as it can happen anywhere. Lack of explanation is not necessarily a flaw in an otherwise clear story. Okonkwo, sent to obtain restitution from the elders of Mbaino, succeeds in bringing back a boy. Thus he wards off the need for Umuofia's making war on Mbaino. This kind of success in peaceful negotiation gives a man prestige in such a community. The boy Ikemefuna lives in Okonkwo's household as his son. He becomes his own son's soon-loved brother. But at the end of two years a majority of Umuofia's headmen consent to what Achebe surely wishes the reader to see as a cruelly primitive, implacable, eye-for-an-eye retribution, imposed by the Oracle and superstitiously believed in. Hadn't Obi averted just such cruelty by bringing the village the useful Ikemefuna? But the innocent boy must after all die. The men take him out into the forest.

Here seems the crux of Obi's – and Achebe's – story. A man should be individually strong by the traditional standard of the 'God within' : his conscience. This is the *Chi* of Ibo theology. Achebe seems to be saying that this standard of the 'God within' is a perennial human standard : it is not one that has recently 'evolved'. But rather than seem weak by the superstitious standards of his fellows, and against the advice of the wisest old warrior-elder, Obi takes upon himself to deal the child who has called him father the fatal blow.[1]

At the funeral of that same old warrior-elder Obi's gun – a symbol of the individual strength, the coveted technical prowess of the white man – 'accidentally' explodes. The explosion kills the dead man's link with the living, his eldest son. Unless this 'accident' is seen as inevitable because Okonkwo is what he is, it may seem merely an unconvincing incident. Actually it conveys the important statement that the ambitious Okonkwo wants more power but has not a strong enough *Chi*, a conscience of sufficient awareness and integrity, to hold it. He fails abjectly to control his modern weapon. Thereby he shows himself unfit not only for true, traditional responsibility but for the even heavier responsibility that further enlightenment and modern lethal instruments impose on men.

[1] Austin J. Shelton's article (*Transition,* 13) 'The Offended *Chi* in Achebe's Novels' takes insufficient account of the subtlety of Achebe's emancipation as a writer.

Obi accepts the seven years' banishment from the village for his crime. He must go to his mother's people. In Umuofia culture a mother's people will always help a son or a daughter in trouble. Here there is tacit comparison between this form of non-vindictive justice and the colder penalties both of the primitive.Oracle and of modern legality. These penalties, Achebe is implying, are both of them often useless and, therefore, evil.

The first white missionaries have arrived in Iboland by Obi's return to Umuofia. One has been killed by the villagers of neighbouring Abame. Umuofia people well know that the killing of any stranger unless in battle is blameful. Killing this one is senseless as well. They have heard more and more of the white man's daring, knowledge, power, and weapons. They envy and desire all these.

More missionaries arrive, this time at Umuofia itself. They are given a piece of the Evil Forest on which to build a Church. This is to be a test of their god. Umuofia people are convinced that the watching Spirits of the Evil Forest will cause the missionaries to die and their power to make converts fail. These missionaries have condemned abandonment of twins, possessing of more than one wife, beating of wives; they have asserted their god to be the 'only god on earth' and Umuofia gods to be 'wicked heathen idols'.

The missionaries don't perish. But their converts are the weak, the unfortunate, distraught mothers of twins, or social outcasts, *osu*. That this question of the Ibo social outcast, *osu*, is an important one for Achebe is clear from his second novel in which the story centres round the struggle of an educated Ibo who has to choose between Clara, the girl he loves, and his village which is outraged by his choice : for Clara is *osu*. Presumably *osu* are outcasts because of some crime or social misdemeanour one of their ancestors has been guilty of. The village Elders attempt to identify themselves with relentless 'natural' laws of punishment : they, the guardians of the community's morals, cannot trust to present mercy and forgive the innocent descendant of an offender. They must hold to implacable logic of judgement. Simple human forgiveness would be thought weak and sliding.

By the missionaries' survival Achebe seeks to show how inevitable it is that cruelty and superstition, even the implacable judgement of Elders, about *osu*, about twins, or about mystic powers of the royal python, must all go down when challenged. They may be challenged by more developed superstitions – as that forgiveness is commanded by the Son of the only God, miraculously born of a Virgin, who rose from the dead, and who will preside at a Judgement Day to decree eternal torment for wrong-doers. Compassion could never be a simple human good? But Christianity must mean more than its superstitions if it is to hold more of the elusive truth. All this indicates the depth of imaginative thought at which Achebe consistently works.

Because of Okonkwo's harshness as a father his son runs away from home. He joins the missionaries. Obi curses him. When the seven years' exile are up and Obi has been helped to rebuild his home in Umuofia, more trouble has arisen between the missionaries and the villagers there. Trouble often arose between missionaries and villagers. Hitherto we have had chiefly the English version. Now we have the African version.

Urged by Obi the villagers burn the Christian Church. The Christians allow themselves to be backed by their military. Messengers of the foreign District Commissioner take six villagers, among them Obi, to a discussion, beat them up, and free them. Obi urges war against the foreigner. Soldiers in numbers descend on the village, to uphold the *pax Britannica* by superior force of arms. Obi sees the villagers have lost heart against the colossus. They won't fight. Rather than give in he goes out and hangs himself.

Thus *Things Fall Apart* is a tragedy, the downfall of a man who was not strong enough to challenge cruel stupidity in his fellows; a man not courageous enough, and therefore not trusted enough, to stand alone for the age-old wisdom of not helping in the slaughter of an innocent boy accepted as a son. The novel illustrates, in Achebe's unadorned prose, not only the gulf that can yawn between the African point of view and the white man's, but also the hiatus that gapes between perennial standards of behaviour true and false.

Achebe's second novel, *No Longer at Ease* (1960), skips a generation. It misses out Obi Okonkwo's son, Isaac, who became a Christian for a reason that was understandable, even valid, but was certainly not strength of belief. *No Longer at Ease* takes up the story again at Obi's grandson, also called Obi. This Obi is a young man growing up in the nineteen-thirties and forties to a Nigeria ready to become independent with new towns, urban-industrial development and the irresistible prospect of material riches for more and more people.

Obi is being educated in the white man's knowledge. He is the hope of his village. He has been to England on the village's money. On his return he horrifies his parents and his benefactors, the Progressive Union of Elders, by having fallen in love, on the boat coming home, with Clara : Clara has been to England too and is a nurse. Innocent, she yet belongs to an *osu* family. By obscure, stupid, and surely unjust, village reckoning, she is an outcast.

Obi comes home to a modern Lagos. There emphasis on money, success, luxury, and class distinctions are of prime importance.

There can be no denying that some Africans took to these so-called American and British values as easily as do most human beings. Desire 'for power in terms of rule or of having your own way, like desire for wealth and physical luxury is latent in people of most cultures judging by the ease with which opportunity for these things is passed on. (We must except cultures such as Bushman, Pygmy, Amerindian, Maori, and some Nilotes : these are relatively uninterested in technological advance and education. But they are said to be dying.) Yet hot on the heels of 'advance' and 'progress', writers like Chinua Achebe sense the need to think again; and – more insight gained – to speak for some 'eternal' values that are to be preferred to some of civilization's more materialist ones. These perennial values are at once beyond, and at the same time part of, what we often, imprecisely, call the 'natural'.

Nigerian village cultures represent the greater extent of the country's life. They are not, of course, its vocal aspect or its growing-point. In Scotland, Wales and Ireland, as well as in many other parts of the Earth, a parallel could be made : rural cultures are far greater in extent than the most press-noisy urban ones. To think only from urban standpoints is to fall victim to many illusions. Thus, Obi's parents and the Elders of his village want him to be a splendid and prosperous man of the town. They have no inkling of what they are asking him to stand against.

Again, the crux of Achebe's second novel is of similar profundity to that of his first. Besides being, overtly, young Obi Okonkwo's story, *No Longer at Ease* is about the confusion of values, not only between 'good' tradition and blind, ugly superstitious tradition, but also between new 'advance' and new corruptions. First Obi gets into debt over taxes, then over his new car, then over sending money to his people. Next he takes bribes. The white leaders are not free from using personal pull in well-disguised, or 'civilized', 'innocent' forms : such as that you are most likely to gain promotion if you go to Church and say you are a Christian, if you let it be known that you have been to a well-known school, or even if your aunt slept with a king. As if unaware that any of these things are not in the deepest sense corrupt, they are supremely critical of the African new officials' form of corruption, their addiction to stark bribery, by money or gifts. Bribery of the overt kind whites feel they have outgrown.

Again and again, in his laconic, flat prose, Achebe shows up the new values. Again he stresses how clarity and charity and strength of mind are needed to keep one's head above the shifting morass of social change. Wisdom and strength of mind might be thought to belong to, to be derived from, bodily bravery. In reality they have only a little to do with physical courage. How can the traditional brave man of action become the modern man of insight? This is what Achebe seems to be asking. Sometimes it looks as if the complacent, white man's offers of progress and his religion have emasculated the black man.

And again, as backdrop to this novel Achebe paints a moving picture of traditional village life under the onslaught of modernity.

But in *No Longer at Ease* the detached, matter-of-fact, confident prose has become lighter : 'We all have to stand on the earth itself and go with her at her pace' : this is Obi thinking after his downfall towards the end of the book. Words put into a chief character's mouth or mind should never be confused with an author's own thought. But this philosophic outlook of Obi's may mean that his creator, too, has accepted the inevitability of modern change. It may also mean that the pitfalls of 'progress' need not be seen as wholly tragic.

In his third novel, *Arrow of God* (1964), Achebe returns to the Nigeria of 1931. This could be looked at as a retreat from facing the struggle at too close quarters in his own generation. But *Arrow of God* is Achebe's richest and most competently constructed novel to date. It may not be the great African novel that Ezekiel Mphahlele is waiting for. But it would not come altogether badly out of a comparison with novels like *Anna Karenina, Madame Bovary,* and *Middlemarch.*

Arrow of God has more resonance than Achebe's previous novels have. It has less comic sense. The chasm between perennial values and the cruelly superstitious, as well as those which are meretricious among the new, is returned to as mortal, tragic; superficial misunderstandings alone are treated as comic.

In a group of six Ibo villages called Umuaro, the ageing Ezeulu, headstrong, ambitious, prosperous, jealous of his power after years of wielding it, is the priest of the most powerful of Umuaro's lesser deities, Ulu :

> In the very distant past, when lizards were still few and far between, the six villages – Umuachala, Umunneora, Umuagu, Umuezeani, Umuogwugwu, and Umuisiuzo lived as different people, and each worshipped its own deity.
> Then the hired soldiers of Abam used to strike in the dead of night, set fire to houses and carry men, women and children into slavery. Things were so bad for the six villages that their leaders came together to save themselves. They hired a strong team of medicine-men to install a common deity for them. This deity which the fathers of the six villages made was called Ulu. . . .
> The six villages took the name of Umuaro, and the priest of

Ulu became their Chief Priest. From that day they were never
again beaten by an enemy. How could such a people disregard
the god who founded the town and protected it? . . .

Thus in their sore need of a god, not against circumstances but
against human cruelty, the villagers united. Their Elders asked the
good medicine-men, called by some 'witch-doctors' but really diviners and often the village conscience, to set up a god. Then the Elders
turned about and declared that the god himself it was who had
created their union; the god it was who now protected *them*. Vil-
agers' sense of community as well as their unity with natural forces
is here brought out by Achebe. Such sense of community and of unity
with nature can be paralleled, of course, amongst remote Welsh,
English and Irish villagers. It is found in most rural areas of the
Earth. In his book *The African Image* Ezekiel Mphahlele takes Dan
Jacobson and Hannah Arendt lightly to task for asserting that
African tradition in its unity with nature made no 'human reality'.
Achebe seems to be saying that a self-aware, individual sense of this
'human reality' is as relentlessly necessary for human living as is the
modern, more scientifically connoted, community sense.

African creation-myths, like all creation-myths, are a patchwork
of guesses both beautiful and crude. More fully than before Achebe
outlines the Ibo ones. Umuaro believes in Ani-Mmo, the spirit-
world, in a High God or Creator, and in an Earth-Mother. The
High God of Umuaro took little interest in his creatures. Earth
Mother could not protect her children's lives or change their fates.
Each Umuaro man's and woman's *Chi*, his 'god within', gave him
his knowledge of good and ill; a man's *Chi*, therefore, might be said
to be the personality made out of his inherited traits, even his destiny.
With a man's *Chi* we may compare that difficult Christian assump-
tion 'free will'. Achebe makes us ponder on all that we do not know
about, as well as what we know about. He persuades us, as novelists
and poets do set out to persuade, towards clearer thought about
what we are all doing here.

Umuaro's gods, lesser than the High One, are like Greek gods :
they are not above jealousy and spite as men are not above these.
In dramatic action Achebe illustrates disagreements, greeds, jealousies, and fears among Umuaro men and women. He gives dialogue
without mincing and proverbs in abundance, revealing the richness
of Ibo culture. By the 'arrow of God', presumably, he means to
indicate the killing by Christianity of Ibo superstitions. But can,
Achebe seems again to be asking, God's Christian creatures solve
the problem of how to live more wisely?

The god of Umuaro's rival village of Okperi is Eru the Magnificent. Eru personifies the universal desire, latent in some maybe, for riches. Eru is the 'one who gives wealth to those who find favour with him'. We are not told how riches are got in traditional West Africa. No doubt riches are got as they are got elsewhere and have been got since the days of the Pharaohs – by prolonged endeavour and by shrewd and sharp long-term plans. Eru's rich priest, Nwaka, excites the jealousy of Eleuzu, priest of Ulu.

When the white man first came to Umuaro, the district, like many another, but by no means like all African regions, had no king. The man 'who aspired to be king must first pay all the debts of every man and woman in Umuaro'. The council of Elders decided that such social responsibility must be the sign of fitness to be a king. No man was found to be as generous with his personal gains as all that. Umuaro remained kingless. Thus, Achebe seems to imply, if rich men cannot shoulder responsibility as heavy as this for their fellows, better no king.

The white man, 'who turned everything upside down', interfered and decided in favour of rival Okperi's land-claim against Umuaro. Eleuzu stood out against his village. In the cause of what he then saw as truth, Eleuzu sided with the white man, agreeing that the land was originally Okperi's.

But as time went on Eleuzu grew, as power makes so many grow, more and more overweening in pride and obstinacy. Achebe draws Eleuzu's character, with its strengths and its weaknesses, in more loving detail and with more warmth than he has yet expended on any of his creations. He shows again the interplay between Umuaro's ceremonies, rivalries, quarrels, cruelties, and the power Umuaro men and women attribute to their gods, ancestor spirits, and priest. Humour is seen in what the black man admired in the white besides his wealth, his weapons, his strength and his knowledge – an ability to 'write word with his *left* hand'.

Blindly the Umuaro villagers fear, as well as admire, the white man's knowledge and force. They conclude all comes from the white man's god. Madly pretending – interpreting – their own god, priest Eleuzu declares it is Ulu's decree to postpone the people's yam harvest; he locks them in the old year for two moons. This haughty cruelty brings famine to his village and his own family.

But not even Eleuzu the priest of a powerful god can stand as a stiff-necked individual. Eleuzu's son dies. The people see this as an unmistakable portent; Ulu has turned against his overweening priest. They abandon Eleuzu. They offer yams to the Church in grovelling hopes that the Christian god will bless the new harvest. Eleuzu in his last days is still haughty and arrogantly opinionated. But he is demented, almost a laughing-stock, though spared knowledge of any 'final outcome'. Does the white man have the 'last' word again? Achebe indicates that – only temporarily, and not by moral superiority – the white man does.

But he does not try to offer any larger-than-life or any over-simple solution to the mortal conflict among human values. The sifting of these issues, his packed and dramatic stories seem to suggest, forms part of life's perpetual challenge to our race.

This writer's fourth novel will be most eagerly awaited.

CYPRIAN EKWENSI A third Nigerian novelist, Ekwensi has written four novels – *People of the City* (1954), *Jagua Nana* (1960), *Burning Grass* (1962), and *Beautiful Feathers* (1963). He also writes short stories; and *An African Night's Entertainment* (1962), is a traditional fable. In his novels Ekwensi uses an urban-sophisticated style.

Jagua Nana is perhaps the best known of the four novels. Jagua Nana is a harlot of Lagos night-life, and tough. Since Lagos has become a modern town, she has learnt to live by what a leading African critic has called her 'down-to-earth common sense'. According to her standards Jagua loves Freddie. Freddie is twenty-five to Jagua's forty-five, and educated – a teacher. The story turns on Jagua's jealousy as he continues his education and career, to some extent with her help; but he comes to love Nancy who is his own age and ready to fight for ordinary marriage. Jagua is left to age and loneliness.

Like all Ekwensi's novels, *Jagua Nana* is modern-western in tone as well as in style. The values, which are fairly superficial, are almost totally urban. Yet the conflict of jealousy in Jagua is what anyone in any culture would understand. The struggle between her way of life and her age that will make that way of life impossible is also understandable. Ekwensi's exuberant drawing of Jagua is disinterested enough not to detract from his portrayal of the genuineness of Nancy's love for Freddie and he leaves us in no doubt about which affection is preferable. Yet Jagua remains by far the most vital character in the book.

Personal conflict just below the character-surface is what interests Ekwensi and what he evokes. He has the liveliest eye for telling yet obvious detail and a 'living', or physical, use of words. There is little traditional background in *Jagua Nana*. The pidgin, used chiefly by Jagua, adds very much to her aliveness. Some people complain it is not 'proper' pidgin. But one virtue of pidgin, evidently, is that it can't be standardized. In all his novels so far, Ekwensi does, beneath a certain superficiality, contrive to extend a little the experience of his readers, though this may be chiefly by virtue of his Africanness.

ONUORA NZEKWU   In *Black Orpheus*, No. II, Omidiji Aragbabalu has compared the Nigerian Onuora Nzekwu's first novel, *A Wand of Noble Wood* (1961) with Chinua Achebe's *No Longer at Ease* (1960). Nzekwu is from eastern Nigeria, and he has written two novels so far. The second of these is *Blade Among the Boys* (1962).

Nzekwu's style, Mr Aragbabalu writes, 'has none of the ease and balance of Achebe's accomplished and beautiful prose'. But then Mr Aragbabalu goes on to discuss, to Nzekwu's advantage, and somewhat against Achebe's, each author's approach to his hero. Both *A Wand of Noble Wood* and *No Longer at Ease* are concerned with a young Ibo living in Lagos, and the entanglements of each with modernity and with native village life. Mr Aragbabalu feels that Obo Okonkwo in *No Longer at Ease* despised both his own people and the townspeople of Lagos. But this very fact supposes and proves – at least to a non-African reader – greater depth in Achebe's characterization. The weight of Achebe's insight about false values both new and old may be responsible for his chief character's lonely isolation. The heroes of both Nzekwu's first and second books are not delineated to any depth, are too much part of their relatives and traditions – to despise, defy, or feel tragically alienated, as modern sons, and not only of African parents, do.

D. O. FAGUNWA   This writer has four novels in Yoruba awaiting translation. All that is yet published in English is an extract, 'The Forest of the Lord' in *A Selection of African Prose, 2* (1964).

NKEM NWANKWO   The youngest of Nigerian novelists is Nkem Nwankwo. Nwankwo's first novel, *Danda*, was published in 1964.

Born in 1936 near the well-known market-town of Onitsha, this young Ibo received his entire education within his own country. He graduated in the English school of Ibadan University and now teaches English in Ibadan Grammar School.

Nwankwo's novel *Danda* is similar to Gabriel Okara's *The Voice* in one respect – it concerns itself wholly with African characters and values. But there is no tragedy in *Danda*. The young man Danda, or 'Rain' as he is nicknamed, is a Peer Gynt, a playboy kind of fellow; he wears bells on his legs, plays the flute, dances, makes love to the flighty youngest wife of the chief, and he escapes by sheer gaiety being taken to task for idleness and shiftless irresponsibility. At the end of this light-hearted book we are left in no doubt that Danda will marry, settle down, and in due course take the *ozo* title, the mark of the senior men of his village, simply by paying for it. He will end up an Elder wise enough to counsel others.

There is nothing deep about the novel *Danda*, and it has many blemishes in construction. Too many threads are left hanging : Danda's brother, for instance, comes into the story, provokes our interest in him, but he disappears without further comment; again we are given to understand that Danda must surely be punished for the heinous fault of making love to the pretty Ekeama under the *ogbu* tree by moonlight; but the matter is not touched upon again. Perhaps we are meant to assume that the chief forgave Danda's seduction. But there are too many unfinished strands and unwarrantable shifts of focus for us to be sure about this. Ibo words are used, but the glossary at the end of the book is not adequate. Yet the novel is high-spirited and very African in the sense that its characters are free from European presences and European inhibitions. Probably *Danda* is close to the traditions of Ibo oral storytelling : certainly most of its lively and inconsequent chapters are short stories rather than architectural parts of a unified novel.

TIMOTHY MOFOLORUNZO ALUKO   In 1959 this author's *One Man, One Wife*, published in Lagos, was the third Nigerian novel to be printed. Reviewing it in *Black Orpheus*, No. 6, Ulli Beier wrote that it concerned conflict between Christian and Shango (Yoruba) ethics; but 'instead of a novel his book has become an harangue that ends with a sermon'. Its 'abusive misunderstanding' of Yoruba culture and its pervading use of clichés were what made Ulli Beier so unusually condemnatory.

T. M. Aluko's second novel, *One Man, One Matchet*, was published in England in 1964. His prose has been commended by a critic in *The Times Literary Supplement* as 'graceful', 'relaxing'; his irony as 'gentle'; the story he tells is called by the same critic 'enchanting'.[1]

Has T. M. Aluko developed the expected African sense of humour? He has. There is a fashionable preference for light irony in the British 1960s. Lightness and laughter are indispensable to any written art. But a novel should also have depth of perception.

Dealing with the wealth and variety of West African novels now coming from the Press means emphasizing yet once more what a novel, as opposed to 'fictional entertainment', is. As chameleon as most art-forms, the novel in advanced cultures has, in recent years, had its appeal challenged by sociological, psychological, and anthropological, case-histories, as well as by films and television. It is a fact that industrial work is so enervating that we turn in leisure to what makes least demands mentally and emotionally. A further fact is that fewer of us in this social era have quiet, or mood, or freedom of self-sufficient solitude, to read a novel in the way in which

[1] November 12th, 1964.

a novel needs to be read. After all, a true novel probably holds a little of the life-blood – if not of a master-spirit – of an articulate and feeling person.

One Man, One Matchet is a competent piece of light fiction. It is full of action, of court-house trials, fraudulent fund-raising, chiefs' meetings, and cut-throat enmities that end, of course, in murder. Its period is that in which power was being transferred from white men back to black men. That this transfer was supposed to be taking place in Yorubaland (Western Nigeria) can be ignored. Dialogue in *One Man, One Matchet*, weighted with Christian phrasing, might belong to almost any Christianized tribal community. But – contrary to what some scholars thought as recently as ten years ago – fear, superstition, and disease, as well as speech itself, have very distinctive shapes in each of the many different districts of Africa. If unique variations are scamped, vital human differences are falsified.

Thus, a subtle denigration lies behind some of T. M. Aluko's 'gentle' irony. When this irony is directed against African characters, sophisticated Western readers may find it funny. They will probably be unaware that a sense of superiority is part of the reason they find irony and humour there. Characterization of this sort is irksome in a novel : irksome because it is as manifestly spurious as the 'evil' of the 'slant-eyed' Oriental agent of bookstall fiction, the kind of fiction found at air and rail termini all over Europe and America; soon, probably, such fiction will be copious at African and Asian stations and airports as well.

A novel is a tale in which, with humour and individual perception, a little more of the infinite labyrinth of our common human nature is traversed. T. M. Aluko's lively fictional entertainment can be read with all but the topmost layer of intelligence cheerfully disengaged.

Two writers of Sierra Leone

ABIOSEH NICOL Born in Sierra Leone, Nicol was educated in Nigeria and read Natural Sciences at Cambridge. He is a short-story writer and a poet of sensitivity and intellect. Two of his best stories are 'As the Night, the Day', and 'The Devil at Yolahun Bridge'. The second story turns on the presentation of the points of view of an African engineer, Oluyemi Hughes, Sanderson, an English colonial officer, and Hounslow, a Kenya-European trader. In this realistic story the decent friendliness of the three men, two white and one black, towards each other shows, at one and the same time, both how tantalizingly possible understandings seem, and yet how far-off they in fact are. A poem of Abioseh Nicol's that promises much, and it is to be hoped, promises more like it, is 'The Continent that lies within us' from Olumbe Bassir's *Anthology of West African Verse*. 'The Devil at Yolahun Bridge' is given in our Anthology; and the poems and stories of Abioseh Nicol may sometimes be heard on the B.B.C.

WILLIAM CONTON Also of Sierra Leone, William Conton has written one novel up to 1964. *The African* is, in respect of tone and language, written with distinction. William Conton's outlook and his one book places this author beside Soyinka, Clark, Peter Abrahams, Ezekiel Mphahlele, Okara, Chinua Achebe, and Abioseh Nicol for width and vision of aim if not of achievement. We are bound to use words such as vision and tone and to measure one writer by another. This does not mean that each writer is not seen in his own right. Nor need it mean that unprofitable comparisons are being made.

The African is the supposed autobiography of Kisimi Kamara, a gifted Hausa from a fictitious West African state. Hausas are Muslim Negroes of Northern Nigeria speaking a Hamitic language. Kamara, from Songhai, tells how he went to study at the University of Durham in Britain. Conton's – or Kisimi Kamara's – account of the visitor's reactions to the country and his dealings with ordinary British people is the most generously understanding of any African's writing up to 1964. English readers cannot fail to be won by it.

Kisimi returns to Songhai. He teaches for some time; then, urged by his idealistic conception of a Pan-African Federation, after independence for Songhai and other states has been achieved, he enters politics.

In his book *The Human Factor in Changing Africa* (1962) Melville Herskovits describes how, in 1953, in Lagos, he attended the session of the Nigerian House of Representatives. On that occasion the withdrawal of members from Western and Eastern Regions broke the existing constitutions and paved the way for Nigeria's Independence seven years later. There is a similarity between these events and that period which William Conton describes, although Conton is a Sierra Leonian.

Years of exhausting and complicated political struggle for freedom from foreign rule were in store for Kisimi Kamara. He becomes premier of Songhai. One reader's respect was won again by Kamara's remaining undisillusioned and without too cynical a worldliness. He left Africa and African events for four or five important years of his youth, to live in a foreign culture. This gives him a scale for measuring his own Africa.

Erisa Kironde, in *Black Orpheus*, No. 10 criticizes Conton, perhaps justly, for attempting to cover, in his book, too long a span of
years, and for touching on too many live issues to go deeply into
any of them. Conton, Erisa Kironde says, refers to 'large and indis-
cribable doses of the materialism of "Western Civilization" ' on his
return : 'we were', he writes 'in danger of losing our direction'. For
Ezekiel Mphahlele, Conton's rediscovery of his own Africa, upon
his return from Britain, tends to romanticism : it is a 'stance that
spoils the author's good writing'. Mr Mphahlele continues :

> Must the educated African from abroad come back to re-colon-
> ize us? Must he walk about with his mouth open, startled by the
> beauty of African women, by the black man's 'heightened sensi-
> tivity'? It's all so embarrassing.

Certainly, it must be embarrassing to an African to hear himself
supposed to have 'heightened sensibility'. African sensibility is of
the run of that of other human beings. Perhaps the point is that
African cultures do not set out to hide 'sensibility'. Western
twentieth-century literature, schooled in two wars, almost always
disguises this quality under a toughly reasoning intellect.

But the memory of the white South African girl with whom Kisimi
Kamara had the beginnings of an understanding in Britain will not
leave him. After a few weeks with her in England, Greta had been
run over and – most unconvincingly, it must be admitted – killed.
Haunted by his loss, Kisimi at last resigns his premiership. He
enters South Africa secretly to find and kill her previous Boer lover
whom he believes responsible for her death in England. When
eventually he finds him, the man is miserably drunk. Kamara's
desire for useless revenge turns – too suddenly for most readers'
credulity – to compassion. This, with lightning stroke – also incredible – frees Kamara from vindictiveness.

Undoubtedly hurdles of plot, probability, and character-motive,
are not surmounted with success by Conton in *The African*. Yet
the story is held by a certain realism joined to an idealistic strength
of mind. These together seem able to include in their scales both
traditional and modern backgrounds and values. The glow, often
tender and humorous, that Conton sheds over both African scenes
and English ones does make conflict between tradition and modernity seem too easily soluble. But not all readers will see this as an
unforgivable fault – overriding Conton's insight and breadth of outlook.

There are other writers, not only of West Africa, but of East
and South as well, whose work is not known sufficiently well to
make any discussion valuable at present.

Chapter 7

THE PRESENT AND THE FUTURE

If all the wide approaches to problems specifically African, 'black consciousness', *Négritude*, or 'the search for the African personality' are put aside, what becomes apparent to the non-African reader, not once but too repeatedly to be missed among African books, is the limpidly-clear style which some African-English writers seem to possess. One result of using this style is that, however urgent the writer's emotion, his prose remains direct and uncorrugated. Such a style might even be called unpretentious.

Among those who have this kinship in prose style are African writers as widely distributed over their continent as Camara Laye, Peter Abrahams, William Conton, Chinua Achebe, Shaaban Robert, James Ngugi, Grace Ogot, and among short story writers, Abioseh Nicol, Ezekiel Mphahlele, Alex La Guma, Cyprian Ekwensi, Alf Wannenburg, and Arthur Maimane. There must be many more among prose writers who have the characteristic. It is not of course wholly instinctive or unselfconscious. The fact that they have a clarity or concrete straightforwardness in common by no means detracts from each writer's individuality of expression. On the contrary, the individuality of each, certainly of those mentioned above, is added to and enhanced. Maybe such style is part of important writers' answers to being confronted by, and being hailed as scions of, an already created literature in an old language.

Among poets the same element of transparency, of search towards simple verbal precision – if it can be called that – is noticeable. Gabriel Okara has it. Rabéarivelo shows it – as, of course, any real poet (or any poet beyond an occasional versifier) must show it. That the quality is one that emerges only from writing in English is not being condescendingly suggested. That Africans are more direct 'by nature' than other writers is equally not being put forward. Shaaban Robert, in both his poetry and his prose, shows the straight-spoken yet humble refusal of easy conviction that is also part of the attitude under review. Wole Soyinka's academic training and John Pepper Clark's have not stifled it in them : they show it but to a much more hidden degree. Soyinka hardly shows it at all to a non-African reader in *A Dance of the Forests*; in his brilliantly funny 'Salutation to the Gut' he is obviously imitating delib-

117

erately the most elaborately referenced styles of varied British academic studies. Among poets such as Efua Theodora Sutherland, Valente Malangatana, and Kwesi Brew, spontaneous directness is also an unhampered expression of convincing, not more than life-size, human feeling.

Amos Tutuola's naïveté stands not altogether alone here. Having a similar physical directness his particular individuality suggests that the characteristic in question has something to do with the closeness that written African prose and poetry still have to Africa's only half-revealed universe of spoken story and verbal poetry; this remains bound up with African communal, chiefly non-urban, living. An effort towards emotional forthrightness (though this last word is rightly suspect at this moment in time) is certainly part of Beja and Shukria poetry, the only oral verse of which the author has any personal knowledge.

The distinguishing feature to be isolated and given attention may be no more than relative freedom from intellectualization or from sophisticated, knowing condescension. If so, such quality is bound soon to be lost, at least lessened. Plainly only decreasing amounts of what is here being allied to naïveté of feeling and thought can be retained in written art of any kind. But need this burgeoning of African literature that we are witnessing cause some African-English styles to forfeit their certain and supreme element of difference? Need any African writer sacrifice his speech-freedom, more than is strictly practical, in face of the tough problems of modern commercial saleability? Onitsha market in Nigeria has been selling for the past ten years novelettes of the domesticated, romantic, sex-stories of the British *Home Magazine* type. In all probability Onitsha market will not stop selling this kind of literature. The Johannesburg magazine, *Africa*, has its 'Lonely Hearts' pages. The columnist of the *Tell me, Josephine* personal advice bureau was acclaimed in English papers as revealing the 'real' Africa. That columnist is now syndicated in America. Certainly he reveals one of the many faces of Africa; and certainly we all recognize that face as kin. But African literature, as David Rubadiri, poet-ambassador from Malawi to the United States, wrote in *Transition* for August 1964, shows such 'a varied pattern of insights and views and an enormous assortment of styles' that perhaps no arid intellectualism need pull it into the dullness of over-competence; any more than a false condescension towards popular intelligence and feeling need debase and vulgarize it.

In the first and second chapters of this book it was suggested that since long before Phoenician seamen first sailed round the African continent at Egyptian Necho's behest, from the days of

Zinjanthropus and *Homo habilis*, through the medieval traffic of East Africa with the Orient, from time to time something richly new comes out of Africa. It was also suggested that European intervention in Africa, since Vasco da Gama rounded the Cape in 1497, may be seen in the healing balance of time as a mutual enrichment : Africans, particularly important rulers such as Chaka the Zulu and Mtesa of Uganda, not only accepted the white man's coming but admired his sea-daring, grasped at his inventions, accepted some but not all his ideas, and wished for civilization almost as much as Europeans imposed it. Both Africans and Europeans have brought to the last century's encounter their dissimilar intrepidities and their so different deviousnesses.

Today, between Anglo-Saxon inventive reasonableness and African generous exuberance, a similar mutual enrichment is visibly taking place. Strengthening and modernizing are prominent, of course, in African politics, economics, and trade – in the last of which European-American interests can no longer seize the major share. But cross-reference is lighting up African and English literature probably more than ever it has done since the fabled days of African Aesop.

African literature and English literature, on the only possible basis, that of equality, have much to offer each other. Perhaps they always will have. Either one does not believe at all in the possibilities of such cross-fertilization; or one believes in it deeply.

PART TWO

An Anthology

Peter Abrahams

from TELL FREEDOM

Joseph the Zulu

Each day I explored a little more of the river, going further up or down stream, extending the frontiers of my world. One day, going further downstream than I had been before, I came upon a boy. He was on the bank on the other side from me. We saw each other at the same time and stared. He was completely naked. He carried two finely carved sticks of equal size and shape, both about his own height. He was not light brown, like the other children of our location, but dark brown, almost black. I moved almost to the edge of the river. He called out in a strange language.

'Hello!' I shouted.

He called out again, and again I could not understand. I searched for a place with stones, then bounded across. I approached him slowly. As I drew near, he gripped his sticks more firmly. I stopped.

He spoke harshly, flung one stick on the ground at my feet, and held the other ready as though to fight.

'Don't want to fight,' I said.

I reached out to pick up the stick and return it to him. He took a step forward and raised the one in his hand. I moved back quickly. He stepped back and pointed at the stick on the ground. I shook my head.

'Don't want to fight.'

I pushed the stick towards him with my foot, ready to run at the first sign of attack. I showed my new, stubby teeth in a tentative smile. He said something that sounded less aggressive. I nodded, smiling more broadly. He relaxed, picked up the stick, and transferred both to his left hand. He smacked his chest.

'Joseph! Zulu!'

I smacked my own chest.

'Lee. . . .' But I didn't know what I was apart from that.

He held out his hand. We shook. His face lit up in a sunny smile. He said something and pointed downstream. Then he took my arm and led me down.

Far downstream, where the river skirted a hillside, hidden by a cluster of willows, we came on a large clear pool. Joseph flung his sticks on the ground and dived in. He shot through the water like a tadpole. He went down and came up. He shouted and beckoned me to come in. I undressed and went in more tentatively. Laughing, he pulled me under. I came up gasping and spluttering, my belly filled with water. He smacked me on the back and the water shot out of my mouth in a rush. When he realized I could not swim he became more careful. We spent the afternoon with Joseph teaching me to swim. At home, that evening, I stood beside Aunt Liza's wash-tub.

'Aunt Liza. . . .'

'Yes?'

'What am I?'

'What are you talking about?'

'I met a boy at the river. He said he was Zulu.'

She laughed.

'You are Coloured. There are three kinds of people: white people, Coloured people, and black people. The white people come first, then the Coloured people, then the black people.'

'Why?'

'Because it is so.'

Next day, when I met Joseph, I smacked my chest and said:

'Lee! Coloured!'

He clapped his hands and laughed.

Joseph and I spent most of the long summer afternoons together. He learnt some Afrikaans from me; I learnt some Zulu from him. Our days were full.

There was the river to explore.

There were my swimming lessons, and others.

I learnt to fight with sticks; to weave a green hat of young willow wands and leaves; to catch frogs and tadpoles with my hands; to set a trap for the *springhaas*; to make the sounds of the river birds.

There was the hot sun to comfort us. . . .

There was the green grass to dry our bodies. . . .

There was the soft clay with which to build. . . .

There was the fine sand with which to fight. . . .

There were our giant grasshoppers to race. . . .

There were the locust swarms when the skies turned black and we caught them by the hundreds. . . .

There was the rare taste of crisp, brown baked, salted locusts. . . .

There was the voice of the wind in the willows. . . .

There was the voice of the heaven in thunderstorms. . . .

There were the voices of two children in laughter, ours. . . .

There were Joseph's tales of black kings who lived in days before the white man. . . .

At home, I said:

'Aunt Liza. . . .'

'Yes?'

'Did we have Coloured kings before the white man?'

'No.'

'Then where did we come from? Joseph and his mother come from the black kings who were before the white man.'

And laughing, and ruffling my head, she said:

'You talk too much. . . . Go'n wash up.'

And to Joseph, next day, I said:

'We didn't have Coloured kings before the white man.'

And he comforted me and said:

'It is of no moment. You are my brother. Now my kings will be your kings. Come: I have promised the mother to bring you home. She awaits you. I will race you to the hill.'

From the top of the hill I looked into a long valley where cattle grazed. To the right, on the sloping land, nestled a cluster of mud huts. Round each hut was a wall built of mud.

'That is my home.' Joseph pointed.

We veered right and went down to it. From a distance, we saw a woman at the gate of one of the huts.

'There is the mother!' He walked faster.

She was barefooted. She wore a slight skirt that came above her knees. A child was strapped to her back. The upper part of her body was naked except for the cloth across her chest that supported the child. Round her neck, arms, and legs, were strings of white beads. As we drew near, I saw that she was young. And her broad, round face was beautiful. Her black eyes were liquid soft. She called out a greeting and smiled. Joseph pushed me forward.

'This is my brother Lee of the Coloureds, little mother.'

'Greetings, Mother,' I said.

'I greet you, my son,' she said softly, a twinkle in her eyes. 'As the man of my house has told you, food awaits. Come.'

'See!' Joseph puffed out his chest. To his mother he said, 'He would not believe when I told him I was the man in our house.'

'He is indeed,' she said.

Circling the hut was a raised platform. We sat on this while she brought us the food; salted fried locusts and corn on the cob. She sat nearby and watched us eating.

'Show the mother,' Joseph said and took another bite at the *mielies*. 'Show the mother you are not circumcised yet.'

I showed her.

'This is strange,' she said. 'Have you no initiation schools?'
'No!' Joseph said.
'Then when do you enter manhood?'
'He does not know.'
'Is it true?' She looked at me.
I nodded.
'He's still a child!' Joseph cried. 'So big and a child!'

Christmas came and it was a feast of eating and laughter. I spent
half my time at home with Aunt Liza and Uncle Sam and the other
half with Joseph and the little mother.

My sixth birthday came. Joseph and the little mother and I
celebrated it by the river.

Then, early one morning, just as the first cold touches crept into
the morning air, Joseph came to our location.

I was washing up when I heard young voices shouting:
'Look at the naked kaffir! Lee's kaffir!'
I rushed out. Joseph came gravely to me.
'I come to take leave, my brother. My father has died in the
mines so we go back to our land.'

He stood straight and stern, not heeding the shouts of the child-
ren about. He was a man. This was the burden of his manhood.
I had learned much from him, so I said equally coldly:
'I must take leave of the little mother.'
'She is a woman. She weeps.'
We ran all the way there. . . .

When the little cart had taken them away, I climbed the hill and
went down to the river. I carried Joseph's two sticks with me. These
were his parting gift to his brother.
'Defend yourself,' he had said. 'I will make others.'

I walked along the river that had been our kingdom. Now, it was
a desolate place. Joseph had been here with me: now Joseph had
gone. Before I realized it, my tears flowed fast. There had been
much between us.

The Peaceful Valley called the Grace of God

In the months after his visit to the city, Jonathan and I had again
and again brooded over the way the white man treated the black.
We had worked it down to Christianity. The white man believed
in God. He had brought God to us. God taught: 'Love thy neighbour
as thyself.' Christ came that we might have life and have it more
abundantly. The Church taught that we were all brothers in Christ,
one with another. . . . And the whites, those who had spat on us and

on others, were all Christians. The equation did not work out. Where was the error? In the religion? In the white people? In us? In God or in man? And how were we to work it out?

Here, in this peaceful valley, the equation worked out. The Fathers who taught us lived up to their teaching. They were good men and they poured their lives into good work. Belief was translated into reality. We were the witnesses.

But we would leave this peaceful valley and go out into the big world. And there, among the whites, it did not work out. It did not work out when whites came to our church. They sat in the front row. What made it so very difficult for us was the fact that the equation did work out with the Fathers and indeed with the Sisters from across the little bridge. But we had proof that the rest of the white Christians of our land were not like the Fathers and the Sisters. If there were any fault that we could lay at the door of the good Fathers and Sisters, it was that they had taught us too well. They had made Christianity a living reality for us, a way of life, a creed to live by, to measure our relations with others by. And the tragedy lay in the measuring.

The equation did not work out. And in the harshness of our young idealism we demanded that it worked out as logically as a piece of mathematics. And it did not.

Where was the error: in man or God?

And so, under the pressure of my own and Jonathan's brooding, I thought of the would-be teacher whose place I was taking and thereby cheating thousands of others.

I wrote to Teka from time to time. He wrote and sent me copies of *The Bantu World*. My poetic efforts had spurred one or two other black boys on. Their poems were published. One of them wrote really brilliant verse. Teka thought he had the makings of a first-rate poet and his letters said this young man and I had to meet next time I got back. Then, one day, I received a note of acknowledgement to a letter of mine. It said that Mr Teka had left *The Bantu World*. He had left no forwarding address. The tone and signature of the letter were those of a European. My last real contact with Johannesburg was gone.

It was customary for boys to be given periodic week-end leave to go out of bounds. Armed with a week-end pass, they usually went to the native location on the fringe of Pietersburg. Jonathan and I decided to have a week-end off.

Father Woodfield's eyes twinkled as we collected our passes that

Friday evening. There was no real need for me to have a pass. I was Coloured. I had a sudden moment of fear as we stood in front of him. Would he say I did not need one? If he did it would be a barrier between me and Jonathan.

Father Woodfield looked from me to Jonathan. The twinkle in his eyes deepened and carried a smile to his lips. He wrote our names on the two printed slips and signed them.

'Thank you, Father,' Jonathan said.

'Thank you, Father,' I said.

'Behave yourselves and be back before "lights out" on Sunday.'

'Yes, Father. Thank you.'

We got a lift on the provision truck early next morning. Perched on the back of the truck, our feet dangling, we swept away in a whirl of choking dust. The truck bumped and bounded over the uneven dusty road. It was so old that its noisy rattle made talk impossible. Through a thick haze of dust, we watched the rolling land sweep away in all directions.

And again I was struck by the aloofness of the land. Just so would a proud, austere man stand on his dignity, relaxed yet aloof. Not stiff, nor bending, just a silent, firm, relaxed presence, commanding respect in just being. Is there a land with the compelling power of this African land? Can any other land be cold and austere and yet tender? How does one tell of such a land, of the feel and hold of it on the hearts and minds of its children?

I turned to Jonathan.

'It is wonderful!'

The rattling truck drowned my voice. His lips formed a word: 'What?'

I shouted louder: 'I love it!'

He shook his head. I waved my arms to take in the land. He shook his head again. I gave it up.

A watery, pre-Spring sun sat above the eastern hills when we got to the wide macadamized road. The dust settled. The rattling and violent shaking of our bodies eased. The truck pulled up. We jumped off and stretched aching legs. The driver took the cap off the boiling water tank. Steam blew out of the engine. He filled it with cold water.

A fine coating of dust covered us from head to foot, turned us into figures of grey dust. Our hair and eyebrows were coated with it. We spat dust, cleared our noses of dust, coughed dust, and blinked dust out of our eyes. We turned dust out of pockets. We scratched our heads and raised dust clouds. We were possessed by great thirst but the motor needed all the water. So we continued on our journey bearing our thirst as best we could.

We passed a few farmsteads. We passed black folk on the road. They walked with the steady, unvarying pace that covered great distances. At last we could see the dorp's church spire far ahead. The truck slowed down as we neared a group of sand-hills some way off the road. We jumped off. We waved to the driver. He waved then accelerated.

We turned off the road and made for the sand-hills. On the other side of the hills, the sand was damp. We found the dampest spot. We dug with our hands and made a deep hole. While water filtered through, we stripped. We shook the dust out of our clothes then dressed again. The hole, now, was half-filled with clear water. We cupped our hands and drank. Then we washed the dust out of our hair and faces. We covered the hole so that others who passed here might find water that had been made clean by the earth. We continued our journey to the little dorp.

We reached Pietersburg a little before noon. It was very much like Elsburg, one of scores of little Boer dorps scattered up and down the land: a station, a church, a few rows of houses that make a few streets, a police station, a post office, and a few shops. A quiet place where life moves quietly, unhurriedly. And nearby, as in Elsburg, as in all the other little dorps, was a location of blacks who worked in the homes of the whites.

We went to the station first. The truck was there but the driver had gone. The truck would be there till late that afternoon. We jumped on the back of the truck and rested. That way we were safe. This was known as the college truck. We had passes to show we had a right to be on the truck. The police could not accuse us of anything. After our rest, we went to have a look at the town.

'We may meet some of the other boys,' Jonathan said. 'Then we can go to the location.'

'Yes,' I said.

'My friends will give us good food,' he said. 'You will like them. They are country people like me.'

'What shall we take to them?'

'Bread,' he said. 'They will like that.'

We walked to the heart of the little dorp.

'It is a nice place,' he said.

'It is,' I said.

'Maybe, one day, we will have little towns like this for ourselves. I prefer it to your big city. There is too much noise in your city and a man cannot think. In a place like this I would be content. Perhaps I would be the teacher at the little school. It would be nice.'

'I want to live on a farm,' I said. 'If I have the money one day, I will buy me a farm.'

E

'But you are of the city.'
'I would still like to get a farm.'
'And the city?'
'I will visit it. But I like to live in a quiet place.'
'You won't have time to write if you are a farmer. Our land is small but my father works all the time, and I, too, when I am at home.'
'Yes,' I said. 'But I will get someone to help.'
'You will need many helpers if it is a big farm.'
'I want it to be very big.'
An open trap drawn by a prancing grey with a shining coat turned a corner and shot past us.
'A beautiful horse,' Jonathan sighed. 'A beautiful horse.'
I had been more interested in the cheerful young couple on the trap. They made a fine picture.
'And I will go around like that,' I said.
'With your wife?' Jonathan's eyes mocked affectionately.
'Why not!'
'You are such a dreamer,' he laughed. Then he grew serious. 'I wonder if a man who is not white can buy a farm.'
I did not know. We carried on in silence along the quiet street. This point of reality had spoiled the illusion. Far ahead, we saw the shops.
'I'll get the bread,' I said.
'I will pay half,' he said.
'I have more money than you.'
'I will pay half,' he said firmly.
We reached the shop.
'Come,' I said.
'I will wait,' he said.
I went in. There were two women, one man and the storekeeper. They all stared as I entered. The man behind the counter smiled at the others then moved slightly to my end of the counter.
'*Ja klonkie?*'
Better behave, Peter.
'A loaf of bread, please, *baas.*'
'You're new here. . . ?'
'Not many of his kind around,' the other man said.
'They prefer the towns,' one of the women said.
They waited for me to tell them all about myself.
'I'm from the college, *baas.*'
'The kaffir college?'
'Yes, *baas.*'
'But you're Coloured, aren't you?'

'Yes, *baas.*'

'Then why are you at a kaffir college?'

Careful, Peter.

'Because my parents want it, *baas.*'

'Let him go,' the second woman said boredly.

The storekeeper reached under the counter. He put a loaf of bread on it and pushed it in my direction. I put my coin on the counter. He took it, counted out the change and put it beside the unwrapped loaf. I gathered bread and money and hurried to the door. As I reached the door I flung myself forward in a dash. Too late, I saw the looming figure of a giant of a man.

The big man's arms shot out and caught me.

'O-O-o-o-p-s!' he grunted gaily.

Then he saw my colour. My feet were off the ground. The laughter passed from his eyes. Disgust contorted his big tan face. He flung me away like one near the point of nausea through touching human waste. I hit the ground bodily. The bread and money went flying.

In a daze, I heard a woman's voice say something about 'church arrangements'. A booming voice, tinged with disgust, rumbled something about a 'black baboon'. I scrambled quickly to my feet. They might come out. Then Jonathan was beside me.

'Come!'

We gathered the bread and money and hurried down the street, back to the station. We did not look back. We got on the back on the truck. I sat shivering.

'Are you hurt?' Jonathan's voice was tight.

'No.' I felt awfully tired and numb.

I looked at Jonathan's face. It was bleak. He avoided looking at me.

'We will go back,' he said. 'I think it is better, heh?'

'Yes,' I said.

We got off the truck and took the road out of the little dorp, the road back to the college. We did not talk. There was nothing to talk about. In the late afternoon, we went off the road and sat on a green hill while we ate the loaf of bread. Then we set out again. My brain began to function once more.

. . . Perhaps the truck would pick us up on its way back. Yes, perhaps it would. The truck rattles. The truck rattles. Yes, damn, the truck rattles. It is no use. Why did he look so sick with disgust? The other wouldn't have mattered if he had not looked so sick with it. Am I really like ordure to him? Only the touch of that could make me feel and look as he did. Only that. Only that. Sick with disgust. Only that. Yesterday I phoned the station. The white man said good-day to me. And I said: 'Please reserve a first-class single coupé for Canon Woodfield.' And he said: 'I will do that. Thank you. Good-bye.' The disgust one feels when touching human waste. A first-class coupé and human waste. White and black. No! The truck will pick us up. You're only making it worse by being so tense, Jonathan. Relax. Let's try to forget it. Not the same as spittle. But that disgust. And the first-class coupé. No! . . .

Savagely, insistently, my mind forced the error of the equation into the peaceful valley called the *Grace of God.*

Late that night I knelt in the dark and empty chapel. I knelt in front of the black statue of my patron saint, St. Peter. I offered him the error Jonathan and I had found in the equation. Why was it so? God had made miracles for white folk, would He make one miracle for one black boy? Would He make it now, please. That bowl of water at your feet, Dear St. Peter. . . .

Jonathan moved from the shadows of a tree as I came out of the chapel. We moved slowly across the silent quad to our dormitory.

We lay awake far into the night, each aware that the other was awake. And our burning hearts ached as only the hearts of the young can.

A shadow now lay over our friendship. The weeks to the half-yearly holiday went heavily.

At last, end of term came. I was packing my case on that last night. At his bed next to mine, Jonathan was also packing.

'Peter. . . .'

'Yes?'

'Are you coming back?'

'No.'

'I thought not. I will miss you.'

'I will miss you, Jon.'

'Have you told Father Woodfield?'

'I can't. I will write to him.'

'Yes. It is difficult. But you must write. He likes you and it will upset him. . . . What will you do now?'

'I don't know.'

'Let us walk for the last time.'

In silence, under the early summer moon, we visited our old haunts.

In the morning, I took leave of my dear friend Jonathan and turned my face from that peaceful valley called the Grace of God.

Chinua Achebe

from THINGS FALL APART

The village crier was abroad again in the night. He beat his iron gong and announced that another meeting would be held in the morning. Everyone knew that Umuofia was at last going to speak its mind about the things that were happening.

Okonkwo slept very little that night. The bitterness in his heart was now mixed with a kind of child-like excitement. Before he had gone to bed he had brought down his war dress, which he had not touched since his return from exile. He had shaken out his smoked raffia skirt and examined his tall feather head-gear and his shield. They were all satisfactory, he had thought.

As he lay on his bamboo bed he thought about the treatment he had received in the white man's court, and he swore vengeance. If Umuofia decided on war, all would be well. But if they chose to be cowards he would go out and avenge himself. He thought about wars in the past. The noblest, he thought, was the war against Isike. In those days Okudo was still alive. Okudo sang a war song in a way that no other man could. He was not a fighter, but his voice turned every man into a lion.

'Worthy men are no more,' Okonkwo sighed as he remembered those days. 'Isike will never forget how we slaughtered them in that war. We killed twelve of their men and they killed only two of ours. Before the end of the fourth market week they were suing for peace. Those were days when men were men.'

As he thought of these things he heard the sound of the iron gong in the distance. He listened carefully, and could just hear the crier's voice. But it was very faint. He turned on his bed and his back hurt him. He ground his teeth. The crier was drawing nearer and nearer until he passed by Okonkwo's compound.

'The greatest obstacle in Umuofia,' Okonkwo thought bitterly, 'is that coward, Egonwanne. His sweet tongue can change fire into cold ash. When he speaks he moves our men to impotence. If they had ignored his womanish wisdom five years ago, we would not have come to this.' He ground his teeth. 'Tomorrow he will tell them that our fathers never fought a "war of blame". If they listen to him I shall leave them and plan my own revenge.'

The crier's voice had once more become faint, and the distance had taken the harsh edge off his iron gong. Okonkwo turned from one side to the other and derived a kind of pleasure from the pain his back gave him. 'Let Egonwanne talk about a "war of blame" tomorrow and I shall show him my back and head.' He ground his teeth.

The market-place began to fill as soon as the sun rose. Obierika was waiting in his *obi* when Okonkwo came along and called him. He hung his goatskin bag and his sheathed matchet on his shoulder and went out to join him. Obierika's hut was close to the road and he saw every man who passed to the market-place. He had exchanged greetings with many who had already passed that morning.

When Okonkwo and Obierika got to the meeting-place there were already so many people that if one threw up a grain of sand it would not find its way to the earth again. And many more people were coming from every quarter of the nine villages. It warmed Okonkwo's heart to see such strength of numbers. But he was looking for one man in particular, the man whose tongue he dreaded and despised so much.

'Can you see him?' he asked Obierika.

'Who?'

'Egonwanne,' he said, his eyes roving from one corner of the huge market-place to the other. Most of the men were seated on goatskins on the ground. A few of them sat on wooden stools they had brought with them.

'No,' said Obierika, casting his eyes over the crowd. 'Yes, there he is, under the silk-cotton tree. Are you afraid he would convince us not to fight?'

'Afraid? I do not care what he does to *you*. I despise him and those who listen to him. I shall fight alone if I choose.'

They spoke at the top of their voices because everybody was talking, and it was like the sound of a great market.

'I shall wait till he has spoken,' Okonkwo thought. 'Then I shall speak.'

'But how do you know he will speak against war?' Obierika asked after a while.

'Because I know he is a coward,' said Okonkwo. Obierika did not hear the rest of what he said because at that moment somebody touched his shoulder from behind and he turned round to shake hands and exchange greetings with five or six friends. Okonkwo did not turn round even though he knew the voices. He was in no mood to exchange greetings.

At this point there was a sudden stir in the crowd and every eye was turned in one direction. There was a sharp bend in the road that led from the market-place to the white man's court, and to the stream beyond it. And so no one had seen the approach of the five court messengers until they had come round the bend, a few paces from the edge of the crowd. Okonkwo was sitting at the edge.

He sprang to his feet as soon as he saw who it was. He confronted the head messenger, trembling with hate, unable to utter a word. The man was fearless and stood his ground, his four men lined up behind him.

In that brief moment the world seemed to stand still, waiting. There was utter silence. The men of Umuofia were merged into the mute backcloth of trees and giant creepers, waiting.

The spell was broken by the head messenger. 'Let me pass!' he ordered.

'What do you want here?'

'The white man whose power you know too well has ordered this meeting to stop.'

In a flash Okonkwo drew his matchet. The messenger crouched to avoid the blow. It was useless. Okonkwo's matchet descended twice and the man's head lay beside his uniformed body.

The waiting backcloth jumped into tumultuous life and the meeting was stopped. Okonkwo stood looking at the dead man. He knew that Umuofia would not go to war. He knew because they had let the other messengers escape. They had broken into tumult instead of action. He discerned fright in that tumult. He heard voices asking : 'Why did he do it?'

He wiped his matchet on the sand and went away.

William Conton

from THE AFRICAN

Liverpool next day was grey, cold, wet and foggy; and the promised land looked most unpromising from the deck of the ship. Once ashore, however, the towering buildings, massed traffic, and attractive shops kept us staring and gaping whilst waiting for our trains to various parts of the country. The sight of white people *en masse* was itself something which required some getting used to; but the thing that took us really aback was our first sight of a white man sweeping a gutter. He was a short, seedy-looking, rather dirty man, with heavy working boots and stained, well-worn clothes, but unmistakably a white man nevertheless; and actually standing right down in the gutter sweeping it, collecting the rubbish on a shovel and tipping it into a wheelbarrow. We stood in utter disbelief, at some little distance from him, expecting him at any moment either to vanish like a gremlin down the nearest drain, or else to turn dark brown. I suppose if you had asked us beforehand who swept gutters in England, we should have replied, after a moment or two's reflection, that we supposed some of the English drains, at least, must have the honour of being swept by white men; for even all the stowaways and workless migrants from Africa and the West Indies could not provide enough labour for so many menial tasks. But no one had prepared us beforehand by any such question; and the sight of that man almost felled us.

'Thank God for bringing me here,' breathed Appiah reverently, the first amongst us to recover his breath. 'I always suspected there was some good reason for my coming to Britain.'

And I think that summed up how most of us felt. We did not lose respect for the white man – very far from it. What we did lose however (and long overdue was the loss), was an illusion created by the rôle the white man plays in Africa: that he is a kind of demi-god whose hands must never get dirty, who must not be allowed to carry anything heavier than a portfolio or wield any implement heavier than a pen. Without realizing it, we had come to think of the white man only in the rôle of missionary, civil servant, or senior business executive, one who was always behind the desk, never in front of it. We saw him as one who always gave orders, never took them, who could have any job he liked for the asking. So to realize that that man was perfectly happy working in that gutter (snatches of his melancholy whistling reached us faintly where we stood) was a most salutary experience. It was now possible for us to like the white man. For before you can like (as distinct from merely admiring or emulating), you must feel kinship, a shared humanity, the possibility of common experiences and destinies. As we resumed our walk past the sweeper, he looked up and grinned cheerfully at us, leaning for a moment on his brush. We waved and grinned back; and in that mute exchange of greetings there was erased in a moment the memory of the behaviour of the stewards on board. The latter had acted as if the gods had decreed that the black man should minister and the white man be ministered unto, and that they were stewards and we passengers only by special dispensation. Our friend the road-sweeper, on the other hand, was so far from harbouring any such notions that he had found time to give us, in his own way, a welcome to Liverpool.

We were soon to find, as countless thousands of colonial students in the United Kingdom must have found, that the Britisher at home is an altogether different creature, and a much more lovable one, than the Britisher overseas.

I found it very difficult to express my gratitude to Joe for the experience of meeting his 'chums' in that humble roadside hut. So much of my future career was to depend on my ability to understand and establish contact with men of no greater education in my own country. I was gratified to find myself capable of being absolutely at ease in their company, and with similar experiences and stories to exchange with them. One hears so much about the gap between the intellectuals of Africa and the unlettered peasant or town dweller there whose vote at the polls is decisive. It is easy to conclude that, as in the Britain of Disraeli's day, 'two nations' are emerging in Africa, with little in common. It was reassuring for me to discover so early, and so pleasantly, that all this was much more a matter of attitudes than of education. Given a sufficiently strong motive for doing so, it was surprisingly easy to feel both interested and interesting in the company of people whose intellectual experiences were very different from one's own, and whose race and social background were even more so. I think it was this episode which helped me more than anything else to seek to cultivate the art of 'being all things to all men', and of deliberately seeking that point of common interest which I believe lay hidden somewhere between myself and every individual I met.

I spent that night comfortably with Joe's friend in Carlisle, and the next morning a newsagent's van drove me out to Keswick. The hostel was not open to members until early evening, but the Warden agreed to keep my rucksack for me so that I could carry out my plan of doing a little climbing and of exploring the lakeside that day. The climbing I very soon decided was too much like hard work, rucksack or no rucksack. The slopes of Mount Skiddaw were much too steep for my liking, and the view improved only too gradually. In the end I decided that the African respiratory tract was not constructed for mountain climbing; and, after having regained my breath, I returned to road level at a leisurely pace. After all, I consoled myself, Lakes Bassenthwaite and Derwentwater might just as well be seen separately as together.

E*

After a meal of bread and peanut butter (the latter was now my last gastronomic link with home, and I ate it on all possible occasions), I went off in search of Lake Derwentwater. Stretches of water against a background of hills had always fascinated me, and I was anxious to see if I could recreate a similar perspective here. I thought of the view back at home from Governor's Beach, whose long, curving golden crescent was set against a magnificent backdrop of dark green. I wanted to look across Derwentwater at Skiddaw, and to get the mountain to form a contrast in tone, colour and dimension with the glassy blue water. I felt like an artist composing a picture in my own imagination, as I made my way to the water's edge; except that I hoped eventually to see the picture I had conceived, not on flat canvas, but in its proper dimensions.

After a little searching I found the vantage point I believed I sought – a tiny headland jutting out from the western shore of the lake, and which commanded an excellent view across it. A few yards from the end of this headland there stood an old beech, and as I reached it with a view to seeking a place to sit, I found I had been forestalled. Sitting on a boulder at the foot of the tree, with her back to its gnarled trunk, was an English girl (as I took her to be), whose long, fair hair fell in carefully arranged tresses to her shoulders, and who wore a red pullover, a tartan kilt, and a triangular-shaped scarf thrown loosely over the shoulders. Her back was towards me; but as I stopped, hesitating as to what I should do, she turned; and revealed a face of such striking appearance that I found myself momentarily robbed of the power to do anything but stare.

It is difficult to describe that face in detail, that face whose image, during the course of the next few months, was to fill all my waking hours and many of my sleeping ones as well. Since arriving at King's, I had met very many English women students, had studied with them, danced with them, and seen many of them come to the Club on Leazes Terrace as guests of the colonial students there, to parties or to a meal. But I had often thought to myself and remarked to others that, their wardrobes apart, there was nothing our girls back at home need fear in competition with these. So often I had heard bitter complaints from our girls that we menfolk in Britain seemed to find British girls so much more attractive, that we did not hesitate to break long-standing promises, and even to disregard clearly expressed parental wishes, in order to make foreigners our wives. As a result the matrimonial market in Sagresa had become increasingly filled with frustrated old maids, who regarded every new foreign bride with thinly veiled hatred.

Cyprian Ekwensi

from JAGUA NANA

He held her hands. He saw the flush come to her face. Instinctively her eyes went to the door. He sat beside her on the bed and took her wrist and laid it in his hand, examining the long and shapely fingers. She turned her face towards him, and, though he could read the cautionary message, he kissed her and her eyelids slid down and the soft eyelashes fluttered against his cheek. The anger was melting away and the world had become sweet with Nancy Oll and her fine skin and bewitching fragrance.

He felt the gentle push and the gentler voice 'You come again, Freddie. You always wantin' dat. Anytime you see me always you wantin' dat one. Is all you like me for, Freddie?'

He slid his fingers along her bare shoulder and into her blouse. There was nothing else he could have done. The blouse was cut to be slipped away. She did not even wear a brassiere and her breast was dancing in his hand.

'De door open, Freddie.' She was hissing now.

He squeezed her again, then went to the door and bolted it. 'Don' fear, Nancy. Nobody fit enter now.'

'But is too hot now, Freddie. Is too hot for doin' anythin'. True. Let it be anodder time.'

'Yes, dear.' He had taken her in his arms and was squeezing her close. Through the drumming in his ears, he heard the last lonely cry of Nancy the girl reaching out for help she must know would never come from the wolfing Freddie. 'Freddie, Freddie – Oh! . . . I beg you, make we keep it till anodder time. If you love me, Freddie. . . . But I not goin' to run. Is for you Freddie. I not goin' to give it to anodder man, while I love you.'

The drumming had become a roar. The fingers were trembling around the buttons, the intricate knots which showered the clothes she had on. He caught his breath. Her superbly tanned and shapely young body stood revealed. He could not help leaning back for a moment and devouring the slim shoulders, full breasts with the long nipples. He kissed them now and they reared into a gooseflesh with a sharp intake of her breath.

'Gently, Freddie, you will rumple me clothes. Me Mama will

know what you done.' She wriggled out of her frock and chemise. Her waist was so slim and her belly so flat that he laid his palm on it to believe what he saw. She had small buttocks unusual for a Nigerian-bred girl, but they were silky smooth with an eel-like electricness that sent shivers of madness through him.

He took that slim waist and marvelled at it and pressed her to him and was entwined in her teen-age athleticness. The heat and sweat, the odour of mating, fused them both in a reeling bout of insatiable lust. She was crying too loud for his comfort.

'Freddie, I die! Kill me, Freddie. I die! . . . Oh God! . . .'

He bit her ear. He felt golden-sweet with this release of his pent-up tensions. The pleasure he had found in Nancy's youthfulness, her sensitivity, came as from a fable. He could not help contrasting her skin which was firm and elastic, with Jagua's flabby and soggy for all the artifice. When Nancy cried, it was because she felt pain or pleasure; not because she had rehearsed it and timed it in advance. Her eyes rolled in ecstasy, and when she sat sobbing after he had had her he was disturbed and he kissed away the tears and smoothed her cheeks. She was genuine. Did genuine mating exist? Freddie asked himself. If only Jagua knew it, this was the greatest betrayal she had ever faced.

'Freddie, tell me you love me.' She kissed him.

'I love you, Nancy,' he murmured between kisses. 'But why you cryin'? You so sweet, I wonder if I jus' dreamin'!'

The tears came up again. He saw them fill the eyes, brown eyes that looked beyond him in a flood of grief. He took a handkerchief and dabbed away the tears and tenderly told her to get up and dress before lying back for a while. She slipped out of the bed and clumsily began putting the chemise over her head. He went and held her hips.

'Where you come from, Nancy?'

'My fadder and modder come here from Freetown, in Sa Leone. Long time. My fadder workin' in de Secretariat before he die. Since den I live with my modder who sen' me to school. She doin' a bit of dressmaking and a bit of bakery – we got a nice shop where we sell cake and bread. . . .'

'So you say your modder know all about we?' He handed her the blouse. She was getting into her knickers, and she held his shoulder to retain her balance.

'I tol' my modder that I love you an' I wan' to marry you. She think I no serious. "Don' forget, Nancy. . . . We comin' a long way, from Freetown. An' if you marry dis Nigerian boy, den you mus' forsake you fadderlan'." So my Mama say, but I don' lissen to her, so she jus' go on talkin'. She tell me dat if I wan' to marry you. I must kill Jagua firs' before I kin get you. I mus' kill Jagua firs'. She talk true, Freddie? Tell me, Freddie, is true dat if I want you Jagua will fight me? Answer me true – not because you and she quarrellin' or anythin'. Answer me true, because I love you, Freddie.'

He looked at the pain her eyes tried to conceal. 'No, Nancy. I not goin' to marry Jagua. At firs' I think Jagua serious with me. But is all lie, lie, lie! She got dis habit of runnin' after men with money. Now if she don' sleep with one man every day, she never feel happy. Den on top of dat, she takin' me as small chil' and she always deceive me under me own nose. If I catch her, she begin to tell long story. I got too much pride, Nancy. But jus' now, it won't be de right thing, if I let her know. Ah mus' wait till ah enter de ship firs'. Till I land in Englan'. Den I will show my hand.'

She threw herself into his arms and he folded her, soft and sweet and dainty. 'But Freddie, what you goin' to do? Jagua put a lot of money on you head. How you goin' to pay back?'

He stroked her hips. 'Easy. Jus' let me reach England and begin to study de law, firs'.'

'You know what, Freddie? I goin' visit your home town of Bagana. Before I cross over to Englan' I mus' go and known Bagana and salute you Fadder and Modder. I will tell Mama to take me wit' her, so she too kin see dat Nigerian man is good for her chil' to marry. Is true we comin' from Freetown, but is here dem born me, and here I go to school. Nigeria is me secon' home.'

Freddie kissed her again; then he heard the loud, insistent knocking on the door.

'Open de door! . . . Freddie, open de door! . . . You hear me? Open de door quick, or I will burs' de door!'

It was Jagua. She would bring the house down on their heads if he did not quickly calm her down. His first impulse was to dart through the window, to pull Nancy after him. But the meshes of the mosquito netting were too fine to allow that. Glancing at his bare legs he reached instead for his trousers, jumped into them, fastening the wrong flap buttons in his headlong hurry. She was banging the door now with a heavier object.

'Just a minute! Wha's de matter, Jagua?'

With one quick glance at Nancy and a finger pressed over his lips, Freddie went to the door and slid back the bolt. Jagua crashed into the room. She lunged straight at Nancy.

'What you doin' in dis room?' she panted. 'You good for nothin'. You call yourself decent gal. What you doin' with my man with de door all locked up and—'

'Is your man, then? Why you runnin' about wit' odder men, you can't sleep in you own bed.'

Nancy's nerve surprised Freddie. He immediately sensed the fight coming and stood on his toes. What a scandalous thing for his teacher reputation. 'I beg you, Jagua. Don' make trouble. Is a misunderstandin'. I goin' to explain.' His words had the reverse effect.

'Shut up, Freddie! Got no business with you – yet!' She turned to Nancy. 'Dis is de poor bastard I got to teach a lesson so dat she will know next time about taking de man of her senior. Nancy, who tell you dat I goin' with odder men?' Her eyes were aflame and Freddie seeing them, went and shut the door. 'Who tell you dat? Answer me!'

'Yousself! Who tell you dat am in de room with Freddie? Why you hurryin' to enter de room. Somebody tell you am here, das why you running and ramming de door with stone.' Nancy was speaking with a spirit which made Freddie want to raise her by the arm and shout: 'Champion! . . .'

'I tell you, Jagwa! I love mah Freddie. He goin' to England and when he coming back he will be my England man!'

'Close you mout', you small pickin'! Who born you to talk to me like dat?'

Jagua sprang at her. 'I goin' to teach you pepper! And you kin go and call you Mama too an' I will give am fire to chop!' Freddie scarcely saw the flash of her hand but he heard the smack and saw Nancy wince and place a hand on her cheek. The two women clinched, and it was Nancy who screamed. 'Oh! . . . Freddie, she bite me! De witch-woman bite me! . . .'

'Bite her back! You got no teeth? Nancy, bite am back good and proper!'

He saw Nancy butt into her and Jagua screamed. Freddie felt a sweet glow at Jagua's humiliation and Nancy's incredible nerve. Quickly he slid between the two women and tried to tear them apart. From both sides blows buffeted his skull and ribs. Jagua landed a good right on his cheek. He seized her by the wrists but with the enraged strength of a jaguar she wrested free.

'Leave me, Freddie. You never gone England yet, and you done begin run after anodder woman! You tink am a fool?'

'I don' run after her, Jagua. What I goin' to do when her modder sen' her to me – an' you run away with other man?'

'What you goin' to do? You done what you mus'! You slept with Nancy. Yes! What kin' young man you be if you don' sleep with such fine gal? You tink Ma Nancy don' know what she doin' to sen' her alone to your room?'

Freddie sneered. 'When you and de three men ride away in de big car, where you go? What you wan' me to do? Sit down and cry?

I must console myself! Das how poor man who no get long car kin console hisself.'

'What concern you wit' Mama Nancy, dat she sendin' her only daughter to your bed? Jagua snapped at him. 'So she sendin' Nancy to you now, so you kin marry her? By de way, Freddie, who help you get passport? Who suffer and bribe de men till dem 'gree to give you passport? Or you don' know about de Government control, how is hard for obtain passport? Why Mama Nancy don't try for you? And who pay for your study and your room in de U.K.? Not me? Where Nancy and her modder hide when I doin' all dis?' She stood arms akimbo, half her blouse torn open, glaring at Freddie and Nancy so young and sweet.

Freddie saw her make straight for one of his suitcases. 'What you want dere, Jagua?' He lunged forward to retrieve the case which contained his passport. 'Jagua, be careful!'

But the maddened woman only turned on him and he felt himself torn asunder as by a lioness. Jagua kicked open the suitcase, rummaged among the clothes till she found the precious document. She took it in her strong hands and tore it to shreds. The document that had cost more than six months of forgery and bribery. Freddie felt the tears tingling under his eyelids. He tried to intervene but she sprang at him, all claws and teeth. A Jagwa woman could be fire. He felt the scarification from the flames. She lifted the suitcase and threw it outside. It fell and split open and his things scattered. A penny rolled away and lodged under the stairs. Freddie stared at that penny. 'Go Englan' now, let me see!' She pointed at Nancy. 'Go with her, and lef' me in Lagos. I jus' an old woman, and you got no use for me. So take your sweetheart Nancy and go!' She took an axe and ran outside. She could wield it with dexterity. Nancy clung to Freddie while Jagua split the boxes open.

All the tenants came down from their rooms but Jagua dared them to come within the range of the axe. She had now belted a cloth across her middle and stood like a fighter when the 'seconds out' bell has just been rung.

'Ah will chop you head if you touch me!' Her magnificent bosom heaved as she stood with eyes burning anger.

'Jealous mad woman!' Freddie hissed. 'You done gone craze with jealousy.'

Olaudah Equiano

from THE INTERESTING
NARRATIVE OF THE LIFE
OF OLAUDAH EQUIANO OR
GUSTAVUS VASSA, THE
AFRICAN. WRITTEN BY
HIMSELF.[1] 1793 (Seventh Edition)

That part of Africa, known by the name of Guinea, to which the trade for slaves is carried on, extends along the coast about 3400 miles from Senegal to Angola, and includes a variety of Kingdoms. Of these, the most considerable is the Kingdom of Benin, both as to extent and wealth, the richness and cultivation of the soil, the power of its king, and the number and warlike disposition of the inhabitants. It is situated nearly under the line, and extends along the coast about 170 miles, but runs back into the interior part of Africa, to a distance hitherto I believe unexplored by any traveller; and seems only terminated at length by the empire of Abyssinia, near 1500 miles from its beginning. This kingdom is divided into many provinces or districts : in one of the most remote and fertile of which I was born, in the year 1745, situated in a charming fruitful vale, named Essaka. The distance of this province from the capital of Benin and the sea coast must be very considerable; for I had never heard of white men or Europeans, nor of the sea; and our subjection to the king of Benin was little more than nominal; for every transaction of the government, as far as my slender observation extended, was conducted by the chiefs or elders of the place. . . . My father was one of those elders or chiefs I have spoken of, and was styled Embrenché; a term, as I remember, importing the highest distinction, and signifying in our language a *mark* of grandeur. This mark is conferred on the person entitled to it, by cutting the skin across the top of the forehead, and drawing it down to the eye-brows; and, while it is in this situation, applying a warm hand, and rubbing it until it shrinks into a thick weal across the lower part of the forehead. Most of the judges and senators were

[1] Eighteenth-century punctuation and occasional eighteenth-century spelling have been left.

thus marked; my father had long borne it : I had seen it conferred on one of my brothers, and I also was destined to receive it by my parents. Those Embrenchés, or chief men, decided disputes, and punished crimes; for which purpose they always assembled together. The proceedings were generally short; and in most cases the law of retaliation prevailed. I remember a man was brought before my father, and the other judges, for kidnapping a boy; and although he was the son of a chief or senator, he was condemned to make recompense by a man or woman slave. Adultery, however, was sometimes punished with slavery or death; a punishment which I believe is inflicted on it throughout most of the nations of Africa : so sacred among them is the honour of the marriage-bed, and so jealous are they of the fidelity of their wives. Of this I recollect an instance – A woman was convicted before the judges of adultery, and delivered over, as the custom was, to her husband to be punished. Accordingly he determined to put her to death; but, it being found, just before her execution, that she had an infant at her breast, and no woman being prevailed on to perform the part of a nurse, she was spared on account of the child. The men, however, do not preserve the same constancy to their wives which they expect from them; for they indulge in a plurality, though seldom in more than two. . . .

We are almost a nation of dancers, musicians, and poets. Thus every great event, such as a triumphant return from battle, or other cause of public rejoicing is celebrated in public dances, which are accompanied with songs and music suited to the occasion. The assembly is separated into four divisions, which dance either apart or in succession, and each with a character peculiar to itself. The first division contains the married men, who in their dances frequently exhibit feats of arms, and the representation of a battle. To these succeed the married women, who dance in the second division. The young men occupy the third; and the maidens the fourth. Each represents some interesting scene of real life, such as a great achievement, domestic employment, a pathetic story, or some rural sport; and as the subject is generally founded on some recent event, it is therefore ever new. This gives our dances a spirit and variety which I have scarcely seen elsewhere.

We have many musical instruments, particularly drums of different kinds, a piece of music which resembles a guitar, and another much like a stickado. These last are chiefly used by betrothed virgins, who play on them on all grand festivals. . . .

Our manner of living is entirely plain; for as yet the natives are unacquainted with those refinements in cookery which debauche the taste : Bullocks, goats, and poultry, supply the greatest part of their foods. These constitute likewise the principal wealth of the country, and the chief articles of its commerce. The flesh is usually stewed in a pan. To make it savoury we sometimes use also pepper and other spices; and we have salt made of wood ashes. Our vegetables are mostly plantains, eadas, yams, beans, and Indian corn. The head of the family usually eats alone; his wives and slaves have also their separate tables. Before we taste food we always wash our hands; indeed our cleanliness on all occasions is extreme; but on this it is an indispensable ceremony. After washing, libation is made, by pouring out a small portion of the drink on the floor, and tossing a small quantity of the food in a certain place, for the spirits of departed relations, which the natives suppose to preside over their conduct, and guard them from evil. They are totally unacquainted with strong or spirituous liquors; and their principal beverage is palm wine. This is got from a tree of that name, by tapping it at the top, and fastening a large gourd to it; and sometimes one tree will yield three or four gallons in a night. When just drawn, it is of a most delicious sweetness; but in a few days it acquires a tartish and more spirituous flavour; though I never saw anyone intoxicated by it. The same tree also produces nuts and oil. Our principal luxury is in perfumes; one sort of these is an odoriferous wood of delicious fragrance; the other a kind of earth; a small portion of which thrown into the fire diffuses a most powerful odour. We beat this wood into powder, and mix it with palm-oil; with which both men and women perfume themselves.

In our buildings we study convenience rather than ornament. Each master of a family has a large square piece of ground surrounded with a moat or fence, or enclosed with a wall made of red earth tempered, which, when dry, is as hard as brick. Within this are his houses to accomodate his family and slaves; which, if numerous, frequently present the appearance of a village. In the middle stands the principal building, appropriated to the sole use of the master, and consisting of two apartments; in one of which he sits in the day with his family, the other is left apart for the reception of his friends. He has besides these a distinct apartment, in which he sleeps, together with his male children. On each side are the apartments of his wives, who also have their separate day and night houses. . . .

Our beds consist of a platform raised two or three feet from the ground, on which are laid skins. . . .

Houses so constructed and furnished require but little skill to erect them. Every man is a sufficient architect for the purpose. The whole neighbourhood afford their unanimous assistance in building them, and in return receive and expect no other recompense than a feast. . . .

Our wants are few and easily supplied; of course we have few manufactures. They consist for the most part of callicoes, earthern ware, ornaments, and instruments of war and husbandry. . . . In such a state money is of little use. . . .

We have also markets, at which I have been frequently with my mother. These are sometimes visited by stout mahogany-coloured men from the south-west of us; we call them Oye-Eboe, which term signifies red men living at a distance. They generally bring us fire-arms, gunpowder, hats, beads, and dried fish. . . . These articles they barter with us for odoriferous woods and earth, and our salt of wood-ashes. They always carry slaves through our land. . . . Sometimes, indeed, we sold slaves to them, but they were only prisoners of war, or such among us as had been convicted of kid-napping, or adultery, or some other crimes which we esteemed heinous. . . .

Our land is uncommonly rich and fruitful, and produces all kinds of vegetables in great abundance. We have plenty of Indian corn, and vast quantities of cotton and tobacco. Our pine apples grow without culture; they are about the size of the largest sugar-loaf and finely flavoured. We have also spices of different kinds, particularly pepper; and a variety of delicious fruits which I have never seen in Europe; together with gums of various kinds, and honey in abund-ance. All our industry is exerted to prove these blessings of nature. Agriculture is our chief employment; and every one, even the child-ren and women, are engaged in it. Thus we are all habituated to labour from our earliest years. Every one contributes something to the common stock; and as we are unacquainted with idleness, we have no beggars. The benefits of such a mode of living are obvious. The West India planters prefer the slaves of Benin or Eboe to those of any other part of Guinea, for their hardiness, intelligence, in-tegrity, and zeal. Those benefits are felt by us in the general healthi-ness of the people, and in their vigour and activity; I might have added too in their comliness. Deformity is indeed unknown amongst us, I mean that of shape. Numbers of the natives of Eboe, now in London, might be brought in support of this assertion; for, in regard to complexion, ideas of beauty are wholly relative. I remember while in Africa to have seen three negro children, two were tawny, and another quite white, who were universally regarded by myself and the natives in general, as far as related to their complexions, as deformed. . . .

Our tillage is exercized in a large plain or common, some hours walk from our dwellings, and all the neighbours resort thither in a body. They use no beasts of husbandry; and their only instruments are hoes, axes, shovels, and beaks, or pointed iron to dig with.

Sometimes we are visited by locusts, which come in large clouds, so as to darken the air, and destroy our harvest. This however happens rarely, but when it does a famine is produced by it. I remember an instance or two wherein this happened. This common is often the theatre of war; and therefore when our people go out to till their land, they not only go in a body, but generally take their arms with them, for fear of a surprise; and when they apprehend an invasion, they guard the avenues to their dwellings, by driving sticks into the ground, which are so sharp at one end as to pierce the foot, and are generally dipt in poison. From what I can recollect of these battles, they appear to have been irruptions of one little state or district on the other, to obtain prisoners or booty. . . . When a trader wants slaves, he applies to a chief of them, and tempts him with his wares. . . . We have fire-arms, bows and arrows, broad two-edged swords and javelins; We have shields also, which cover a man from head to foot. All are taught the use of these weapons. Even our women are warriors, and march boldly out to fight along with the men. . . .

As to religion, the natives believe that there is one Creator of all things, and that he lives in the sun, and is girded round with a belt, that he may never eat or drink; but according to some, he smokes a pipe, which is our own favourite luxury. They believe he governs events, especially our deaths or captivity; but as for the doctrine of eternity, I do not remember to have ever heard of it : some however believe in the transmigration of souls to a certain degree. Those spirits, which are not transmigrated, such as their dear friends or relations, they believe always attend them, and guard them from the bad spirits of their foes. . . .

We compute the year from the day on which the sun crosses the line; and, on its setting that evening, there is a general shout throughout the land. . . .

We practised circumcision like the Jews, and made offerings and feasts on that occasion in the same manner as they did. Like them also our children were named from some event, some circumstance, or fancied foreboding, at the time of their birth. I was named *Olaudah*, which, in our language, signifies vicissitude, or fortunate also; one favoured, and having a loud voice, and well spoken. I remember we never polluted the name of the object of our adoration; on the contrary, it was always mentioned with the greatest reverence; and we were totally unacquainted with swearing, and all those terms of abuse and reproach which find their way so readily and copiously into the language of more civilized people. The only expressions of that kind I remember were 'May you rot', or 'may you swell', or 'may a beast take you'.

. . . One day when all our people were gone out to their work as usual, and only I and my dear sister were left to mind the house, two men and a woman got over our walls, and in a moment seized us both; and without giving us time to cry out, or make resistance, they stopped our mouths, and ran off with us into the nearest wood. Here they tied our hands, and continued to carry us as far as they could, till night came on, when we reached a small house, where the robbers halted for refreshment, and spent the night. We were then unbound, but were unable to take any food; and, being quite overpowered by fatigue and grief, our only relief was some sleep, which allayed our misfortunes for a short time. The next morning we left the house, and continued travelling all the day. For a long time we kept the woods, but at last we came into a road which I believed I knew. I had some hopes of being delivered; for we had advanced but a little way before I discovered some people at a distance, on which I began to cry out for their assistance; but my cries had no other effect than to make them tie me faster and stop my mouth, and then they put me into a large sack. . . .

. . . In fact[1] I had a great desire to read the Bible; . . . but not having a convenient place for retirement, I left the house in the day, rather than stay amongst the wicked ones; and that day, as I was walking, it pleased God to direct me to a house where there were an old sea-faring man, who experienced much of the love of God shed abroad in his heart. He began to discuss with me; . . . and in the memorable hour there came in a Dissenting Minister; . . . He then invited me to a love-feast at his chapel that evening. . . . When the wished-for hour came I went. . . . I was much astonished to see the place filled with people and no signs of eating and drinking. . . .

But when they spoke of a future state, they seemed to be altogether certain of their calling and election of God; and that no one could ever separate them from the love of Christ, or pluck them out of his hands. This filled me with utter consternation intermingled with admiration. . . . Their language and singing &c. did well harmonize; I was entirely overcome and wished to live and die thus. Lastly, some persons in the place produced some neat baskets full of buns, which they distributed about; and each person communicated with his neighbour, and sipped water out of different mugs, which they handed about to all who were present. This kind of Christian fellowship I had never seen, nor ever thought of seeing on earth. . . .

After this I was resolved to win heaven, if possible. . . .

---

[1] Whilst Olaudah lived in London.

Alfred Hutchinson

from ROAD TO GHANA

I was no longer Alfred Phiri, the Nyasa returning home. I left Alfred Phiri behind with the government report which had been my companion on the lake steamer. Now I was Alfred Hutchinson with a passport and a ticket for Ghana.

The taxi hooted again and Mbutta and I stumbled out of the sleeping house. In the half-light before sunrise the palms threw up their arms in a flutter of despair. And the shuttered windows of the houses held their secrets intact.

Abongo came out of the Princess Hotel grumbling and rushed back to get something he had forgotten. The inevitable camera was slung over his shoulder. We picked up Mgaya but while we were still a distance from the airport the taxi got a puncture and for a moment I was bewildered. An R.S.P.C.A. van pulled up. It was taking a dog to the plane. We clambered in, leaving the taxi driver jacking up the car.

In the small talk of people seeing off a friend I could sense my friends' sadness of parting. Abongo, who had forgotten his Press ticket, obtained permission to go with me to the plane. Another moment of parting had come; another moment of the many moments of parting on the road. We shook hands and Mbutta gave me a copy of Richard Wright's *Black Power*, a book dealing with pre-independence Ghana. The glass door opened and swung closed. Abongo crouched low like a hunter and snapped furiously. On the steps I waved back to my waving friends.

The plane roared and swung northwards to Nairobi. I was the only passenger and the Belgian hostess called it my plane. She went and sat with two members of the crew and chatted and laughed. The clouds shredded and knotted into drifting knolls. For a while we flew over what seemed to be the sea and then over red earth with the even redder traceries of roads. I turned to *Black Power* in the power of the heaving plane.

The air hostess touched my shoulder. To the left rose Kilimanjaro. At the height we were at it looked like a mound whose base and top was lost in the clouds. The people stopped their chatter and I remembered how the men on the Nyasaland train had done the same as we passed under the gaze of Mlanje.

John Rake, a young white reporter for *Drum*, met me at Nairobi. Abongo had telephoned him to say that I was passing through. Over cups of coffee I answered his questions and posed for a photograph or two.

A number of people joined the plane at Nairobi, including an Indian businessman going to Usumbura in the Belgian Congo. One of the passengers, a woman, had lost her typewriter and the plane waited for a few minutes. The typewriter was found and we continued on our way.

In a matter of hours I had covered distances which would have taken days or weeks to travel. In the evening I should be at Leopoldville at the other end of Africa, and the following night in Accra.

We had lunch at Entebbe. I had attached myself to the Indian businessman. Then, flying south-westwards we were for a long time over Lake Victoria, studded with pocket-sized islands. We left the lake after that, skirted the high mountains of Ruanda-Urundi and touched down at Usumbura beside a lake.

There was an immigration and customs' check at this outpost of the Belgian Congo. I pushed my travel document, a mass of stamps and signatures, towards the immigration official. He scratched his head and called another official. They spoke for a while and I suppose they must have said that it was all right. Then my baggage was missing. The air hostess raised a storm. She set the little place fluttering. After a frantic search it was discovered in the plane. It came limping out. The strap of Hazel's bag was broken and the bundle of blankets had come undone. The customs' official made two rapid crosses and did not bother to ask me if I had a gun. Then the things were rushed back to the plane. The Indian businessman came round to say good-bye.

A member of the crew came up to me. He asked if I would mind giving my seat to some people who wanted to be together and showed me to another seat. I got up. The group of men were probably a team. They wore blazers and spoke animatedly all the time.

An early-middle-aged European was sitting next to me reading *The Saint in New York*. I had thrown my lumber jacket over my knee and was reading my book. It was hot.

'It's very hot,' he said. 'Put your jacket on the rack.'

'They may not like it,' I said.

I had not thought of it before, but I gave that as the reason. The rack was heaped with jackets and other things.

'Why not?' You're a passenger like anyone else.'

'It's all right on my knee.'

I was tensing slowly. A few minutes later he looked up from his book.

'Where do you come from?'

'Johannesburg.'

'Oh well, not everybody thinks like those whites. Where are you going?'

'Accra.'

'The Dutch and their apartheid. There's too much tension in South Africa,' he said.

'You'd like it – it's a wonderful country for whites.'

Suddenly I wanted him to take the responsibility for South Africa, with her exemptions and privileges for the white man; responsibility for the battered passless man, the crying Indian woman, and Moyo taking sprouting potatoes home from a Delmas farm.

'No. Not for me,' he said, waving his hand.

'It's a paradise for the white man,' I said, my bitterness mounting.

I pressed South Africa on him but he steadily refused to accept her.

'Not all Europeans believe in the South African way of life, you know.'

'Really?' I said, laughing. 'It seems that Europeans have two moralities, one for whites and one for Africans.'

He was working for a firm of timber merchants with branches in the Federation and the Congo. He complained of African backwardness and I replied that it had suited the whites to keep Africans backward.

'You know, you're the first African I've spoken to,' he said.

He said it as if it were a compliment. But I did not scream at him. I laughed. What could I say?

'The trouble with Africa is that there is no unity – no common language or religious bonds, no Christianity or Islam.'

'Christianity in Africa is a farce. In South Africa everything is done in the name of Christian civilization. It's synonymous with white civilization – white supremacy. I don't think we need those bonds. But Africa is united – united against white oppression, in her rejection of the white man.

'That's racialism,' he said.

'I don't think so. My grandfather was a white man.'

I remembered Chisiza in the sweltering hold of the *Ilala* jettisoning everything. We talked on for a while. He said he had been in China for many years and that the Chinese were proud of their

race. Then we fell silent and turned to our books, and except for one
or two odd remarks were silent for the rest of the journey to Leopoldville.

The Pan-American plane from Johannesburg to Accra was due
at eight the following night. I had half-a-crown of Rhodesian
currency and a day to wait. What should I do? My neighbour on
the plane came up to me.

'What are your plans?'

'I suppose I'll wait somewhere,' I said.

'Sabena or Pan-Am will have to put you up,' he said. 'Take the
bus to the Regina Hotel.'

He got into a taxi and drove away. An old Englishman with
a stack of passports complained all the time. He was going to Accra
and had had the same trouble all the time : the airlines were unwilling to pay for accommodation. The bus swept the wide empty
streets to the luxurious Regina Hotel.

I pushed my ticket and passport at the receptionist. She looked
at them, at me, and consulted a friend. She broke into excited
French. I shook my head.

'Speak English? Who will pay?' she said.

She was thin and comical.

'I don't know – Sabena or Pan-Am,' I said.

'There's always trouble. People come here and the airlines won't
pay.'

She picked up the telephone. She 'ellooed'. She did not get
through. She got through. She hung up and shrugged her shoulders.
The reception hall had emptied.

'Sabena says Pan-Am must pay. Pan-Am says Sabena must pay.'

I shrugged my shoulders too. It did not matter. If I got a room
that would be fine, if I didn't I should find somewhere to while
away the night. But I should be on the plane the next night. The
receptionist took up the phone again. She shouted at somebody and
hung up flustered.

'What are you going to do? Can you pay for a room?'

I produced the half-crown. She laughed and I laughed too.

'The cheapest room is one pound ten,' she said. 'What are you
going to do?'

'I'll wait outside.'

'You can't do that.'

'Why?'

'You can't sleep on the pavement. It's not nice.'

She got hold of the phone again. She hung up, shrugging her
shoulders.

'I've tried my best,' she said, shrugging finally.

'I know – thank you.'

The knowledge that I should be in Accra the following night sounded like a gong. A sense of victory was welling up in me. I turned to go.

'I'll give you a room at one pound ten and a voucher for seventy francs. If Pan-Am or Sabena don't pay, I will.'

'I'll send you the money from Accra,' I said.

She wrote out a voucher and called a porter. I followed the porter through a maze of corridors to my room and followed him back for the seventy-franc meal. I ordered carefully, adding up all the time. After the meal I went back to my room.

I had done it. It came almost as a surprise that I had made it. The knowledge suffused my being like the afterglow of a warming thought and filled myself and the room with achievement. I felt unashamedly heroic. Then I remembered Patrick Van Rensburg, the young Afrikaaner who had been stationed in Leopoldville and who had resigned from the diplomatic corps because he felt he could not defend the Union's racialist policies. When he had returned to South Africa he had joined the Liberal Party and had grown to love the African locations. He must have come to the Regina Hotel many times. I relaxed. I had made it.

The receptionist was at the desk next morning and she directed me to the Sabena offices. Huge American cars swept the wide streets, their horns blaring. I mixed with the magnificent Congolese women and waved away Africans selling tourist booklets and paintings. The sun beat down on the city and its aspiring sky-scrapers. I lost my way, stopped people and repeated 'Sabena' until I reached the offices.

'Pan-Am must pay,' said the man. 'You're travelling Pan-Am tonight – they must pay.'

It was hopeless. I sauntered back to the Pan-American offices next to the Regina Hotel.

'There's some trouble about paying,' I said to the fat Belgian woman at the office. 'I'm from Sabena and they say Pan-Am must pay.'

She telephoned the receptionist next door.

'We'll pay,' she said. 'Will you take the bus to the airport?'

'Yes.'

'It leaves here at seven.'

A tropical storm whipped the city in the afternoon. The hotel attendants in their puce uniforms rushed out with enormous umbrellas to rescue people from their cars. It was brief and torrential. It left ripped leaves on the streets and singing water. And as suddenly as the storm had come a sharp astringent sun came out.

I shall be in Ghana tonight. The knowledge burns like stars in a rain-washed sky. The last lap of many laps. The straight lap to the goal. The plane we are waiting for will take me to the end of the road. African policemen with rifles slung on their shoulders patrol the airport and chase away the boys selling paintings and tourist books. They catch one who pleads and laughs and the passengers laugh with him as if it were in play.

There are Africans waiting for the plane. Africans with 'southern' airs and faces. Once, long ago, I had wanted a 'northern' face, a face that would take me on the first lap of the road to Ghana. Now I needed no face but my own.

Four hours, twenty minutes' flight to Accra. The last four hours and twenty minutes of a journey that has taken nearly two months. How different is the end from the beginning. How different the boosting plane from the desert train; the runaway train; the sweltering cabin; the bus pounding all day long and all day long.

The plane heaves like the mighty heart of a woman and shoots into the night. It is the beginning of the end; the end of the once unknowable miles of the road to Ghana. Nothing must happen now. Nothing can happen. I find myself gearing for nothing to happen. But for a moment, glancing outside, I imagine that the plane is on fire.

The young white woman in the seat in front turns round and smiles. She speaks German to her husband who is balding on top. She asks where I come from and where I am going. She is going to visit her people in Germany. They are from Windhoek, she and her husband and a little girl with an armful of dolls, and a baby sleeping in a basket. I tell her my story which she touches with her smile. The cigarettes my friends had bought me in Dar-es-Salaam have run out. The hostess takes my Rhodesian half-crown and brings me a packet and some change.

We sit quietly as if turning things over in our minds. And I remember the things that have happened in the last two months. How Mweli once said that he would tell the people in Nyasaland that the way was hard. The plane bounces like a ball in the pockets of emptiness as we ride into a storm. The stars rise and fall. But I know that it is the very last lap and nothing will go wrong.

Somewhere in the night there is Hazel. I try to reach her to tell her that I am nearing the end, as I tried to tell her that I had left in the shushing train, when her face fragmented and fell to bits. I try to tell her that the end is near and that everything will be all right.

The first lights of Accra wink below and the engines ease off, relax. I am filled with gratefulness. Grateful that there is in the world a place like Ghana. Grateful for the sheltering arm.

The plane hits the tarmac and rises like a half-startled bird and settles down. The young woman turns round and smiles. This is the end of the road, the very end of the road to Ghana.

I am filling in the form and the young immigration officer is talking.

'Welcome to Ghana. The Sudan was waiting for you.'

There are details on the form I cannot fill, could never fill, and he takes the form and across its back he writes – EXEMPTED.

'Hutch, I'm glad you've come,' says Mary Louisa Hooper in her caressing American drawl. 'We were beginning to wonder if you got the ticket and would catch the conference. Hutch, I'm *real* glad.'

I am again looking for the road to Ghana in my sleep. My mother and my brothers, George, Sydney and Victor, are walking towards our house. And I know that at home, on the rise, the police are raiding for Hazel. I ask: 'Where is the road to Ghana?' And Victor replies: 'You must plunge deep into the hippo and croco-dile pool . . . sink in oblivion of water. On the other side is the road.'

I hide behind a tree, apprehensively looking at our house where the police are searching for Hazel. I shush my mother but she begins to dance, Swazi-wise, stamping her feet in youthful ecstasy, and sings: 'You are beautiful – I bore you. . . .'

Noni Jabavu

from THE OCHRE PEOPLE

When I saw *Umfana* with my stepmother that day, I had remem-bered my great surprise a day or two before that, on noticing among the small sheaf of annotated postcards my father took out of his waistcoat pocket, a snapshot of the dog and my mother. I had taken it a few weeks before her sudden death. She had been transplanting seedlings with the dog beside her looking on, front paw uplifted.

At last I heard *Sis'* Nompumelelo murmur, for once not at the top of her voice. '*uTitshala* means, Ntando, that you are mistaken to expect *not* to feel resentments on your first visit home under the new order. You are bound to feel them; so do not struggle; admit that you do, and face them – the only way to conquer them, eliminate the poison inside. The struggle to conceal and suppress is useless. It will only fester whereas it must be cast out. We must pray for you to be given patience even in this atmosphere of haste and hurry.' At that I could hold back no more and burst out. *Sis'* Nompumelelo leaned forward : 'O, Noni – take care.'

My voice rose, I suppose; I was overwhelmed by all kinds of things big and small that *I* knew at that moment were trivial : like 'the banishment' of old family photographs, that for instance of my eldest sister (whom I had never known), taken as a baby before she died in the great 'flu of the First World War and whose picture had never never been moved. When Teacher interrupted with a sibilant 'Hush !' the room was suddenly deafeningly still. He uttered the little cluck that people make when in a dilemma, '*Kwek!*' But it only set me off again and I became carried away by the stream of my own interpretation. Whatever my stepmother had done in our house seemed to reflect on my mother and the old order of our life. I did not stop to remember the intricacies of my relationship with my late mother, its ups and downs, or of how Aunt Valetta had suggested when I went to her that a mother's task to *train* her children could never be unalloyed joy on either side; 'whereas with fathers, distance renders them immune. And in this man's world of ours, they have the advantage; to his offspring a man *can* be a source of pleasurable emotions if, like your father, he is indulgent and kind and beautiful to behold as well. He will be feared, rightly, but also adored'. I thought of none of that. My mother now occupied a special place in my feelings. But I could only express all this in futile terms for it was a jumble in my mind, and I could only harp on goods and chattels, the introduction to our house of new ones, dismissal of familiar old ones. I was unable to consider the deeper levels with which the Mzamanes were concerned. I knew that I was being stupid, wrong-headed, but could not stop.

Teacher took on a stern voice, the way you do to ward off hysteria in someone you are fond of. 'Now look here. Your tastes are naturally late-Mama's tastes – those of new-Mama are bound to be different, you know that. Must we treat you like an idiot? Why must you conclude that father is in league with her, with anybody, to erase the memory of the old home life? How can you let yourself think like that? *Kwek!* Don't you realize – don't you *allow* for the fact that men are helpless in these chattel matters? Pictures, vases, chairs, crockery – all those things are women's province. She is trying to make father comfortable in *her* way. *u*Jili could not interfere, even if it occurred to him to do so.'

I could think of no answer to that and only trembled. Teacher leaned forward, an expression of anxiety on his face and asked point blank, 'Have you said any of this to *anyone* at home? I shook my head. I saw him breathe deeply, as if relieved. 'Ah. Then at least war has not been declared.' There was a pause.

But his wife said uneasily, 'It may not be war but people feel, *know* in the bowels.' He interrupted her, leaning back now, and thoughtful : 'Of that Ntando is aware. MamSwazi and the old man naturally know. Nontando, do not *your* bowels tell you of the hurt your hostility causes her?'

It was no use, I now fell headlong down the slope and shrieked out a sentence.

There was a terrible silence. It was as if somebody else had cried out, not me, for I was bowled over by the words I had uttered. It was the unforgivable, a thing that 'should never be spoken even when one *may* speak' – as people say, since permitted freedoms have their rules and beyond a certain point the expression of certain emotions and irrationalities is taboo because it puts too great a strain on the peace that is essential for social balance. 'Words cannot be recalled, therefore those who heard what you should not have uttered are embarrassed when confronted with you' is a saying dinned into your ears from childhood, that you may try to regulate your behaviour according to an ideal.

Mzamane shifted uneasily in his seat. At last he murmured, hoarsely this time, *'Kwek!'* I did not know what to do. I saw him surreptitiously glance at his wrist-watch. It suddenly reminded me of the cousins who were coming to take me dancing. He looked at his wife and whispered, *'Kwek! Yint' eyizak'th'wani le?* What is to be done?'

She did not answer. I found I was shivering now, in spite of the sparkling fire. And, as if at the end of his resource, he finished, *'Impi ye* dance will be here before we can straighten this mess.' I tried to collect myself – and realized, to my astonishment, that I was feeling partly relieved, some of 'the poison' had that moment been 'cast out'. At the same time, my discomfort was acute, acute. What about the ethical offence I had committed in gaining relief? Could I hope they would forgive, erase from their minds the words they should not have heard? Was it too much to pray that they might ascribe my error in uttering them not to viciousness but to 'the mixed behaviour of these days' that he had talked about? I struggled in a state of contradictions, knowing I deserved nothing.

Sis' Nompumelelo took over. Her mind worked on a practical level as well as on his more analytical planes. She started on a series of concrete suggestions. As I listened I could not help thinking that she and her husband had 'inherited' some of my parents' capabilities : they saw people's ordinary problems, however personal, as reflections of 'our changing society'.

Suddenly I heard *Sis'* Nompumelelo call me *'Sis wam'* – the dignity of the title that our ages prescribed that *I* give *her*. I was moved almost more by that than by anything that had been said so far. Was it not an instinctive offering – conciliation, concern, delicacy, affection? Much later, wondering at the effect of so gentle a gesture I remembered our old washerwoman when she had turned to soothe the feelings of the little boy who carried my parcel; she had made a similar approach when she had called him. *'Bawo wam* – my father'. But at that moment, I realized only that I had not after all put myself beyond the pale as I deserved; that I was to understand that my impulsive, hideous utterance was erased from their minds, they would continue as if they had not heard my unspeakable threat never to like, let alone want, a new mother. I could breathe again, pay more successful attention to the rest of what she said. And when she had finished, how I longed to say I did indeed agree with their sentiment – was it not common sense, decency? But I could not trust myself to speak, only nodded, able to look not at them but ahead of me, into the fire.

Traditional

THE ENGLISHMAN AND HIS PET ANIMALS

(*translated from the Bulu by the Rev. A. N. Krug*)

Once upon a time there was an Englishman, and he used to go hunting and shoot game near his home. There came a day that all the game there was finished. So he said, 'Now I perceive that all the game animals in my own home forest are finished; so I think I will go and hunt over in Germany.' He went to tell his father and his mother of his plan, but they objected and said, 'No, you must not go there.' But he was persistent, and again he said, 'I am going.' So they at last reluctantly consented. So he took his gun, and his cartridge box and his travelling bag, and started on the way to Germany.

As he was going along the way he saw a large female chimpanzee, which was carrying its child. When he was just about ready to shoot the mother chimpanzee with his gun, the mother chimpanzee left the young chimp there and ran away into the forest. The young Englishman took the young chimpanzee with him as a tame pet. He went on some distance farther, and he saw a large female gorilla, and it also was carrying its young. When he was getting ready to shoot the mother, it also left its young and ran into the forest. So he took the gorilla as a pet. As he went on still farther he saw a mother leopard with its young, and just when he was ready to shoot the mother leopard, she left the young leopard and ran into the forest. So the Englishman took the young leopard also as a pet with him, Thus he had three pet animals, a chimpanzee, a gorilla, and a leopard.

At last he arrived at his destination. He told the people there, 'I have come here to find a woman to marry,' and they said to him, 'There is a woman in yonder house you may marry.' So he first took his three pet animals to a small house near by. After that he went to where the woman was in the house, and told her his errand; and the woman fell in love with him. But the woman also said to him, 'There is only one trouble here, and one evil thing, for I have had many lovers before you came, but there is a large and fierce animal here that kills them.' The Englishman replied, 'I surpass all men in knowing how to shoot animals, so this fierce animal will not do anything to me.' The woman again told him, 'That fierce animal is in the habit of coming at midnight.'

As soon as darkness had come the Englishman made his plans and waited and was on guard for the approach of the animal. When it was just about midnight that fierce animal did come. When the Englishman heard it come, and while it was still some distance away, the Englishman went and found a good place to wait for it. When it came near he shot it with his gun and it died. He ran in haste and cut off its tail and he gave that tail to his pet animals; and they kept the tail safely with them. After this the Englishman went back to his house and laid down to sleep.

When the soldier, who was always guarding this woman, heard the report of the gun, he came and ran swiftly to the place where he heard the gun, and there he found the animal dead. So the soldier made a plan, and said, 'I will go and kill that Englishman, and after that I will marry this woman.' For the father of this girl had said, 'Whoever kills this fierce animal, he will marry my daughter, and he need not give any dowry either.' So the soldier quietly went into the house of the Englishman, and found him asleep and cut off the head of the Englishman. After this the soldier hastened to the father of the girl and told him, 'I have killed the fierce animal which used to kill the young men and lovers of your daughter.' The father of the girl asked him, 'Which part of the body did you shoot at?' and he said, 'I wounded it in the side of the body.' The father said, 'My men will bring in the body in the morning.'

When the day had dawned the three pet animals said : 'Where is our master who brought us here?' So they all three went to the house where their master used to stay. When they came to the house they asked the girl, 'Where is our master?' and the woman said, 'He has been killed, there lies his corpse.' At first the pet animals were in great trouble and perplexity and did not know what to do. But soon the chimpanzee said, 'I can put his head back on his neck,' and the other said, 'Go ahead, and put it on indeed.' And he put the head back on the neck. The gorilla now said, 'I can bring him back to life,' and the other said, 'Go ahead and do it.' And the gorilla did this. But still the Englishman was not able to talk. So at last the leopard said, 'I am able to make a magic charm, so that he will be able to talk.' They all said, 'Go ahead and do it.' So the leopard made the magic charm, and right away the Englishman asked them, 'What are you all doing here?' They answered, 'You had been killed, but we have brought you back to life again.'

After this the Englishman took a bath and put on his best clothes and went and told the father of the woman, 'I have killed the fierce animal.' But the father would not believe him, and said, 'The soldier has come and he told me that he himself killed it; why do you come here like this and lie to me?' The Englishman said, 'That is not true, and I will prove to you that I myself killed the animal.' So the man asked him, 'What part of the body did you shoot at?' And he replied without hesitation, 'I shot at it as it came towards me, from the front, and hit it in the face.' The father of the woman had meanwhile sent his men to bring in the carcass of the animal, and when the men came with the body, and the man who had the daughter very carefully looked where the shot had hit it and killed it, they found that it had been hit in the face just as the Englishman had said. So the father of the girl and all the people agreed without dissent that the Englishman had killed the animal. So they gave him the woman in marriage.

Soon after this the Englishman took his wife and his three pet animals and started on the road back to his home country. When

F

he arrived at the place where he had caught the young leopard, he released it, and let it go free; when he came to the places where he had taken the gorilla and the chimpanzee he also released them and let them go free. At last he arrived at home again, and he had the beautiful woman whom he had married as his wife. As far as we know they lived happily ever after.

Alex la Guma

from A WALK IN THE NIGHT

Michael Adonis slouched over to the window and stared out through a gap in the dusty colourless curtain and the grimy panes. Beyond, the roofs of the city were sprawled in a jumble of dark, untidy patterns dotted with the scattered smudged blobs of yellow. Hanover Street made a crooked strip of misty light across the patch of District Six, and far off the cranes along the sea front stood starkly against the sky.

He turned away from the window, anger mixing with headiness of the liquor he had consumed and curdling into a sour knot of smouldering violence inside him. The old man was pouring wine into the sticky glass, the neck of the bottle rattling against the rim so that the red sloshed about and wet his knuckled fingers.

'There you are, Michael me boy,' he chuckled, breathing hoarsely. 'Nothing like a bit of port to warm the cockles of your heart.'

He held the glass up, his hand shaking, slopping the liquor, and Michael Adonis took it from him with a sudden burst of viciousness and tossed the wine down, then flinging the glass back into the old man's lap. The thick, sweet wine nauseated him and he choked and fought to control his stomach, glaring at the wreck on the bed, until the wine settled and there was a new heat throbbing in his head.

'A bad mood,' the old man quavered, and poured himself a glass-ful. He drank it, the wine trickling down his stubbly chin, and gasped. He cocked his head at Michael Adonis and said : 'You shouldn't get cross over nothing. What's the matter with you?'

'Aw, go to buggery.'

'Now, now, that's no way to talk. We've all got our troubles.'

'Ya. Bloody troubles *you* got.'

'God bless my soul, I've got my troubles, too,' the old man said, with a sudden whine in his voice. 'Here I am and nobody to look after an old man.' Tears of remorse gathered in his pale, red-rimmed eyes, and he knuckled them with a tangled skein of dirty cord that was his hand. 'Look at me. I used to be something in my days. God bless my soul, I used to be something.'

Michael Adonis lit a cigarette and stood there looking at the old man through the spiral of smoke. He said : 'What the hell you crying about. You old white bastard, you got nothing to worry about.'

'Worry? Worry?' the old man whined. 'We all got something to worry about. He mustered himself for a moment and shook a dried twig of a finger at Michael Adonis. 'We all got our cross to bear. What's my white got to do with it? Here I am, in shit street, and does my white help? I used to be an actor. God bless my soul, I toured England and Australia with Dame Clara Bright. A great lady. A great actress she was.' He began to weep, the tears spilling over the sagging rims of his eyes and he reached for the bottle again. 'We're like Hamlet's father's ghost. I played the ghost of Hamlet's father once. London it was.'

'You look like a blerry ghost, you spook,' Michael Adonis said bitterly. He jerked the bottle from the old man's hand and tipped it to his mouth and took a long swallow, gagging and then belching as he took the neck from his lips. His head spun and he wanted to retch.

The old man said : 'Don't finish the lot, boy. Leave some for old Uncle Doughty'. He reached frantically for the bottle, but Michael Adonis held it out of his reach, grinning and feeling pleasantly malicious.

'Want a *dop*, Uncle Doughty?'

'Oh, come on, man. Don't torment your old dad.'

'You old spook.'

'Give us a drink, give us a drink, sonny boy.'

'What was that you were saying about ghosts? I like ghost stories.' Michael Adonis grinned at him, feeling drunk. He waggled the bottle in front of the decayed ancient face with its purple veins, yellow teeth and slack mouth, and watched the tears gather again in the liquid eyes.

'I'll tell you what,' the old man whined hopefully. 'I'll recite for you. You should hear me. I used to be something in my days.' He cleared his throat of a knot of phlegm, choked and swallowed. He started : 'I . . . I am thy father's spirit; doomed for a certain term to walk the night. . . .' He lost track, then mustered himself, waving his skeleton arms in dramatic gestures, and started again. 'I am thy father's spirit, doomed for a certain time to walk the night . . . and . . . and for the day confined to fast in fires, till the foul crimes done in my days of nature's . . . nature are burnt and purged away. . . . But. . . .' He broke off and grinned at Michael Adonis, and then eyed the bottle. 'That's us, us Michael, my boy. Just ghosts, doomed to walk the night. Shakespeare.'

'Bull,' Michael Adonis said, and took another swallow at the bottle. 'Who's a blerry ghost?' He scowled at the old man through a haze of red that swam in front of his eyes like thick oozing paint, distorting the ancient face staring up at him.

'Michael, my boy. Spare a drop for your old uncle.'

'You old bastard,' Michael Adonis said angrily. 'Can't a boy have a bloody piss without getting kicked in the backside by a lot of effing law?'

'Now, now, Michael. I don't know what you're talking about, God bless my soul. You take care of that old port, my boy.'

The old man tried to get up and Michael Adonis said, 'Take your effing port,' and struck out at the bony, blotched, sprouting skull, holding the bottle by the neck so that the wine splashed over his hand. The old man made a small, honking, animal noise and dropped back on the bed.

Somewhere up in the damp intestines of the tenement a radio was playing and Willieboy climbed up the worn, sticky staircase into a crescendo of boogie-woogie, past the stark corridors with their dead-ends of latrines staring back like hopeless futures.

The electric light on the last floor flickered but did not go out, clinging determinedly to life as if it refused to be overwhelmed by the decay spreading around it. Willieboy walked down the corridor in the struggling glow and reached the door of Michael Adonis' room. He tried the handle. It was locked and he rattled it calling out softly. Willieboy rattled the doorknob again and then scowled and turned away from the door. He walked a little way back towards the stairs. He thought, maybe this old poor white will part with some start. And he turned to the room of the old Irishman.

Tapping on the door he said, 'Hey, Mister Doughty,' speaking with his ear close to the panel of the door. When he received no reply he rapped a little louder, calling again. Then he turned the knob and looking in, looked into the dead blue-grey face of the old man, and it glared back at him, wide-eyed, the stained, carious teeth bared in a fixed grin, with the suddenness of a shot from a horror film. . . .

Raalt said : 'Nobody kills anybody on my beat and gets away with it. No bloody bastard.'

Looking again at the corpse, the driver said : 'A white man, too. What would a white man be doing living in a place like this?' He looked away from the corpse and around the room, wrinkling his nose at the smell of vomit, wine, decay.

Raalt said nothing, but unbuttoned the flap of his pocket and took out his notebook. He glanced at his wrist watch and then began to write in the book. The driver said, a little impatiently : 'I had better get onto the wireless.'

Constable Raalt looked up at him from his writing with his hard grey eyes and then said, grinning : 'Very well. Get the station on your beautiful wireless and tell them to send the detectives. Also give them my greetings and best wishes. Also a blessed Christmas.'

The driver glanced at his eyes, shook his head and went out. Constable Raalt wrote again in his notebook and through the writing thought, I wonder what she's doing now, the *verdomte* bitch, I'll break her neck if I catch her at something. He finished writing and then went to the door of the room. He had become oblivious of the sour smell in the room and it was now merely a smell, like stale tobacco or the smell of disinfectant in the police station.

The people gathered in the corridor, near the upper landing, gazed back at the constable, some of them nervously, some with surreptitious boldness, all with the worn, brutalized, wasted, slum-scratched faces of the poor. They saw the flat grey eyes under the gingerish eyebrows, hard, and expressionless as the end of pieces of lead pipe, pointed at them.

'Now,' he said coldly. 'Now, where is the woman who is supposed to have screamed?'

The people on the landing and in the corridor said nothing, looking away, and Constable Raalt thought, These bastards don't like us; they never did like us and we are only tolerated here; I bet there are some here who would like to stick a knife into me right now.

He said, sneering : 'What's the matter? She didn't do it, did she?'

The man, John Abrahams, laughed a little and said : 'They won't say a thing, *baas*. You know how it is.'

'No, I don't know how it is,' Raalt told him. 'You tell me how it is.'

'Well, *baas*. . . .'

'Alright, forget it, man. What's your name, anyway?'

'John Abrahams, *Konstabel*. I told *baas*.'

Raalt wrote it down in his notebook, together with the address. 'What is the name of the man inside?' Gesturing with his head towards the door of the room where the body lay.

'Mister Doughty,' the man Abrahams said.

'Doughty? What sort of a name is that? How do you spell it?'

'I don't know, *baas*. We just call him Mister Doughty.'

'Doughty,' Constable Raalt repeated. 'What a peculiar name. These people have bloody peculiar names.' Then he remembered that the body was that of a white man and he asked : 'What was he doing here? How did he get here?'

'He lived here a long time,' Abrahams replied. 'He got a pension and he was in the big war. I heard him talk about it once.' He added with a grin, 'Drank like hell, too.' He looked down at his feet when Raalt stared at him.

'Now,' Raalt said, when he had written down the old man's name in his notebook without bothering to try to spell it correctly : 'Tell me, how did this man look you saw running away.'

Before Abrahams could answer Frank Lorenzo said to him from the crowd in the corridor : 'You've said enough already, Johnny.'

Constable Raalt raised his head and looked at Frank Lorenzo, his grey eyes bleak. He said : 'Listen, *jong*, you seem to have a lot to say. You had a lot to say downstairs, too. Do you want to be arrested for intimidating a witness and defeating the ends of justice?'

Frank Lorenzo did not understand these high-sounding phrases but he sensed the threat. Still he met the constable's eyes holding them with his own, until he felt his wife tugging at his arm, pleading : 'Franky, don't get into trouble, please. Remember . . . remember. . . .'

'Alright,' Frank Lorenzo said sullenly. 'Alright.' He looked across at Abrahams for a moment and then looked away again.

Constable Raalt said : '*Pasop*,' to him and then to Abrahams : 'Now, then. Come on.'

'Well, *baas*,' Abrahams hesitated, feeling a little nervous and embarrassed now. 'Well, *baas*, you see I didn't execkly see. . . .'

'Oh,' Constable Raalt said, his voice hard. 'You didn't exactly see. What exactly did you see?'

'Well, *baas*, he was just a boy. One of these young rookers that hang out on the corners. I can't say execkly. . . .'

John Abrahams was now beginning to feel the effect of the abrasive stares of those around him and his bravado commenced to collapse, falling from him like dislodged coloured paper decorations. He shuffled and stared at his feet and fingered his nether lip, trying to salvage some of the disintegrating sense of importance.

'Listen, man,' Raalt told him. 'If you don't want to talk now you can still be forced to appear in court and say what you know before the magistrate. So make up your mind.'

John Abrahams collapsed completely and said quickly : 'He was just a young rooker, *baas*. He had on a yellow shirt and a sports coat and had kinky hair. That's all I seen, *baas*, true as God. That's all.' He looked around helplessly and cried out : 'Well, I got to tell what I saw, mustn't I ?'

The crowd was silent and Constable Raalt, writing in his notebook again thought. They hate us, but I don't give a bloody hell about them, anyway; and no *hotnot* bastard gets away with murder on my patrol; yellow shirt and kinky hair; a real *hotnot* and I'll get him even if I have to gather in every black bastard wearing a yellow shirt.

He said, his grey eyes narrowed with rage : 'Alright, the rest of you can bogger off. Abrahams, you stay here and wait for the detectives.'

'Can't I go, *baas*?' Abrahams asked, whining now.

'No, God, *jong*. I said wait for the detectives.'

He added to his thought, Detectives; I can look after my own troubles; that boy and his detectives.

He stared at the crowd in the corridor, his eyes like pieces of grey metal, and they started to disperse, slowly trickling away. Frank Lorenzo looked again at Abrahams and spat on the floor, then walked down the corridor with his wife. Constable Raalt returned his notebook to the pocket of his tunic and buttoned the flap. He waited for the detectives to arrive, and began to think again of his own wife.

Willieboy lay flat on his face, thrusting his body into the hard, unyielding surface of the roof. He felt the rough corrugated iron against his chest through the shirt and coat, and the touch of something cold and metallic against his chin. There was a sour taste in his mouth and his head ached badly. Also, he was out of breath and his chest heaved and jerked from the wild dash down the street and the scramble onto this roof. There was a smell of cat droppings and urine around him. But he noticed none of these things for the cold clutch of fear deep down inside him.

He had dodged the police many times before, but never like this; neither had he been shot at, and he was afraid. He shivered suddenly and his face puckered in the dark, the tears forming in his eyes. He thought, What they want to chase me for? What did I do? I did nothing. I did nothing. What they want to chase me for?

Lying there in the dark he felt the chill of his fear that was colder than the touch of metal or the breeze that had come up over the city.

He thought again, What did I do? I never did nothing. His mind jumped and he saw his mother standing over him, shouting : 'You been naughty again.' He was seven years old and had been selling the evening paper. The sub-agent for whom he hawked the papers had paid him the few pence commission he had earned and he had bought a big parcel of fish and chips instead of taking the money home. He had not eaten since early that morning, and then only a bowl of porridge without milk or sugar and a slice of stale bread, and by evening he was very hungry. He had gone home to the ramshackle room in a tenement with the smell of fish about him and when he could not produce his commission his mother slapped his face and shouted : 'You naughty little bastard.' She slapped him again and again so that his head jerked loosely on his shoulders and his face stung from the blows. He wept through the pain.

His mother beat him at the slightest provocation and he knew that she was wreaking vengeance upon him for the beatings she received from his father. His father came home drunk most nights and beat his mother and him with a heavy leather belt. His mother crouched in a corner of the room and shrieked and whimpered for mercy. When his father was through with her he turned to Willieboy, but sometimes he managed to escape from the room and did not return until late in the night when the father was snoring drunkenly and his mother had cried herself to sleep. His mother, unable to defend herself against her husband, took revenge for her whippings on Willieboy.

Now he lay on the rooftop and heard her again, saying : 'You naughty little bogger.'

He raised a hand and wiped the tears from his eyes. I've got to get away, he told himself, I've got to get away. I don't want to be shot. Please don't let me get shot.

He lay quite still and listened for sounds on the roof. Somewhere below people were shouting and talking, a jumble of words. But he was not concerned about them. He peered ahead around the end of a projection that crossed the roof in front of his face, searching for any sign of the policeman. Once he heard the crunch of a boot on the corrugated iron and fear leapt in him and he tried to force himself into the hard metal under his body. That law's somewhere out there waiting, he thought. What they want to chase me for? I did nothing. You should not have run, he told himself. Soon as you run they come for you. Well, I did nothing, I can give myself up. They kick the lights out of you. You think they going to chase you all this way and on top of a roof and then just let you go? Us poor bastards always get kicked around. If it's not the law it's something else. Always there's somebody to kick you around. What kind of blerry business is that? he asked himself with remorse.

Then he heard the policeman's footsteps blundering around on the iron of the roof as he came forward and Willieboy sprang to his feet in fright and dashed for the far end of the row of rooftops.

Constable Raalt had been crouching against an old and disused water tank, waiting for some sign of the boy. He knew for sure that the boy was somewhere on that row of roofs and he waited for him to show himself. Constable Raalt was determined to take his time about this. He had his quarry trapped and he was quite sure that he would conclude the hunt successfully. He crouched there in the dark and smiled with satisfaction.

The water tank was on his left and a few feet to his right was a pigeon loft. He could hear the soft rustling sounds that came from inside it and smell the odour of bird-lime. Below in the street the crowd was moving about and growling. For a moment he wondered what had happened to the driver, but he thrust the thought quickly from his mind along with every other thought and concentrated coldly on what he had to do there on the rooftops.

After a while he decided that he would move forward a little. He did not want to turn on the flashlight because he was enjoying this stalk in the dark. He took a long step forward and his face struck a clothesline, the taut, stretched wire causing him to step back stumbling on the corrugated surface of the roof.

He cursed and ducked under the wire and it was then that he saw the dark form of the Coloured youth spring up from behind a projection ahead of him and start off, bounding across the roofs.

Raalt flung himself forward, firing as he did so. The flash of the pistol made a bright flare of light for a second and the bullet struck a drainpipe and sang off. Then Raalt was running across the roofs, his boots drumming the surface.

A roar went up from the crowd in the street below and a woman screamed shrilly. Raalt pounded on, leaping projections, holding his head low to evade the clothes-lines. He saw the boy poise himself for an instant on the edge of the far wall and drop out of sight.

Willieboy struck the asphalt below and the shock of the awkward drop jarred through his body. A hot stab of pain seared through an ankle and he screamed with pain, then he was stumbling and hobbling crookedly into the middle of the street with the crowd breaking back ahead of him. Then he saw another section of the mob split and the patrol van sweeping down on him.

He turned with fear and despair disfiguring his face, hearing the van screeching to a halt and seeing Constable Raalt drop expertly from the roof he had left. He stared bewilderedly about him. Then with the policemen moving on him from the front and back he crouched like a fear-crazed animal at bay and shouted hysterically at the one with the gun :

F*

'You ... boer. You ... boer.'

He cursed Constable Raalt, unloading the obscenities like one dumping manure and then reached frantically for the pocket where he carried the sharpened kitchen-knife.

Before his hand reached the pocket and before he could discover that the knife was not there Constable Raalt fired again.

The bullet slapped into the boy, jerking him upright, and he spun, his arms flung wide, turning on his toes like a ballet dancer.

Camara Laye

from THE DARK CHILD

(translated by James Kirkup)

Of all the different kinds of work my father performed, none fascinated me so much as his skill with gold. No other occupation was so noble, no other needed such a delicate touch; and, moreover, this sort of work was always a kind of festival : it was a real festival that broke the monotony of ordinary working days.

So if a woman, accompanied by a go-between, crossed the threshold of the workshop, I would follow her in at once. I knew what she wanted : she had brought some gold and wanted to ask my father to transform it into a trinket. The woman would have collected the gold in the placers of Siguiri, where, for months on end, she would have crouched over the river, washing the mud and patiently extracting from it the grains of gold. These women never came alone : they were well aware that my father had other things to do than to make trinkets for all and sundry; and even if the making of jewellery had been his main occupation, they would have realized that they were not his first or his only customers, and that their wants could not be immediately attended to.

Generally these women required the trinket for a certain date, either for the festival of Ramadan or for the Tabaski; or for some other family festivity, or for a dance ceremony.

Thereupon, to better their chance of being quickly served, and the more easily to persuade my father to interrupt the work he had in hand, they would request the services of an official praise-singer, a go-between, and would arrange with him in advance what fee they would pay for his good offices.

The praise-singer would install himself in the workshop, tune up his cora, which is our harp, and would begin to sing my father's praises. This was always a great event for me. I would hear recalled the lofty deeds of my father's ancestors, and the names of these ancestors from the earliest times; as the couplets were reeled off, it was like watching the growth of a great genealogical tree that spread its branches far and wide and flourished its boughs and twigs before my mind's eye. The harp played an accompaniment to this vast utterance of names, expanding it and punctuating it with notes that were now soft, now shrill. Where did the praise-singer get his information from? He must certainly have developed a very retentive memory stored with facts handed down to him by his predecessors, for this is the basis of all our oral traditions. Did he embellish the truth? It is very likely : flattery is the praise-singer's stock-in-trade! Nevertheless, he was not allowed to take too many liberties with tradition, for it is part of the praise-singer's task to preserve it. But in those days such considerations did not enter my head, which I would hold high and proud; for I used to feel quite drunk with so much praise, which seemed to reflect some of its effulgence upon my own small person.

I could tell that my father's vanity was being inflamed, and I already knew that after having sipped this milk-and-honey he would lend a favourable ear to the woman's request. But I was not alone in my knowledge; the woman also had seen my father's eyes gleaming with contented pride; and she would hold out her grains of gold as if the whole thing was settled : my father, taking up his scales, would weigh the gold.

'What sort of trinket do you desire?' he would ask.

'I want. . . .'

And often it would happen that the woman did not know really what she wanted, because she would be so torn by desire, because she would have liked to have many, many trinkets, all out of the same small quantity of gold : but she would have had to have much more than she had brought with her to satisfy such a desire, and eventually she would have to content herself with some more modest wish.

'When do you want it for?' my father would ask.

And she would always want it at once.

'Why are you in such a hurry? How do you expect me to find the time?'

'It's very urgent, I can assure you,' the woman would reply. 'That's what all women say, when they want an ornament. Well, I'll see what I can do. Now are you happy?'

Then he would take the clay pot that was kept specially for the smelting of gold and pour in the grains; thereupon he would cover the gold with powdered charcoal, a charcoal which he obtained by the use of plant juices of exceptional purity; finally he would place a large lump of the same kind of charcoal over the whole thing.

Then, having seen the work duly undertaken, the woman, by now quite satisfied, would go back to her household tasks, leaving her go-between to carry on with the praise-singing which had already proved so advantageous to her.

On a sign from my father, the apprentices would start working the two pairs of sheep-skin bellows which were placed on the ground at each side of the forge and linked to it by earthen pipes. These apprentices remained seated all the time, with crossed legs, in front of the bellows; at least the younger did, for the elder would some-times be allowed to take part in the craftsmen's work and the younger – in those days it was Sidafa – only had to work the bellows and watch the proceedings while awaiting his turn to be elevated to less rudimentary tasks. For a whole hour they would both be working the levers of the bellows till the fire in the forge leapt into flame, becoming a living thing, a lively and merciless spirit.

Then my father, using long pincers, would lift the clay pot and place it on the flames.

Immediately all work would more or less stop in the workshop : actually while the gold is being melted and while it is cooling all work with copper or aluminium is supposed to stop, for fear that some fraction of these less noble metals might fall among the gold. It is only steel that can still be worked at such times. But workmen who had some piece of steel work in hand would either hasten to finish it or would openly stop work to join the other apprentices gathered round the forge. In fact, there were often so many of them at these times pressing round my father that I, the smallest, would have to get up and push my way in among them, so as not to miss any of the operation.

It might happen that, feeling he had too little room to work in, my father would make his apprentices stand well away from him. He would merely raise his hand in a simple gesture : at that particu-lar moment he would never utter a word, and no one else would, no one was allowed to utter a word, even the go-between's voice would no longer be raised in song; the silence would be broken only by the panting of the bellows and by the faint hissing of the gold. But if my father never used to utter actual words at this time, I know that he was uttering them in his mind; I could see it by his lips that kept working while he bent over the pot and kept stirring the gold and the charcoal with a bit of wood that would keep busting into flame, and so had to be constantly replaced by a fresh bit.

What were the words my father's lips were forming? I do not know; I do not know for certain : I was never told what they were. But what else could they have been, if not magical incantations? Were they not the spirits of fire and gold, of fire and air, air breathed through the earthen pipes, of fire born of air, of gold married with fire – were not these the spirits he was invoking? Was it not their help and their friendship he was calling upon in this marriage of elemental things? Yes, it was almost certainly those spirits he was calling upon, for they are the most elemental of all spirits, and their presence is essential at the melting of gold.

The operation that was going on before my eyes was simply the smelting of gold; but it was something more than that : a magical operation that the guiding spirits could look upon with favour or disfavour; and that is why there would be all round my father that absolute silence and that anxious expectancy. I could understand, though I was just a child, that there was no craft greater than the goldsmith's. I expected a ceremony, I had come to be present at a ceremony, and it really was one, though very protracted. I was still too young to be able to understand why it was so protracted; nevertheless, I had an inkling, beholding the almost religious concentration of all those present as they watched the mixing process.

When finally the gold began to melt, I used to feel like shouting, and perhaps we would all have shouted if we had not been forbidden to make a sound : I would be trembling, and certainly everyone else would be trembling as we sat watching my father stirring the mixture, still a heavy paste in which the charcoal was gradually being consumed. The next stage followed swiftly; the gold now had the fluidity of water. The guiding spirits had smiled on the operation !

'Bring me the brick !' my father would say, thus lifting the ban that until then had kept us all silent.

The brick, which an apprentice would place beside the fire, was hollowed out, generously greased with Galam butter. My father would take the pot off the fire, tilt it carefully, and I would watch the gold flowing into the brick, flowing like liquid fire. True, it was only a very sparse trickle of fire, but oh, how vivid, how brilliant ! As the gold flowed into the brick, the grease would splutter and flame and give off a thick smoke that caught in the throat and stung the eyes, leaving us all weeping and coughing.

It occurred to me later on that my father could easily have re-linquished all the work of smelting the gold to one or other of his assistants : they were not without experience in these matters; they had taken part hundreds of times in the same preparations and they would certainly have brought the work to a successful conclusion. But as I have told you, my father kept moving his lips! We could not hear those words, those secret words, those incantations which he addressed to powers that we should not, that we could not hear or see : this was essential. Only my father was versed in the science of conjuring the spirits of fire, air and gold, and conjuring evil spirits, and that is why he alone conducted the whole operation.

By now the gold would have cooled in the hollow of the brick, and my father would begin to hammer and stretch it. This was the moment when his work as a goldsmith really began. I noticed that before embarking on it he never failed to stroke stealthily the little snake coiled up under the sheep-skin; one can only assume that this was his way of gathering strength for what remained to be done, and which was the most difficult.

But was it not extraordinary, was it not miraculous that on these occasions the little black serpent always coiled up under the sheep-skin? He was not always there, he did not visit my father every day, but he was always present whenever there was gold to be worked.

Moreover, it is our custom to keep apart from the working of gold all influences outside those of the jeweller himself. And indeed it is not precisely because the jeweller alone possesses the secret of his incantations; but also because the working of gold, besides being a task of the greatest skill, is a matter of confidence, of con-science, a task which is not undertaken excepting after due reflection and experiment. Finally, I do not think that any jeweller would re-nounce the opportunity of performing such a task – I ought to say, such a spectacle! – in which he can display his abilities with a virtuosity that his work as a blacksmith or a mechanic or even as a sculptor is never invested with; even though in these more humble tasks his skill is no less wonderful, even though the statues which he carves in wood with his adze are not insignificant works!

The snake's presence came as no surprise to me; ever since that evening when my father had talked to me about the guiding spirit of our race, it had ceased to surprise me; it was quite natural that the snake should be there : he had knowledge of the future. Did he impart any of that knowledge to my father? It seemed to me quite obvious that he did : did he not always warn him of what was going to happen? But I had another reason for believing implicitly in the powers of the little snake.

The craftsman who works in gold must first of all purify himself, that is, he must wash himself all over and, of course, abstain from all sexual relationships during the whole time. Great respector of ceremony as he was, it would have been impossible for my father to ignore these rules. Now I never saw him make these preparations; I would see him address himself to his work without any apparent preliminaries. But from that moment it was obvious that, forewarned by his black guiding spirit in a dream of the task that would await him in the morning, my father must have prepared for it as soon as he arose, and had entered his workshop in a state of purity, his body smeared with the magical substances hidden in his numerous pots full of secret potions. So I believe my father never entered his workshop except in a state of ritual purity; and that is not because I want to make him out as being better than he is – he is a man like any other, and has a man's weaknesses – but always when it was a matter of ritual he was uncompromisingly strict.

The woman for whom the trinket was being made, and who would often have looked in to see how the work was getting on, would come for the final time, not wanting to miss anything of the marvellous sight as the gold wire, which my father had succeeded in spinning, was transformed into a trinket. She was here now, devouring with her eyes the fragile golden wire, following its tranquil and inevitable spirals round the little metal cone which gave the trinket its shape. My father would be watching her out of the corner of his eye, and sometimes I would see the corners of his mouth twitch into a smile : the woman's avid attentiveness amused him.

'Are you trembling?' he would say to her.

'*Am* I trembling?' she would ask.

And we would all burst out laughing at her. For she *was* trembling! She was trembling with covetousness for the spiral pyramid in which my father was inserting, among the convolutions, tiny grains of gold. When finally he terminated the work by placing at the summit the largest grain of gold, the woman would jump excitedly to her feet.

Then, while my father was slowly turning the trinket round in his fingers, smoothing it into perfect shape, no one could have displayed such utter happiness as the native woman, not even the praise-singer, whose trade it was to do so, and who, during the whole process of transformation, had kept on singing his praises, accelerating his rhythm, increasing his flatteries as the trinket took shape, and praising my father's talents to the skies.

Indeed, the praise-singer participated in a curious – I was going to say direct, effective – way in the work. He, too, was intoxicated with the joy of creation; he declaimed his rapture, and plucked his harp like a man inspired; he warmed to the task as if he had been the craftsman himself, as if the trinket had been made by his own hands. He was no longer a paid thurifer; he was no longer just the man whose services each and anyone could hire : he had become a man who creates his song under the influence of some very personal, interior necessity.

When my father, after having soldered the large grain of gold that crowned the summit, held out his work to be admired, the go-between would no longer be able to contain himself, and would intone the douga – the great chant which is only sung for celebrated men, and which is danced to only for them.

But the douga is a tremendous chant, a provocative chant, a chant that the go-between would not venture to sing, and that the man for whom it is sung would not venture to dance to, without certain precautions.

My father, forewarned in a dream, had been able to take these precautions as soon as he got up; the praise-singer had taken them as a matter of course when he had made his bargain with the woman. Just as my father had done, he had smeared his body with magic lotions and so had rendered himself invulnerable to the bad spirits which the douga would undoubtedly stir into activity, invulnerable also even to his fellow praise-singers who, jealous perhaps, were only waiting to hear the chant, the note of exaltation and the loss of control which that exaltation entails, to cast their evil spells upon him.

At the first notes of the douga, my father would rise and utter a cry in which happiness and triumph were equally mingled; and brandishing in his right hand the hammer that was the symbol of his profession, and in his left a ram's horn filled with magic substances, he would dance the glorious dance.

No sooner had he finished than workmen and apprentices, friends and customers in their turn, not forgetting the woman for whom the trinket had been created, would flock round him, congratulating him, showering praises on him, and complimenting at the same time the go-between, who found himself laden with gifts, gifts that are almost the only resources he has in his wandering life, that he leads after the fashion of the troubadours of old. Beaming, aglow with dancing and the praises he had received, my father would offer kola nuts, that small change of Guinean civility.

All that now remained to be done was to redden the trinket in a little water mixed with chlorine and sea-salt. I could go now : the ceremony was over ! But often, as I was leaving the workshop, my mother, who might be in the yard pounding millet or rice, would call me.

'Where have you been?' she would ask, although she knew very well where I had been.

'In the workshop.'

'Oh, yes, your father was making something out of gold. Gold! It's always gold!'

And she would pound furiously the helpless bowl of rice or millet.

'Your father's ruining his health! You see what he's doing.'

'He's been dancing the douga,' I would reply.

'The douga! The douga won't stop him ruining his eyesight! And you would be better off playing here in the yard instead of going and breathing the dust and smoke in the workshop!'

My mother did not like my father to work with gold. She knew how harmful the soldering of gold can be : a jeweller can wear his lungs out, puffing at his blow-pipe, and his eyes suffer by being so close to the intense heat of the forge; and even more perhaps from the microscopic delicacy of the work. But even if there had been no danger in it, my mother still would have disliked this sort of work : she held it in suspicion, for you cannot solder gold without the help of other metals, and my mother used to think that it was not honest to keep the gold which was saved by its alloys, although this was the accepted thing; and she, too, was quite prepared, whenever she took cotton to be woven, to receive in return a piece of cloth of only half the original weight.

. . . Kouyaté and Check had been my school-fellows in the primary school at Kouroussa. They were both quick-witted and particularly gifted in mathematics. I can still remember how, when the master had barely finished dictating us a problem, they would both of them jump up and take him the finished sum. This amazing rapidity used to fill us all with wonder, but also used to fill me with discouragement, even though I always used to get my own back in French. But from that time onwards, despite – or perhaps because of this competitive spirit – we had been friends : but it was a friendship such as only very young schoolboys know – not very well founded, and impermanent.

Our real friendship did not begin in fact until after I had left our home-town to study in Conakry, and Kouyaté and Check had left to continue their studies at, respectively, the High Schools of Popoda and Dakar. We exchanged numerous and very lengthy letters, in which we used to describe our life at school and compare notes on our lessons. Then when the holidays came we met again in Kouroussa, and we soon became inseparables.

At first our parents had not looked upon our friendship with any great favour. Either we used to disappear for whole days, forgetting meal-times and the meals themselves, or else we used to stay in the compound, so that at meal-times there would be two unexpected guests. Such behaviour was undoubtedly a little free-and-easy. But this disfavour did not last long. Our parents soon realized that if we disappeared for two out of every three days, the two guests would put in an appearance only on every third day; and they soon accepted the very fair and judicious rotation we had put into practice without consulting them.

'But couldn't you have told me?' my mother used to say. 'Couldn't you have given me notice, so that I could have prepared something special?'

'No,' I would reply. 'Our sole wish was, precisely, that no one should make any special preparations for us. All we wanted was the usual daily meal.'

In the summer holidays which came at the end of Kouyaté's and Check's third scholastic year – and at the end of my second year, since I had lost a year in hospital – I saw my two friends again; they had gained their teaching certificates and were waiting to be given posts. If their success did not surprise me, if it corresponded with everything I expected of them, nonetheless it gave me great pleasure and I congratulated them warmly. When I asked after their health, Check replied that he felt very worn-out.

'I worked hard,' he told me, 'and just at the moment I have not quite got over it. I'm worn out.'

But was he merely 'worn out'? He looked ill and his face was drawn. A few days later I took advantage of being alone with Kouyaté a moment to ask him if he thought it was simply overwork.

'No,' Kouyaté told me. 'Check is sick. He has no appetite and he is losing weight; besides, his stomach is swelling.'

'Should we not warn him?'

'I don't know,' said Kouyaté. 'I think he's noticed it himself.'

'Isn't he doing anything for it?'

'I don't think so. He is in no pain and perhaps he thinks it will gradually get better.'

'And if it gets worse?'

We did not know what to do. We did not want to frighten Check, and yet we felt that something should really be done about it.

'I'll speak to my mother about it,' I said.

But as soon as I began to talk to her about him, she stopped me.

'Check Omar is seriously ill,' she said. 'I've been watching him for several days. I really think I should go and warn his mother.'

'Yes, do,' I said, 'because he's doing nothing about it.'

Check's mother did what was always done in the circumstances :

she consulted the medicine-man. They prescribed massage and infusions. But these remedies had scarcely any effect : his stomach continued to swell, and his face looked grey. Check was not alarmed.

'I'm not in any pain,' he said. 'I haven't much appetite, but I don't feel any pain. It will probably go as quickly as it came.'

I don't know whether Check had very great confidence in the medicine-man; I rather think he had very little : we had by now spent too many years at school to have complete faith in them. Yet our medicine-men are not charlatans : many of them have great knowledge and can perform real cures; and certainly Check was aware of that. But he must have realized that this time their remedies were not working; and that is why he said, 'It will probably go as quickly as it came,' putting more faith in the passage of time than in massage and infusions. His words cheered us up for a few days, then, with brutal suddenness, they lost their comforting quality, for Check really began to suffer. He now had violent attacks of pain, and he used to weep in agony.

'Look,' Kouyaté told him, 'the medicine-men have been no use to you; come with us to the dispensary !'

We went there. The doctor sounded Check and sent him into hospital. He did not say what was wrong with him, but now we knew that it was a serious illness, and Check, too, knew it. Would the white doctor succeed where our own medicine-men had failed? Evil is not always overcome by good, and we were filled with anxiety. We kept watch in relays at Check's bedside; we would watch our poor friend writhing on his bed. His stomach, swollen and hard, was cold like something already dead. Whenever the attacks grew worse, we would run distractedly to the doctor : 'Doctor ! Come quickly !' But no medicine was of any use; and all we could do was to take Check's hands in ours and press them hard so that he would not feel all alone in his pain, and say to him, 'There, Check ! . . . There ! . . . Be brave . . . it will pass.'

All week we stayed at his bedside : his mother, his brothers, my mother and the mother of Kouyaté. Then towards the end of the week, Check suddenly ceased to suffer, and we told the others to go and rest. Check was now sleeping peacefully, and we did not dare to awaken him. We watched him sleeping, and a great hope began to spring in our hearts. His face had grown so thin that all the bones stood out, but his features were no longer drawn, and his lips seemed to be smiling. Then gradually the pain came back, the lips ceased to smile, and Check woke up. He began by dictating to us his last wishes. He told us how we should share out his books and to whom we should give his banjo. His voice was now getting fainter and fainter, and we could not always catch the end of his words.

Then he said good-bye to us once again. When he stopped speaking, it was not far off midnight. Then as the dispensary clock finished the twelve strokes, he died. . . .

I feel as if I were living through those days and nights again, and I do not believe I have ever spent more wretched ones. I wandered aimlessly here and there; we both, Kouyaté and myself, wandered around as if we had lost our wits, our thoughts full of Check. To have lived so many happy days . . . and then for everything to be over ! 'Check. . . .' I kept saying to myself; we both kept saying it to ourselves; and we had to restrain ourselves from saying his name out loud. But his shade, his shade alone accompanied us. And when we managed to get things a little clearer in our minds – and we could not see things too clearly – we saw him in the centre of his compound, laid out on a bier, laid out under his winding-sheet, ready to be laid in the earth; or it was in the earth itself, laid out, at the bottom of his grave, his head raised a little, waiting for the covering of planks to be placed over him, then the leaves, the great mounds of leaves, and finally the earth itself, so dark, and so heavy.

'Check ! . . . Check ! . . .' But I could not say his name aloud : you must never lift up your voice to address the dead. And yet, at night, it was almost as if I *had* lifted up my voice to speak with the dead : suddenly, he would be standing before me. And I would wake up, my body bathed in sweat; I would be seized with fear, for, if we loved Check's ghostly shade, if his shade was all that was left to us, we feared it almost as much as we loved it, and we no longer dared sleep alone, we no longer dared to face our dreams alone. . . .

Camara Laye

from THE RADIANCE OF THE KING

(*translated by James Kirkup*)

Clarence watched the dancers for a long while. It was the first time he had witnessed one of the native dances, and the novelty and strangeness of this rather barbaric spectacle were such that he could not take his eyes away from it.

'They are dancing well,' he said at last. One of the black giants at his side looked him up and down in an unfriendly manner.

'You call that "dancing"?' he said bitterly. 'I call it "hopping", nothing more.'

'Well, yes, they *are* hopping,' thought Clarence. "They *are* hopping, but they're dancing, too; that must be their way of dancing.'

'They don't know the first thing about dancing,' the black man went on. 'They. . . .'

But he did not finish his sentence. He spat contemptuously on the red earth.

'You wait a while, yes, you wait, and you'll see some real dancing when the king. . . .'

'Will the king be here soon?' asked Clarence.

'He will be here at the appointed time,' answered the black man.

'What time will that be?' asked Clarence.

'I've just told you : at the appointed time.'

'Yes, I know. But exactly what time will that be?'

'The king knows!' replied the black man. He spoke the words abruptly, cutting short the interrogation.

'Can I have offended him?' Clarence wondered. 'I don't think I said anything that might have upset him.' He looked back at the dancers, but found he could see them much less clearly : the red cloud seemed to have grown considerably denser.

'I came here in order to speak to the king,' he said.

'So you want to speak to the king?' said the black man, looking Clarence up and down a second time.

'That is what I came for.'

'But it's unheard-of!' said the black man. 'It's absolutely unheard-of. Young man, do you think the king receives just anybody?'

'I am not "just anybody",' replied Clarence. 'I am a white man.'

'A white man?' said the black man.

He made as if to spit, but stopped himself just in time.

'Am I not a white man?' cried Clarence.

'The white men do not come here, on the esplanade!' retorted the black man, using the same abrupt tone of voice as he had used before.

'No, this esplanade would not be the place for white men to put in an appearance,' Clarence thought bitterly. 'They wouldn't let themselves be shoved around by all these black men; they would more likely be sitting in their villas, where it was cool, or else playing cards and sipping iced drinks on the veranda of the hotel.'

And he saw again in his mind's eye the spacious veranda with its neatly arranged tables and its swaying fans, its striped awnings and its black waiters in their white jackets putting bottles of wine to cool in buckets of ice. Only a week ago, he had been sitting on the veranda, playing cards and drinking brandy; he was calling his partners by their Christian names and ordering the black waiters around, free with his tongue, and bitingly witty. . . . But now he was no longer at the hotel. . . . Would he ever go back there? . . . No, he would never go back there, because if he did they would all turn their backs on him. There was not one of these white men whom he did not owe money to, money he had lost at cards and, moreover, money he had borrowed at a time when he still had hopes of getting on his feet again, and – what foolish hopes – of breaking his run of bad luck.

Luck! . . . it was enough to make you die of laughing. He didn't like cards! He never used to touch cards! But it was like this : all the white men who went to that hotel were gamblers and they had more money that they knew what to do with. . . . More than they knew what to do with! . . . What was it to them, the money he owed the white men? They could lose it at a single throw of the dice and never feel the loss! But because he owed it to them, he who had never had very much money, who no longer had any money, they had insisted harshly on being paid, not of course because they set any store by it but merely in order to humiliate him. . . . That was why he was living now in a sort of negro caravanserai; yes, a sort of caravanserai, that was all you could call it; you couldn't truthfully call such a hovel an hotel. Maybe he was being too generous in calling it a caravanserai, because it was really a. . . . No, no! he would not distress himself by calling it to mind again; he felt sick at the mere thought of it. . . . The only hope left to him – the last chance! – was to be taken on in the king's service.

'I shall present myself to the king as soon as he arrives,' he said.

The black man beside him sniggered.

'Do you really mean that?' he asked.

Once again he looked him up and down, with an even unfriendlier expression on his face than on the previous occasions.

'The guards won't even let you go near him!' he declared.

'Then what shall I do?' said Clarence. He suddenly felt overwhelmed with weariness. . . .

'Perhaps I shall put in a word for you,' said the black man.

'What – *you*,' cried Clarence.

He looked at his neighbour in amazement : he was an old man, poorly clothed; a tall man, no doubt, like all those in the front rank, but dressed in rags – a sort of beggar.

'But you are a beggar,' he said.

'That is true : begging and soliciting – that's my trade,' said the black man. 'It's not an easy life; I began to learn the trade when I was very young.'

'A fine advertisement you would be!' thought Clarence. If the guards were going to stop him, a white man, from approaching the king, with all the more reason they would stop this black man in his disgusting rags from addressing him. The man was obviously nothing more than an old fool.

'Your clothes are shabby,' said the black man all of a sudden.

'But they aren't in rags,' retorted Clarence.

'I was especially careful not to say they were in rags,' went on the black man. 'No, they aren't in rags, yet – but they're already very shabby.'

A few moments went by, then he continued :

'It won't be long before they're in rags.'

'In rags?' cried Clarence.

He looked down at his clothes, at his jacket and his trousers. They were made of coarse linen. Would the material wear so very badly? Perhaps in this climate and with all this red dust, it would not wear so well as in Europe.

'It's good material,' he suggested.

'Listen,' said the black man, 'I know you don't think much of me but never mind, I'll put in a good word for you.'

'*You'll* put in a good word for *me*?'

He felt a quick surge of anger. What! *Him*, a beggar, a negro, 'put in a good word' for *me*? The phrase stuck in his throat. He was asking no favours of anyone. He would offer his services to the king; he was willing to do some kind of work, provided it was honest and he received adequate remuneration for his services. *He* wasn't going begging! . . . But he swallowed his rage : he was on his beam ends, and had lost the right – the right or the luxury – to be angry; he owed money even to that native innkeeper who was in charge of the caravanserai! This creature had more than once cast a covetous eye on Clarence's apparel and had even insinuated that he might accept them in exchange for the price of a bed. 'Of course, I wouldn't want *all* your clothes,' he added, 'only one of the less important items – the jacket, the cap, or the trousers. It's not absoluely essential to wear both a jacket *and* trousers,' he added. 'Many natives wear nothing more than a shirt!'

As if Clarence would walk round in his shirt-tails after that! At the moment, all his worldly goods were the clothes he stood up in. Of course, he had two trunks full of belongings, but they were being held by the white hotel-keeper who had refused to give them up, and was keeping them as security for the unpaid hotel bill. The only things Clarence had been able to take away were his razor and a piece of shaving soap : not even his shaving brush – he had to lather his face with his fingers! . . . No, he no longer had the right to anger. 'I've still got the right,' he told himself, 'but I no longer have the means to put my anger into effect. . . .' The means! Is that what one's 'rights' were? . . . Apparently! And that was why this black beggar had taken the liberty of saying he would 'put in a good word' for him.

'How ludicrous!' thought Clarence. A fresh wave of anger swept through him, but this time it was anger against himself, and anger whose sole object was to castigate his own pettiness. Why had he turned on the beggar just now? The man had said nothing amiss. He wasn't much to look at – with his ragged clothes, he certainly wasn't much to look at – but he was certainly someone who had knocked about a bit, and so must know a thing or two.

'It's not right,' began Clarence.

'Well, any child knows that,' the beggar said.

'Yes, any child,' replied Clarence, 'but if. . . .'

He broke off. He had been going to say: 'But if you had not pointed it out to me, perhaps I should never have realized it.' And at that moment it suddenly dawned on him that ever since the beggar had offered to speak on his behalf, the beggar had not uttered another word, except of course when he spoke about what any child would know. In the meantime, the beggar had kept completely silent; he had made no allusion whatever to any kind of 'right'. . . . Yet it was as if he had been speaking all the time. . . . Could it be that the beggar had the power of entering into the thoughts of others? He might very well have that power! Perhaps he was a bit of a witch-doctor; lots of beggars are given that way. . . . Oh, no! If this man had really been a witch-doctor, he would have been in the procession with the king on a day like this. . . . 'Are you a witch-doctor?' Clarence rehearsed the phrase in his head, but just then a louder roar rose from the waiting crowds and interrupted his train of thought.

This great roar was followed almost at once by piercing cries : the young dancers, that the royal guards were driving along in front of them with whips, surged forward rapidly towards the edge of the esplanade. It did not seem as though their tragic cries were to be taken seriously; it was partly the lash of the whips that caused them, and partly the primitive delight in uttering them. Besides, the dancers had no sooner reached the crowd than they became part of it, adhering to it and falling silent. They were drenched in sweat, their naked bodies were steaming with sweat and spattered with red earth from head to foot. They were panting hard. Their sudden approach had the effect of turning the front rank of spectators into the second rank. This did not affect their view as these dancers were hardly more than boys, whereas the black men in the front rank were all giants; but from the point of view of cleanliness, it was another matter. This earth, this red dust, an almost oily sweat, could not be kept off the spectators' clothes. However, no one made any protest at this defilement, apart from the beggar who, dressed as he was in rags which could hardly be made any the worse, angrily addressed the dancer who had placed himself in front of him :

'Don't you dare touch me!' he cried, 'or I'll give you a good hiding.'

The boy drew swiftly to one side, as if the beggar's words had scorched him.

'Stand here,' said the dancer who had taken up his position in front of Clarence.

He seized his companion, putting his arm round his neck and drawing him close.

'I trust we are not obstructing your view?' he asked Clarence.

'Not at all,' replied Clarence. 'But mind you don't press against me : this is the only suit I've got, and you are both covered with dust and sweat.'

'Don't worry,' the young dancer assured him, 'we'll soon have stopped sweating.'

'The sun will have dried us before the king arrives,' said the other.

'They're liars, both of them,' growled the beggar, beating the earth with his stick. 'A pair of downright liars.'

'We can stand somewhere else if you like,' said the second of the two dancers.

'No, stay where you are,' said Clarence. 'You're not in my way.'

But his nose was on a level with the tops of their heads, which gave off a strong smell of rancid grease.

'Does your hair always smell as strong as this?' he said.

'It always smells like this until it gets dry. The sooner we've finished sweating, the sooner our hair will be dry.'

'I wonder how they think them up, all these tales they tell you,' the beggar said.

Clarence lifted his head, but the odour of grease, the stuffy odour of wool and oil was very penetrating, and he could not escape it. A faint drowsiness came over him : he closed his eyes, and his head lolled forward. . . .

'Come on,' the beggar was shouting, 'wake up!'

'Is it time?' asked Clarence.

'It's the appointed time,' said the beggar.

But the esplanade was still empty. . . . Then it was suddenly alive with galloping horses that came to a halt, rearing up on their hind legs, only a few feet from the front of the crowd. They were strange horses, all caparisoned and panoplied and wearing layers of petticoats, and some of them had even been dolled up in silken trousers. The eye was so much taken by all these trappings that it was some time before the rider himself could be made out. Yet they were proud figures, seated with almost insolent assurance in their saddles, and bearing lances that whirled and flashed in the sun. They were enveloped in long, flowing robes and on their heads were turbans curiously decorated with acorns and surmounted by high, round hats with broad brims.

Clarence wondered if the king himself might be among them : the king might easily have been one of these magnificent horsemen. But if he *was* there, what were the signs, the insignia by which he could be recognized? And Clarence's eyes went from one horseman to another. But how was it possible to make out anything clearly? The cloud of red dust, which had settled a little since the dancers had left the track, had become denser than ever with the arrival of the horsemen.

'Don't get excited!' said the beggar. 'All these are nothing but petty rulers who have come to do homage to the king. . . . The king. . . . But how could anyone fail to recognize the king! . . . He is. . . .

He was at a loss for words. Perhaps he realized that there are no words to express what the king is.

'He is . . .' the beggar began again.

But a sound of drums and trumpets drowned his voice. Kettle-drummers were marching towards them, in splendid array, drumming away bravely on their drums, the male drum on the left, the female drum on the right. They were followed by trumpeters who, with grotesquely distended cheeks, were blowing long ivory horns. Their vehement music seemed to be utterly without meaning, as if it were simply a loud din that had to be flung against the barrier of heat, against the sky; but it was obviously more than that, more than just a queer, haphazard noise, for the beggar announced suddenly :

'They are heralding the king's approach!'

'Yes,' said Clarence, 'That's what I gathered.'

'No you didn't!' said the beggar crossly. 'You didn't know *what* it was. Those drums are talking drums. They announce the king's approach and they say that he is king of kings. . . . It's only the white man's music which is devoid of meaning.'

Prince Modupe

from I WAS A SAVAGE

I 'become clean'

Circumcision is ritual among our people and is performed in the Bondo Bush where all youth go at puberty. The word Bondo means strength. A child learns in the Bondo Bush that his strength and security come from being a part of his tribe. Before one enters the bush school he is a member of his family. Just before he comes to the bush school, he is made to realize that the entire community is concerned with his conduct and responsible for it. During the time one is in cult training, his concept of family is extended to include all of the tribe. The boys of his age-group who are trained with him become like actual brothers. A strong lifelong bond of brotherhood is felt among them. The group circumcision ceremony is a physical symbol of their spiritual oneness. Afterwards, if one does an evil thing, it is not only oneself and one's family who are harmed; the entire tribe is wronged, and particularly one's own age-group.

I was happy when the day came for me to go to the Bondo Bush. I was tired of being pointed at by the older boys and ridiculed as 'unclean'. My mother seemed sad about my going, a thing I could not understand.

The Bondo Bush was held in an enormous clearing cut out of dense forest, fenced with tall stakes driven side by side into the earth. Lamina and I reached it after walking the better part of a day through the rain and over rough terrain. In the entry to the Bondo was an enormous monstrous-looking figure. I clung to Lamina, chattering with fear.

A horde of boys about my age swarmed out of the gate offering me fruits and nuts, symbols of brotherhood. They were laughing and happy and seemed unconcerned about the frightening figure which guarded the entry. They surrounded me and swept me past the awesome figure. I had one glimpse of Lamina as I left him. He looked almost as tearful as my mother.

In the Bondo Bush we learned everything which our elders thought we needed to know in order to become men of the tribe. I knew that the masked figures who had us in their charge were men, not spirits. I even knew their names. But when these revered men wore the sacred masks, I no longer thought of them as men. They became the soul-stuff or our ancient tribal dead, come back to the Bondo to mingle their strength and their wisdom, their power, with those of us who were just becoming alive as part of the tribe.

The plant life around any village is highly important to the community. Our food, clothing, the roofs of our shelters, the medicines, the spices, the well-being of the people derive largely from the things that grow in the earth. A medicine-man may be thought of as a specialist in roots and herbs and plants, but every individual must know the commoner uses of plants. Therefore a great emphasis was placed in the Bondo schooling on botany.

We also learned the names our people have given the stars and the constellations, and the stories about them. We learned to track and to hunt game, to identify and to imitate the sounds of the jungle creatures. We learned that silences as well as sounds are significant in the forest and how to listen to the silences.

It seems to me now that this insistence upon the deep silences in order to become attuned to the rhythms of earth was one of the most distinguishing phases of our Bondo training. With all their might, most of the learners tried to hypnotize themselves into a sort of religious coma, a closer contact with God. Deeply felt silences might be said to be the core of our Kofon religion. During these times, the nature within ourselves found unity with the nature of earth. This is not 'closeness to nature' but rather an immersion in the common nature which pervades all life – plants, animal, human.

Sex education is given great emphasis in the Bondo. Those who know only a little about the puberty rites of Africa have called them lascivious and indecent. I will explain what we were taught, and why.

The first thing we were made to understand is that the finest service a tribesman can perform is to continue himself in his children. After we were taught our *duty* of perpetuation, and that it is a sacred duty, we were taught the rules governing it.

We were taught that the manner of growth in a girl is that she is sealed and that no man may break this seal until the girl is given him for a wife with the consent of her family and his. If one of us were to break this seal for our pleasure, we would disgrace ourselves, our family, our entire age-group, the tribe. Even if the monstrous act went undiscovered until the girl's marriage, it would become known then, the marriage cancelled, the girl brought to public trial, her duty then being to name the man who had despoiled her.

Three such trials had been held within the memory of our people and they were reviewed for us. In two cases evidence was presented which indicated previous physical injury. In the third case, the girl's family thought she was guilty and made no defence. She was banished from the tribe. Death would have been a kinder sentence. There was simply no place for an ostracized person to go.

The hunter who throws his spear too soon does not live to throw again. This tribal saying applies to love as well as to war and to hunting.

We were told how to deal with a woman when the season of waiting was past, how to behave so that our seed might grow and our people flourish.

The girls in adolescence had a similar bush school and were taught comparable things, the sacredness of their bodies, what to expect at marriage, how to please the man who would become their husband, the importance of children. Girls were brought from their section of the Bondo and the secret parts of their bodies shown to us, ours to them. I underwent no end of torment when my body was used as demonstration, but I was soon over my curiosity about sex. At times we were allowed to mingle freely with the girls on the Bondo reservation in order to test our strength of will.

Great emphasis was placed upon personal cleanliness, not only as a habit of life but as a symbolic part of our 'becoming clean'. Life to a tribal African is synonymous with religious living. His beliefs come into play in the smallest detail of his life. We believe in one Supreme Being but we do not visualize this Being in the image of man. We feel this Being as soul-force or spirit-energy manifesting itself in all life. We believe in life after death, an active life, in which the spirits of ancestors participate in all important tribal affairs. This has been called ancestor worship, but we do not deify our ancestors, nor any human. We venerate their memories and feel their influence active among us as long as they are remembered. In the Bondo, we were taught that by emptying our minds, by making our minds void of all sensation, the spirit-force of the Supreme Being could fill us. This was easier to achieve after the exhaustion of physical exertion, so we danced to the drums day after day.

As the climax of the Bondo Bush, the circumcision rites, neared, we danced until it seemed that it was the power of the drums that lifted our feet. The glory of manhood was in the beat of those drums.

Thirty of us were considered spiritually ready for the ceremony. We ate certain herbs and were bathed in herbs. We were told that when one's turn came, he needed to stop dancing only long enough for the slash of the witch-doctor's knife and the binding of a leaf; that pain lives in the mind and that we need give it no room.

Nude, we danced in a circle, the Bondo priest in the centre, flashing the blade of the circumcision knife so its surface glinted in the sun. The older warriors and elders formed a flanking circle around us, dancing in place.

The drums beat louder and faster, so fast it was almost impossible for the feet to hold the beat. The priest whirled close to us, back to the centre, close again, back. We were all moving so fast the scene was like a heat blur to my eyes. Then the drums slowed a little to a pace, still rapid, at which the priest could do his work.

The chanting began. The priest leaped towards a boy. As instructed, the boy ceased dancing. The priest, dancing in place, cradled the boy's penis in one hand. With the other hand he brought the knife slashing down and across in a single sweeping motion. A medicine-man was quickly at the boy's side, wiping away the blood and wrapping a special leaf around the organ. The boy continued dancing, picking up the beat from the others who had not stopped. The priest was back in the centre of the circle. All of this had been done rhythmically, cleanly, expertly, without cessation of movement by any but the boy.

Two more boys were inducted. Then the priest leaped towards me. I was trembling and I clamped my teeth so I would not shame myself by crying out. I stopped dancing. The drums seemed to be trying to lift my feet against my will.

The priest's hand grasped my person. His other hand flashed through the space between us. I knew a great fear of pain but I knew no pain. There was only a brief stinging sensation. I was no longer one of the 'unclean'.

The priest was back in the centre of the circle before I felt the medicine-man wiping away the blood and applying the leaf bandage.

I caught the step. I no longer needed to resist the pull of the drum! I danced with the others. But now it was different. I was a member of the sacred Bondo, a man of my tribe!

White, good, and gold

Finally, the white man arrived. My first sight of him was a delightful relief. He did not appear to have demon quality and although his belly was large, it was not out of proportion to his head like the termite queen's. The only part of him that was much out of scale was his feet, which were encased in leather. For some reason, I had believed from childhood that to be a real man one had to have a large belly and big feet. This fellow had both and he looked human besides. Furthermore he was not really white as milk is white, not the portion of him which showed, at least; he was more the colour of leather. Most of him was covered; the black coat hung down past his knees, and the short sturdy neck was bound with a band of cloth which was really white. His lips appeared like nothing more than a faintly red slit in his face and his nose seemed bird-beakish long and thin. His wife and a little girl-child were with him, and they too were encased in clothing. The child had hair which hung to her shoulders and was the colour of gold. It was in curls like shavings from the chisels of our wood-carvers, not springy and crisp like mine. The three were led across the clearing to the royal stool where my grandfather sat waiting for them. The elders, the witch-doctors, and the head warriors moved forward with them as they advanced to stand before the chief. The rest of us, out of custom, remained in the background, not pressing too close. I longed to hear what was being said and I had a great desire to touch the golden curls of the little girl. I could see from the gestures and various groupings that the traditional courtesies were being exchanged. Grandfather sat his stool with grave dignity. There was a waiting-to-see in his posture as the missionary placed gifts at his feet. Everyone gaped in wide-mouthed wonder. Some of the little boys scrambled up trees and perched on branches for a better view. Much as I would have liked to do the same, I was too mature for that kind of behaviour. All I could do was quietly and slowly to edge my way towards a more advantageous position.

Finally, stools were brought for the man and his family. If the stools had not been fetched, it would have meant lack of approval of the missionary's manners and lack of further interest on Grandfather's part. The interview would have been over. Although I did not know it, my future hung on that nod of my grandfather's head. If he had not approved the seating of our guests, I would not now be writing this story. I would not be writing anything, anywhere, nor reading either. All I knew of writing was that the small group of Moslems who lived in one quarter of our town had symbols for their beliefs marked on paper, but they did not read these; they had them sewed into leather packets which they wore as good-fortune amulets. All that interested me at this moment was getting closer to the heap of gifts at Grandfather's feet.

When I had wormed my way into view of them, the objects seemed to be new things and there was glitter among them. They did not have the earth quality of our own artefacts. I later came to know these things as a Bible, a camera, a mirror, a kaleidoscope, shoes, a high hat, cigarettes, matches, tinned goods, shiny trinkets, and cotton goods. There was something else which may need a bit of explanation – a keg of whisky. We had palm wine to drink, a mild fermented brew of palm sap, but we had never heard of distilled liquor. In time I was to learn that the particular missionary who visited us belonged to a denomination which makes a distinction between temperance and abstinence. Their ministers are allowed to drink and to smoke, but not to excess. I suppose our visitor thought that mellowing our minds towards his words was a worthy use of whisky.

The photographs which the man brought showing bridges and cities, trains, boats, big buildings, were not impressive to us even when we were allowed to view them at close range. Having had no experience with the diminished scale of things in a photograph, we gained no concept of magnitude. But there were other pictures which disturbed me deeply. They were bright depictions of heaven and hell, which I later learned were made expressly for mission use. In them all the bright angels hovering over the golden streets had white faces. The tortured creatures in hell with the orange-red flames licking over agonized, contorted bodies all had black faces! Some of the fire-seared damned seemed little boys about the age I had been when Tongo and I broke the Foula pot.

The missionary spoke to us through his interpreter. He denounced our old ceremonious life, the rituals, especially sacrifice. He said that we worshipped wood and stone and carved images. This was not accurate, but no one was impolite enough to contradict him. Any-way, it would have been too difficult to make a stranger understand. For a moment there was deep silence. Someone coughed. An old man shuffled his feet. An elder next to me rumbled in his throat. I turned my head and saw that it was Grand-uncle D'gba. I switched my attention back to the missionary, wondering why Grandfather allowed him to go on insulting everything we held sacred and valuable. I could see that Grandfather was trying his best to fol-low the spirited ranting of the white man. His expression was puzzled and he was trying his best to understand. Perhaps the *juju* would be clearer to us than the speech.

The crowd became restless. All this talk-talk! Their politeness held out, but they shifted their weight on their feet, squirmed a little, rustled quietly. Finally, the harangue ended.

The missionary picked up the mirror, made a few twists of his wrist as though gathering up the invisible power in the vicinity of it, and gazed into the glass. Grandfather leaned forward, watching closely. The white man proffered the shiny handle to Grandfather. My grandfather, who had always been considered a brave man by his people, jerked back away from it. Then, warily, he accepted it. He did not gaze into it at once. It was plain that he feared the thing. The missionary spoke reassurance.

The crowd tensed. Grandfather had to go through with what he had started or forfeit pride. He looked into the mirror. A cry of surprise escaped from his throat. He turned the handle, looking at the back, and saw his reflection disappear. When he turned it to

the front side, there he was again! He spoke to his brother D'gba.
I do not know whether he did this because he knew his brother was
opposed secretly to these goings-on and hoped to convince him by
the new wonders, or whether the mirror simply seemed a wondrous
thing to show one's brother.

D'gba reluctantly approached, his face contorted with scorn.
An order from the chief was an order, brother or not. Every muscle
in his body spoke of his aversion to the command but he dared not
speak against it. Grandfather handed D'gba the mirror, pointed at
the image in his hand. D'gba howled and fell to the ground, the
mirror in his hand. He laid the fearful thing in the dust and smashed
it with his fist. Perhaps he thought to liberate his trapped self from
it, to get his face back. The thing broke, cutting his hand. Blood
dripped from him as he stood up.

Blood has mystic significance to an African. Blood is life-stuff;
life drips away with blood. A tribesman will endure enormous welts
and bruises without a whimper if the skin is not broken, but let
someone draw blood, even a bead of blood from a faint scratch, and
the matter takes on enormous proportions and gravity.

While an excited murmur ran through the crowd and D'gba examined his red-dripping hand, the missionary spoke quickly and
emphatically to Grandfather. Grandfather nodded and gave us the
verdict. What had happened was due to D'gba's resentment of the
white man's god. D'gba had been punished, as we had all seen. The
white man's god was capable of punishments far beyond this. What
was the loss of a little blood compared to having to spend all of the
time not yet come rolling in the hot flames of hell? A black devil
with horns kept the fires tended. D'gba disappeared, holding his
wounded hand at the wrist.

The missionary followed up his initial triumph with a tin-opener.
With great flourishes he opened a tin of beans and ate some of the
contents to show they were not poisoned. He offered some to
Grandfather, who tasted a small portion and then larger portions,
approving the flavour of this wonderful *ewa*, beans not cooked, yet
ready to eat, coming all together from a shining 'pod' which was
hard like iron. The other articles were shown, demonstrated, explained. Grandfather was enchanted with the kaleidoscope, reluctant
to put it down.

The missionary preached while the portions of whisky were doled
out, first to the chief and the elders, then to each villager in turn
as they formed in line. Grandfather jerked his head at the first taste
and coughed, but after the second attempt he was smacking his lips
and requesting more.

A long time was required for the end section of the queue to come

G

abreast of the keg. The young men had to defer to the elder ones in this as in all things, and many of the elders, after downing their allotments, would slip back into line with their age-group for second helpings. Probably the missionary was too busy working up to the mass conversion to notice this. In any case, as many as drank and drew away and returned found themselves mellowed and ready to give themselves up to the new faith.

I noticed that Grandfather's eyes became bloodshot. When he stood up to walk he no longer moved with slow dignified royal steps. Uncertainty swayed him from side to side, but he wavered towards the diminishing keg. His purpose was certain even if his feet were not. I did not know what drunkenness was so I attributed Grandfather's condition to his body's being possessed with the power of the new *juju*. I saw him waving the Bible in the air as he announced that we accepted the new religion for our own. It was true, then, I concluded, that the white *juju* was superior to our own. Its power had caught D'gba and drawn blood, its power had transformed Grandfather, its power produced the wonderful objects the missionary had brought, its power warmed the belly, so the men said who had swallowed the sacred elixir from the keg. The only one of the older men who could not testify to that was D'gba. He did not take part in the drinking, nor was he to be seen in the throng.

Grandfather invited the white man to stay to dinner and for the night. The invitation was accepted. The women and children retreated to start the cooking and evening tasks. Great fires were lighted in the compound and the warriors gathered around them. Good food was brought, steaming hot. I stayed as close to the missionary and his family as I dared. My eyes lingered on the little girl with the golden curls. I reasoned that she must be immensely wealthy to have gold-stuff for hair. It was because of her father's *juju*, of course, that this wealth had come to her and to her family.

Grandfather and the missionary came by the tree where I was standing in shadow. The missionary cleared his throat, hawked, and spat. They passed on. The spittle lay in the dust almost at my feet. It had been part of the body of this powerful, wealthy, celestial being. Would not the essence of these attributes be in this part of him, now separated from his body? I kneeled reverently beside the damp spot in the dust and touched it with a stick. No sound nor smoke came from it as I half feared. This gave me confidence to touch the dampness with my finger. I picked it up, cupping it in my hands. I was sure that some of the white man's power now belonged to me. But how to keep it? The answer to that was to swallow it. It would then become part of my body just as the body-stuff of the leopard became part and one with the initiate into the Pende-

Pende society. Glowing with anticipation of wonderful things to come after absorbing this small portion of power-essence, I swallowed it. Perhaps if enough of this potion were obtainable, my hair would turn to gleaming gold-stuff like the little girl's. I stood up, waiting tremulously for some change to work within me. I had felt as a leopard when its blood flowed with mine. Now I waited to feel as a god. Nothing happened. Had my skin lightened a shade? I could not tell in the dark. I felt at my hair. No, nothing had changed except this one thing : for the first time in my life I felt doubt about the desirability of a brown skin and kinky hair. Why did gold grow above the faces of little white girls, who according to the pictures sprouted shining wings as soon as they went to live in the glorious compound of worthy Deads, a compound glowing with gold under their pale little feet? How could they smile with what seemed a mother-love delight as they peered down over the edge of the golden compound into the fiery pit, deep and wide enough to hold all the *doomboos* the Yolos had ever consumed? But the fiery pit did not hold *doomboos* waiting to be caged. It was filled with black people who might have been Sousous. Why did the horned demon who banked the fires of hell have a black face like us? Why did he twist his mouth with laughter while he seared the flesh of small boys who were as black as himself?

Perhaps the real reason why my limbs trembled and my hands shook was that a little of the pride and glory which I had felt in being a Sousous youth had gone out with the light of this eventful day !

Thomas Mofolo

from CHAKA THE ZULU

The Death of Noliwe

. . . And then Isanusi said : 'Think well, Chaka. What has been done by my servants can be undone, but that which I will do through the blood of Noliwe, your woman, even I cannot undo. What will be done will be done for ever. So I will ask you yet again.

'Tell me the truth that is in your heart and fear nothing. Which do you choose – Noliwe, or the chieftainship?'

And Chaka answered, 'The chieftainship.'

At once, all Isanusi's sadness left him and gave place to joy, and he said : 'You have answered like a man after my own heart : I have no patience with one whose thoughts change. But you are a chief, and your answer is the answer of a chief. Today I know what you are and I shall work with a heart even more joyful than before. You have known how to choose the path along which you will walk and the way in which you will live on earth, and when you die your kingdom will have no limits. And greatest of all – the splendour of your famous and glorious chieftainship will last for ever and ever.' Isanusi then drew Chaka to him and they went outside, and Isanusi looked up at the sky and pointed to the stars : 'The number of your fighters will soon be greater than the number of the stars in the heavens. Among the tribes you will shine as does the sun when no clouds cover it. And before you the tribes will disappear, for the blood of Noliwe will bring you wealth beyond count.'

The reader can imagine Chaka's feelings when he was told these things by Isanusi. But matters remained as they were for a few days and nothing was done; they were waiting till near the time when Chaka should go down in the morning to the river.

On the evening before Chaka was to go down to the pool he went to Noliwe, taking with him a long needle of the kind used for sewing grain baskets. He found her sitting alone with only her maid, and as soon as he entered the maid went out. There was a fire of wood burning and its dancing flames provided a bright light which lit up the hut.

Chaka approached her. He took her in his arms and kissed her and then asked what was wrong with her. Noliwe answered, 'Chaka my lord, your face is sad and your voice sorrowful. What has disturbed you?' Chaka said that nothing had disturbed him except that he had been annoyed by some fool during the daily war exercises.

They continued thus, speaking happily and exchanging kisses, when suddenly Chaka pressed his strong hands upon Noliwe's mouth and pushed the needle into her body under the arm. Then he turned her on her side and raised up the part where the needle had gone in so that no blood might flow from the wound and be wasted on the ground.

When Noliwe was on the point of death her eyes looked into his and she said : 'Chaka, my loved one, you who are now my father, who are Jobe, who are Dingiswayo, who are. . . .' At that moment her life went out, and her pure spirit joined Dingiswayo in the place of glory above. When Noliwe was quite dead, Chaka felt within himself something like a heavy stone falling, falling, till it rested on his heart.

He ran outside, but he saw nothing, except only the face of Noliwe on the point of death. His ears were stopped and he heard nothing except Noliwe's last cry. When he recovered he found himself with Isanusi in the hut, and Isanusi was saying words of praise : 'Now your name has been written among the number of our chiefs, the great and the mighty.'

The poor girl who had been with Noliwe when Chaka entered was killed; it was said that she had not spoken when Noliwe was ill, so that Noliwe died and none knew of it. And Ndlebe spread the story that it was this girl who had bewitched Noliwe. Isanusi had now taken from Noliwe the thing he wanted to take (what it was we do not know), and he prepared it as he alone knew how, and the next morning he went with Chaka to the river, and Malunga and Ndlebe were there. And when they returned Isanusi made haste to go to his own home.

So died Noliwe, sister of Dingiswayo.

Ezekiel Mphahlele

from DOWN SECOND AVENUE

The class teacher said I was backward. The principal said I was backward. My aunt said I was backward. So said everybody. Mother didn't know. I had no choice but to acknowledge it. So when I was placed in Standard Three instead of continuing from Standard Four, it didn't occur to me that they might be wrong.

I found rather big boys, and realized that I was one of the smallest. So I felt consoled. I was in a class of about eighty. In the half-yearly test I took 77th position in our class. Everybody at home shook his head tolerantly and they said they knew how poor country schools were. It was no surprise to them. 'Wonder is you get any position at all,' one of my uncles said.

I scraped through to Standard Four. They called the class teacher by the nickname of 'Kuzwi'. A corrupted form of his real name. A stocky, conservative little tyrant, Kuzwi. He caned at the slightest provocation or whim.

He'd run to ring the morning starting bell when he knew that we were far from the school grounds; just so that we might be late and satisfy what I regarded as something like a neurotic desire to whip. If you were number 50 in a test, and number 51 in a subsequent one, Kuzwi caned you for 'walking backwards', as he put it. If you cycled to town when you might have walked the distance, Kuzwi came upon you with both feet. 'Learn to walk', he said. One day he thrashed me severely. I had come to school with a pair of trousers he had seen torn the previous day. When he asked me who had mended it I said my aunt had. The punishment I got was for not mending the trousers myself. I cried and cried, thinking how unjust he had been. It seemed that I could never stop sniffing. Every time I thought of the injustice the flood-gates of my tears opened again.

At recess Kuzwi gave me tea from his flask. I took it but felt ashamed because I wanted to hate him and now his tea was making it difficult at the outset. Kuzwi was a terror in arithmetic. I was too dense to master figures and his ability to work out examples at a terrific speed, coupled with his inevitable cane, did not encourage us the slower ones to do better. I hated the subject more and more and even imagined I hated him. I hated his 'short methods' and his grand display of one 'trick' after another. I hated myself for utter clumsiness with figures. I disliked the way he patted the clever ones on the back.

But for a reason no one could ever explain, this little man was hardest on his niece, Fluenza. She lived with him and it was common talk that he was taking it out on her for what she had done wrong at home. It conjured up a number of dark little stories which fascinated the bigger boys and made us, the cubs, giggle.

'What kind of man is this?' I asked Flu'.

'I don't know.'

'He puzzles me and frightens me.'

'I'm not frightened of him any more.'

'Does your mother know about it?'

'I've no mother, no father.' And she laughed as she said so, with her poignant face that looked as if she would cry any moment.

'Does he beat you as much at home?' Fluenza looked at me with pain in her eyes. I was sorry I had asked. In a sense, I felt that we two were allies, if only passive sponges for tyranny.

The happiest day for us was when we passed out of Kuzwi's hands – to Standard Five. We were going to a thin, pale-faced, coughing teacher who had rusty teeth.

'Moloi! Just look at that!'

'What's it?'

'Those people up there.' I pointed to a high building under construction in Church Street.

'C'mon, Eseki! We're going to be late for bioscope!'

I stood still, amazed at such a structure; it might topple over soon and crush us under it. I was a little frightened.

'C'mon, you sheep! 'Sthat first time you see a building?' He was impatient.

He was my next door playmate; and he always stood on my side when the other boys threatened to get tough with me. He was full of bouncing spirits and liked to sing aloud at his home so that his voice resounded down the street.

The building seemed as high as any mountain in the northern Transvaal. It conjured pictures of some of these mountains. I had once feared standing at the base of them, lest they flatten me out. But in the city the fear often turned into wonder, although I knew the country fear was sitting quietly somewhere and at any moment the dark creature might begin stalking my tender self.

'Don't you think it'll fall over soon, Moloi?'

'Don't be silly. These white people are clever, chum.'

'But there are some of our people up there, too.'

'It's the white chaps that do all the thinking here.'

'What d'you mean? Up in the north where I come from it's the Blacks who do all the work.'

'This is not the north, chum.'

'But Blacks are Blacks and whites are whites all over.'

'But I'm telling you the whites do the thinking here.'

'Like the one that gave me a hot clap at the market this morning?'

'Yes, chum.' Then Moloi laughed till he couldn't sit up any more. He had very large ears and they were the very expression of the gaiety in this boy. I pushed the four wheeled cart very hard and then jumped on to the edge while it rolled down-street.

I found myself laughing aloud. That was a stinging slap I had got from the large palm of the 'Market Master'. He wasn't the Market Master in fact. He was a caretaker or something like that; but we called him Market Master. He was huge enough to symbolize the man who to us controlled such a big place as the city market.

We had been picking up stray carrots, overripe tomatoes and so on to eat in between drives to the suburbs. The 'Market Master' swooped down on us. By the time I saw the white dustcoat flapping next to me, he had struck out with his big paw and the blow at the back of my head sent me sprawling on all fours. A whip cracked on another boy somewhere ahead of me. We scattered. Moloi had loaded our cart with a white customer's vegetables and we set off for the suburbs.

All the way to Sunnyside in the morning I was confused. I wondered whether this was the sort of life one was to continue to live until one's death. . . .

After laughing, as the cart glided nicely on good tarred road, I felt both hungry and depressed. And somehow I seemed to be travelling along a long, long winding road that promised no destination; just like those red roads of my earlier years, where the dust far ahead of you told you the end was not yet. Was it to be thus in the city?

Soon, however, we forgot our hunger, weariness, everything else, lost in the exciting moments of the movies. We always had a large bill for fourpence. Often they showed four pictures and a serial chapter on one programme. Those were the days of silent films : the days of Hoot Gibson, Tom Tyler, Frankie Darro, Buck Jones, Tex Maynard, Tim McCoy; the days of funny actors like Harold Lloyd, Richard Talmadge, Larry Simon, Charlie Chaplin, Buster Keaton and a host of others.

We stood on chairs to cheer our screen heroes. A piano played a medley of noisy tunes which, however, made superb background music. The other boys relied on me to read the dialogue and titles on the screen aloud so that they might all follow the story. I felt really big and important and useful because I could read fast – as fast as the slow tempo of life in those years made it necessary.

'But how do you read so fast?' Moloi would ask me.

'Just like that,' I would answer, smiling mysteriously.

'No use asking you anything,' he would say, genuinely disgusted.

The truth of it was that I used to pick up any piece of printed paper to read, whatever it was. It became a mania with me. I couldn't let printed matter pass. I felt inferior to most of my class at school. I was pretty poor in English, which was the medium of instruction. I read, and read, till it hurt. But I also got a good deal of pleasure out of it. And I felt proud because I was overcoming my backwardness.

Often I didn't have money for the movies. Then one of the boys would pay for me, just so that I should read for them. I managed to be heard above all the din from the audience accompanied by the klonk-onk from the piano, which was constantly playing during the performance.

St Peter's church was one of the most beautiful African churches in the Transvaal Province. It was long and had four chapels on the sides. Domestic workers from Rosettenville and the neighbourhood and residents from nearby mine compounds attended St Peter's on Sunday afternoons.

Brother Roger was boarding master of St Peter's. A strict but open-minded man. He caned very hard, I understood; I was happy not to cross his path. He invited several white men to come and lecture to us on various topics. St Peter's boys and girls were allowed the freedom to debate on any kind of subject. For the first time in my life I felt a sense of release. Brother Roger was always clean-shaven and he never grew his hair long. He moved about with a long light and graceful stride, one hand holding up his cassock and the other hanging mid air like an actor sweeping on to the stage. He was all energy and vitality, and when he laughed his mirth seemed to sap the blood from his lips and left a tinge of bloodless yellow around them.

'I suppose you think you're marvellous,' he was fond of saying to a boy. Or 'I'll smack your bottom. . . . How's the old cow getting on? (meaning my mother). . . . Hullo you crooked old thing! (to annoy the ageing Latin mistress who walked with her head tilted one side). . . . Why can't you stop making that horrid noise, you old geezer? (to the stout lady of St Agnes's girls' hostel, who coughed so violently in church that she always went into one of the chapels during a service). . . . It's just frightful the way you boys behave when girls enter the hall. . . .' His prefects were always right as far as he was concerned.

I hadn't the slightest idea what high-school education was for, so for a long time I was bewildered. Mathematics, physics and chemistry were utterly new to me. The First-Form boys and girls just grinned and admired the teachers and cuddled in the grandness of the atmosphere – an atmosphere in which pupils ahead of us gloried in chalking out geometry riders and figures on the nearest board they could find. And then they ganged up to watch the heroes solve the riders.

'You'll never be able to do mathematics, my boy,' the African mathematics master often said, exasperated. It pained me because I knew, as much as he was generally acclaimed, that he was an ex-cellent teacher, if rather impetuous. I was easily the best in English and Latin, and managed to keep up a respectability in the first position in mid-year and promotion tests. I discovered I could only understand when I stayed in class after school hours and worked out constructions, riders, and equations, slowly, at my own pace. I retained a loathing for arithmetic with all its stocks and shares and dividends and percentages.

For the first time in my life, when I was at St Peter's, an aware-

o*

ness was creeping into me : an awareness of the white man's ways and aims. There was complete harmony between us and the white teachers at school and between them and the African staff. And yet no one, Brother Roger or the Principal, or the Community fathers, ever said anything about the attitude they thought we should adopt towards whites and white authority outside school. Slowly I realized how I hated the white man outside the walls of St Peter's.

I had many times before in Pretoria seen tanned Afrikaners supervise African road gangs. A white man stood, with hunched shoulders, hands in the pockets, speaking his instructions with the aid of a trembling index finger. I had taken it for granted that he ought to be there and getting work done by merely pointing a finger. But now when I came upon similar road workers, I was filled with impotent anger.

There was a double-decker bus service for Europeans between Rosettenville and the city. Coloured passengers were given a limited corner upstairs. Always. Some white conductors tolerated a few Africans as well. Others didn't. So in most cases we walked the distance or used a most irregular tram service reserved for Africans. A schoolmate and I took a chance on a bus in town to return to school on a Saturday afternoon. We had already gone out of the city when the conductor came. He glowered at us beneath an ungainly cap that didn't contain his unruly hair.

'What do you want here?' the young bear growled.

'We're going to school,' I said, showing my school pass.

'This is not for Kaffirs.'

'We're Coloureds,' said my mate.

'Black as Kaffirs and you tell me you're Coloureds !' said the young bear. I didn't see any one of the European passengers turn to look back. I was struck by their hard backs and hard red necks.

'Step down !' the young bear said, pressing a button near the door.

The bus came to a stop and we stepped down and walked back to school, about four miles. The only thing we ever said to each other, my schoolmate and I, was a long 'Ya !' Every step I took that afternoon seemed to accentuate the pulse of my anger against the whites and my hatred of them.

Sunday afternoon was outing time every week. The head prefect moved with us to the neighbouring hill, and the head prefect of St Agnes's, the girls' section brought up the rear with her charges. I was walking with two friends, also Pretorians, along the left curb but on the tarmac. Two whites on a motor-cycle came tearing down in the opposite direction. The driver came straight at us and we jumped on to the pavement.

'Voetsek, you Boers !' I shouted impulsively. They turned back.

The head prefect came to inquire. They reported the matter to him, and he wouldn't listen to our version.

'Do you want us thrown out by the European people from this place?' the stocky Yorkshire head master said to two of us (the other boy had talked himself out of it). 'What? If you're going to swear at Europeans they'll do it, what?'

One of the biggest senior boys called Zephania – known to everyone as 'Zeph' – was the fire-brand of the school. He was big and bony and wore large mine boots of which he polished only the bull-dog-looking nose. Our uniform consisted of khaki shirts and shorts for daily wear, and he really looked grotesque as he strutted about on the debating platform, predicting doom to South African white rule and British imperialism. 'A nation is no nation without arms' was his popular heroic line. At first it was all a jumble of words to me when political debates went on. Gradually, as I listened, I was beginning to put into their proper places the scattered experiences of my life in Pretoria. Poverty; my mother's resignation; Aunt Dora's toughness; grandmother, whose ways bridged the past with the present, sticking to neither at any one time; police raids; the ten-to-ten curfew bell; encounters with whites; humiliations. But I only succeeded in reconstructing the nightmare which in turn harassed my powers of understanding.

In 1935, the first year at St Peter's, I had two Coloured friends. Thomas came of an African father from my tribe and a Coloured mother. A lovable and intelligent chum. He had compulsions that made him want desperately to touch everything he passed – a tree, a wall, a desk, somebody's nose. Thomas would stop what he was saying if he thought there was something he had to touch. And then he pressed his finger or the tip of his shoe and looked up as if in a trance, and as if the object he was touching relieved him of a burden. If gutters were charged with electricity we knew it through Thomas and kept clear of such places. He was always talking about a girl of his whose photograph he kept on his person all the time. He swore he was going to marry her. There was nothing uppity about Thomas, nothing like most Johannesburg Coloureds with their superior airs. He always said what made him such a thorough-going optimist was the fact that his upper lip was a little thicker than his lower one, and that the fact that my lower lip was slightly longer than the upper, was responsible for my pessimism.

The other Coloured friend was Peter Abrahams, now a writer of note. I remember him vividly talking about Marcus Garvey, taking it for granted we must know about him. And dreamily he said what a wonderful thing it would be if all the Negroes in the world came back to Africa. Abrahams wrote verse in his exercise books and gave them to us to read. I admired them because here was a boy writing something like the collection of English poetry we were learning as a set book in school. I remember now how morose the verse was : straining to justify and glorify the dark complexion with the I'm-black-and-proud-of-it theme.

James Ngugi

THE WIND

Karanja stood outside the door of his hut and looked across the courtyard, across the field and beyond the valley to the opposite ridge. Women going to the river; boys trotting after a multitude of cows and goats, going to herd them; far beyond the ridge, a hut that belonged to his friend, Njoroge, could be seen with smoke sinuously curling to heaven. In his hut, a murmur of drunken voices could be heard. It was still early, too early for work but not for drinking.

But Karanja did not feel like drinking for he was thinking and reviewing the events of the past months since the advent of the White Missioners. Yes – they had come in their midst and disrupted the tribal order and tranquility.

They had brought a new religion, a religion that taught men to turn from their true God – Murungu – God of Gikuyu and Mumbi. Their sons and daughters had been stolen and were being stuffed with a new order – a new order that would upset the old and bring the wrath of God on them all. Their daughters would not be circumcised. And who would pay goats and cows for a girl that was not circumcised? Was this what had been predicted by Chege Kibiro, the Gikuyu Prophet of old? '. . . and there shall come a people with clothes like butterflies.' Yes. That was the prophecy of a Great Gikuyu Seer. And now it had happened.

'What shall we do?' Karanja stood there, irresolute, a thousand thoughts crossing his mind. He gazed still, into space, unseeing, heedless of anything : just like a man in a vision. He saw a tribe that had been – a tribe that had a sacred code of behaviour unchanging, invincible, unviolable. The tribal rites and customary observances kept the tribe pure and strong, tilling its soil and grazing its cattle and goats.

Slowly he saw the tribe and its sacred rites crumbling down, bowing before the new order. He saw the tribe swallowed and buried. The tribe was no more – the tribe that had been and now was not. Famine and pestilence had done their worst and in their wakes came the white man's religion and his government. And fear gripped his whole being. He trembled all over – fearing – fearing something that was not *fear*, a thing he did not know.

'No! We must act! The white man must *go* – must be killed before it is too late. . . .' Calm. His way was now quite clear. He must save the tribe. He was its 'Saviour'.

With a new determination, he re-entered his hut. The warriors and the other elders who had collected in his hut were still drinking. And there Karanja, a tall figure with a slightly drooping back and sharp eyes deeply embedded in the sockets, stood, towering over them all. Quietness prevailed in the hut as Karanja with a new sense of mission, to help him, declared death to all those who were followers of the new religion. Not a sound could be heard except for a solemn murmur of assent that greeted his speech.

Scouts were to be sent all over the country to various *kraals* and arouse the people. Those who could not see the new threat must be made to see it. A day of reckoning would be fixed, but before the attack on the Siriana Mission Station, they must put out those who had contaminated the sanctity of the tribal rites and followed the new order.

Lots were cast. His friend Njoroge would be the first victim and he, Karanja, with three other warriors were to bring about the execution. Not a muscle moved. Only his hand convulsively clutched the post against which he was leaning as the full demand and implication of this new decree expanded by him, became fully known to him. Njoroge was his friend – had been his friend since they were children. Childhood adventures and plays; little places they had been together; confidences and secrets they had exchanged – all these and other things passed through Karanja's mind, though his face remained black and expressionless.

What could he do? How could he save his friend and at the same time carry out his mission – the mission of purifying the Tribe? Two forces began to fight for ascendency in his heart – the sweet bond of friendship and the sacred call of his tribe. But wait! Was he not a 'saviour' with a mission? How could he shirk his duty? His sacred call demanded Njoroge's blood to quench the wrath of ancestral spirits. Njoroge must die. . . .

It was the hour of night and except for a star – a lone guardian of the heavens that twinkled in the sky, it was all darkness.

The murmuring stream that divided Njahi-ini Ridge where Karanja came from and Mukoro Ridge went on its course incessantly while a small breeze slightly swayed the bullrushes that lined its banks. No stir, no sound and except for the quiet breathing of the four warriors who were lying in ambush for Njoroge, nothing seemed to have life. Karanja and one other warrior sat on one side of the path and the other two, on the other side. Karanja was to give the warning for attack.

Soon the serenity of the scene was broken by a figure of a man who was whistling and singing alternately,

> *Lead Kindly Light,*
> *Amid the encircling gloom*
> *Lead thou me on. . . .*

It was Njoroge – Njoroge coming to his doom. Karanja's fierce and unfeeling resolution and determination to shut the pleading voice of friendship was shaken. He began to tremble and in his heart cursed the hour he was born, the hour he had met Njoroge and the hour the white man came. Perhaps the tribe was unfeeling – perhaps it had no heart. But what could you do? You could not live outside the tribe. . . . A tear dropped down as he remembered the treachery he had used in inciting his friend of many years to his doom. For a minute, he was undecided, irresolute.

No! he would not give the word. He had a heart to feel the wrong. Njoroge must not die. So he stood up ready to warn Njoroge, but it was too late! A groan that curdled his blood and Njoroge's last cry of anguish 'The Wind Will Tell' – long remained ringing in Karanja's head. The other two warriors had acted without orders.

Karanja was quiet and for a long time stood gazing at the prostrate body of his friend. Great fear seized him and he could not move!

'Let's go brother. . . .'

He must do something. But what? They buried Njoroge near the stream, in the bush. But even as they trudged home, and even as the wind came, Karanja could hear a voice singing, 'Lead Kindly Light'. Lead, lead, 'the wind will tell,' lead, tell, and soon the singing became a fused mass of incomprehensible words – 'Telleadwind-lightell. . . .'

He could not sleep and from side to side he wriggled in his bed made of grass, covered with a smooth cowskin. To the mud wall he turned. Dumb. No comfort. He tried to close his eyes but they would not close. He tried to shut out all thoughts and stay as if his senses were drugged, but one thought would persistently torment him – Njoroge his friend was dead, was dead and he Karanja was the architect of the scheme that had extinguished the flame of life. Or was it the tribe?

Then it dawned on him. His plan would not do. It would only bring destruction and complete annihilation of his tribe. He was not the saviour of his tribe, could not be a saviour of a tribe. For had he not himself violated the tribal rites that demanded fairness and no spilling of blood, innocent blood? And what had been the words of the same Seer – Chege?

'. . . *beware of shedding blood – innocent blood, for the wrath of Murungu shall be on the evil doer, the murderer. . . .*'

Yes and he was one. For though he did not strike Njoroge, yet, it was due to him, his treachery and incitement, that blood had been shed.

'Oh, what must I do? I have sunk my tribe. . . .'

A thousand thoughts crossed his mind. He must run away from his people, his clan, Mberi and from his tribe. He was a curse to his tribe and to its rites.

The wind blew. Slowly at first, but then it began to blow in earnest. Harder and harder it blew and its noise was like a mighty fall. The thatch on the roof of his hut was blown off, one side of it.

And harder and harder it blew drowning every noise except a sweet singing voice – so sweet and clear! The voice became louder and louder until its words could be clearly heard. And the words sent Karanja's blood freezing in his veins. For even as he sat on the floor preparing for escape, he could hear Njoroge's voice singing – Lead kindly light . . . but no! It was not Njoroge's voice; a thousand voices had joined him and they were all singing—'Lead kindly light. . . .'

This was not his place! He must go! Taking his sword he went out and began to run. He ran and ran hard. The voices followed. The harder he ran, the harder the wind blew and nearer the voices, until 'their' words became fused together into one word – Light. But he could not tell. He could only hear the one word – Light. Then he realized all at once that the God of Gikuyu and Mumbi was a God of light and not darkness! The Gikuyu tribal rites stood for purity, light and peace – not bloodshed. And he ran harder still, down the hill to the stream where they had buried Njoroge's body.

He did not know what he wanted. But he took the dead body and putting it on his shoulders began to run along the stream. Running! Panting! He came to a raised bank and thought he would take a rest. Then he would go to the mission, give them 'their' body.

But he did not want their help. He had found the Light. He would then go to the Government Guard Post. . . . He and the dead body were a curse to the tribe.

As he sat there, the word 'light' persistently rang in his mind and his heart felt like singing. He tried—

'Lead kindly light. . . .' But Who?

His tribal God, the White Missioners or the white man's Government?

'Who is there?' a voice asked. It was unexpected. Fright. Perspiration. Quickly he took the body and ran. His legs missed the ground and now he went down. . . . Splash. Darkness. And for him the wind and voices stopped. . . .

Mr Gerard, the Missioner, heard the splash. Whoever had fallen, that was the end, for he must have fallen off the famous Mukau Rock. Just now he was tired, for he had gone so late to see a sick man in Njoroge's Kraal. He would, however, come back in the morning.

Abioseh D. Nicol

THE DEVIL AT YOLAHUN BRIDGE

Sanderson twirled his fountain-pen slowly round between the fingers of one hand and drummed with the other on the desk before him. His eyes wandered to the distant green hills of Kissiland that marked the boundary between his district and the next. He looked again at the form in front of him, printed on Crown Agents' paper, and read it to himself for the tenth time. 'District Officer's Annual Report West African Colonial Service (Confidential).' The blank space below looked wider than ever. Since McPherson, his Senior District Officer, had gone home on leave, he had kept postponing writing it. He had received a gentle reminder from Headquarters' Secretariat a few days ago. He felt he really must get down to it this afternoon.

'Momoh!' he shouted. The young West African clerk came out of the adjoining office.

'Bring me all the Annual Reports you can lay your hands on.'

'There are about fifty, sir,' Momoh said with some trepidation, 'but I can bring them all if you want them,' he added hastily.

'Bring the past ten years, then.'

When the Reports arrived he glanced through them. He could not believe that anyone bothered to read them. What would happen, he wondered, if he sent, say, the 1936 Report verbatim with the name of a sub-chief altered here and the name of a village there; or, say, a blank form which some cryptic remark like 'Confidentially (as requested) the Africans have not changed much over the past year, but my fellow Europeans in the station have altered beyond belief. Pale hesitant inexperience, for example, in many cases has slowly but steadily given way to an incredible sunburnt competence.'

No, wit was not appreciated in high places. Could he start on an historical note? Or on an anthropological one? He decided against that. He had better stick to the familiar essential things instead – new roads, the increase in trade, and the shift of the young from the village to the towns. Now to begin.

'Excuse me, sir, I have not yet read out to you your appointments for the week.' Momoh had appeared through the doorway and was standing in front of his desk.

Sanderson suppressed a cry of impatience as he remembered that he had impressed on the clerk the importance every Monday morning of reminding him of his week's appointments. He could easily look them up himself, but he was trying to train Momoh to a high pitch of secretarial efficiency and, besides, it gave him a secret pleasure to pretend he was a vast administrator with numerous and important appointments. Momoh himself enjoyed the whole business intensely. He was a short, stocky youth with an alert face and boyish enthusiasm. His breast-pocket was always full of finely sharpened pencils and fountain-pens with different coloured ink.

'All right, Mr Momoh, read them out.'

Momoh cleared his throat and read in a slightly sing-song voice. First, there was the annual inspection of the local secondary school. This was run by a nervous, leathery Irish priest and it had to be inspected every year before receiving the Government grant. The inspection was a formality; for education officers came round from time to time during the year to see that the standards were maintained. Then there was the semi-official engagement, the following night, to lecture to the local African club.

'Will you be there, Mr Momoh?' Sanderson asked him, and at once regretted doing so lest his clerk should regard it as an official command.

'Oh yes, I shall be there certainly, sir,' Momoh said earnestly. 'Things like that,' he continued, 'contribute to a man's uplift of the mind.'

'Well, I don't think this will,' Sanderson remarked dryly. 'Still, continue.' On Thursday there was to be the visit of the P.W.D. Headquarters' engineer. Momoh had put into operation the simple procedure required – the rest-house to be got ready, the file for maintenance and repair of Government buildings to be gone through, and new requirements determined or invented; the Government lorry to be made ready in case that of the visiting engineer broke down on the way to Kissy or when returning from it. Sanderson looked through the list, initialled his approval, and asked Momoh the name of the engineer.

'Mr O. E. Hughes, sir,' Momoh replied with a slight smile which puzzled Sanderson at the time, but which he remembered afterwards. One of our Celtic brethren, Sanderson thought to himself. Aloud he said, 'Right. Thank you very much,' dismissing the clerk.

'Now, about Hughes,' he said, half aloud to himself.

He could not place him; the name did not sound familiar. Must be new, he thought, and decided to look him up in the most recent Senior Staff List. He ran his finger down the column of the Senior P.W.D. Staff until he came to the Hs. Ah, there it was, Hughes, Oluyemi Egbert. Oh, that was it, he was an African. That was why he had never heard of him before. He whistled softly to himself. By jove, there might be complications. Usually, visiting members of the senior staff were taken to the European Club in the evenings they spent in Kissy. He began to go through the list of members in his mind one by one, trying to picture what their reactions would be to an African guest. Then he wondered for a moment, a little shamefacedly, whether it was not he who had started making excuses and finding reasons before anything happened. But no, he decided, it was his duty to make sure beforehand that there were no incidents, because if there were he would have to make a report and probably bear the unspoken blame from Headquarters. He wondered whether it would not be wiser to ask old Mr Thomas, the Senior African clerk, to entertain Hughes. At last he made a decision – he knew what he would do. He would ask Hughes to dinner at his bungalow and he would ask Hounslow, the agent of a large firm, to make up a third. Hounslow was English but born in East Africa, son of a Kenya settler. He would show by that that he had no prejudice. With the problem solved he turned to work with a lighter heart but with a mild sense of dissatisfaction.

Hughes arrived promptly after lunch. He was a tall man, probably in his early thirties, with a small military moustache, close-cropped hair, very dark skin, and even, white teeth, but he was completely unsmiling, and very polite. He shook hands with Sanderson, accepted a seat, refused a cigarette, and got down to business almost immediately. He listened to Sanderson carefully, made notes, and asked one or two questions. Sanderson called to Momoh to bring in the files. The clerk brought them in, put them down, and was going away when Sanderson stopped him suddenly, remembering his smile of pride, and introduced him to Hughes, who smiled pleasantly and briefly, shook hands and turned back to the files. Sanderson found this politeness and efficiency uncomfortable at first, and tried to soften the atmosphere with a joke here and there. But Hughes either did not understand or pretended he did not understand. At the end of a couple of hours most of the work was finished, and Sanderson asked Hughes what he would be doing that night. Then, feeling that the African engineer might regard it as an unwarrantable intrusion into his privacy, he added hastily, 'because I'd like you to come to dinner with me.'

'Yes, thank you, that will be nice,' Hughes answered, putting away his notes and getting up. Sanderson was a little disappointed that he had not shown more enthusiasm. Hang it all, he thought, I don't suppose many Europeans would ask him as I have done, but perhaps he is political and is accepting out of a sense of duty. Besides, he probably guesses why I asked him to come to the bungalow. 'You are sure you can manage it, by the way,' he said aloud.

'Oh, yes, thank you, that will be very nice,' Hughes repeated. 'I'll go and see the other official buildings now, and will be with you this evening. Good-bye, then, for the present,' he added. Sanderson walked with him to the door and they shook hands again while Momoh looked on admiringly.

Hounslow appeared at eight at Sanderson's bungalow and mixed himself a drink. He shouted through the door to Sanderson who was changing in his bedroom.

'Is anyone else coming tonight?'

'Hughes, the new assistant engineer,' Sanderson shouted back.

'What's he like? Does he come from Swansea, look you man?'

'No, he is an African – Mr Oluyemi Egbert Hughes.'

There was a pause.

'Are you there, Hounslow?' Sanderson asked anxiously after a while.

'Yes, I am,' Hounslow replied through the door. 'Why didn't you tell me this before?'

'Because, frankly, I wasn't sure whether you'd come.'

'Are you afraid, Sanderson, of facing an educated black alone?'

'No, not at all, but I thought it would be good experience for you, my lad. It will correct some of your slave-driving ideas.'

'I am afraid he and I won't find much to say to each other,' Hounslow replied. 'Pity the club's closed to-night or I would have escaped before he arrived.'

Sanderson opened the door and entered the lounge-cum-dining-room. 'The club's closed?'

'Yes,' Hounslow said, 'a peculiar situation has arisen. We've run out of drinks through bad management,' he added. 'Why, were you going to take your Mr Hughes there?'

'The idea had occurred to me,' Sanderson said, feeling relieved and somewhat guilty.

'There's no end to what you wallahs in the Administration will do to show your damned official broad-mindedness.'

He lit a cigarette and sank moodily into a chair. 'I wish I had brought my black missus with me,' he added, smiling reminiscently. 'She's a fine girl, you know,' he continued enthusiastically. 'Don't know what I'd do without her.'

'No, you certainly aren't bringing her : Mr Hughes looks very respectable. And you're going to behave nicely to him, too.'

'Yes, teacher. Is he political?'

'I shouldn't wonder,' Sanderson answered. 'They all are, these chaps, you know, although they've got to conceal it when they're in the Service.'

'Shouldn't be surprised if he supplies copy to nationalist newspapers. However, we must move with the times,' Hounslow said resignedly. 'He'll probably get drunk and start smashing bottles,' he added hopefully.

In fact, they were all a little unsober before the evening was out. Olu Hughes appeared looking very smart in a light tropical suit and a black bow-tie.

'Oh, I forgot to tell you not to dress,' said Sanderson.

'Oh, that's all right,' Hughes replied.

Hounslow and Hughes were introduced to each other. The African said, 'How do you do.'

Hounslow nodded. Neither shook hands. Sanderson mixed them drinks and made conversation about his garden.

They moved over to the other side of the room and sat down to chop. Sanderson waited for Hughes to begin before he himself started. Hughes waited for Sanderson because the latter was more senior in the Service, and in any case the array of knives and forks was a little confusing. Hounslow began as soon as the *hors d'œuvres* were placed in front of him. Then Sanderson put his knife and fork on his plate and passed Hughes the salt. Hughes took it and began to eat. Hounslow concentrated on the food and ate gloomily and slowly, now and again addressing a remark to Sanderson. Hughes, perhaps noticing this, turned slightly to Sanderson and spoke to him exclusively of his afternoon's work. Towards the end of the meal Hounslow, talking about rising prices, turned to Hughes and said, 'How are your people managing, Mr Hughes, with all these rising prices? I suppose they're finding European food and clothes not quite so easy to maintain as they thought, eh?'

Hughes chewed his food silently for a few minutes. The silence became unbearable. Hounslow, beginning to frown, thinking he had been snubbed, was going to repeat his question in a louder voice. Sanderson, thinking the African was annoyed, was preparing to say something tactful. Hughes sipped some water, then, turning to Hounslow, said, 'Yes, they are finding European food and clothes hard to maintain.' Then he continued eating. Hounslow was not sure whether sarcasm was meant, and searched the African's face unsuccessfully for a sign. Sanderson said something about the rise in the cost of living hitting all classes, high and low, except the very rich, of course. 'Among which I dare say none of us is numbered. Let's go in and sit in more comfortable chairs and have coffee.'

Hounslow decided to relax, for he did not want to be boorish. Moreover, he was curious to know what Africans really thought; for he had never had the opportunity of talking to an African in such an atmosphere of equality. He addressed questions now and again to Hughes about what Africans thought on this or that matter, until the latter replied quietly that he was afraid he had been so busy lately that he had rather lost touch with the opinions of his people. Hounslow glanced sharply again to see whether any offence had been meant. Trouble is, he said to himself, you can never tell when these educated natives mean to be insolent or not. They all wear this damned mask of politeness; have not the courage of their convictions. But as the evening wore on and another bottle of whisky was opened, the atmosphere became more convivial. Sanderson turned to Hughes suddenly and said, 'You trained at home, didn't you? I mean in Britain. Where were you? London?'

'Yes, I was in London for most of the time, at one of the big Polytechnics near Oxford Circus. I lived in digs at Cricklewood and came up to the College every morning by bus.'

'Did you have good digs?' Sanderson asked.

Old Varsity men swapping reminiscences, Hounslow thought, a little contemptuously, stretching himself out on the chair easily. He will soon ask him, 'What was your first fifteen like?' and the darkie will say, 'Actually the forwards were not bad, a bit slow at passing perhaps, but not bad at all; we once drew with Rosslyn Park.' He helped himself sternly to some more whisky.

'I found a room eventually,' Hughes answered, 'after having

several doors slammed in my face. It was quite a comfortable room
and the landlady was a blonde, decent soul.'

Sanderson smiled. 'What a turn of phrase you have,' he said. 'But
seriously, apart from the lodgings problem, did you enjoy your
time in England?'

'Well, I didn't at first,' admitted Hughes, 'but later on I wasn't
sure. It's the uncertainty of one's reception in England that con-
fuses a lot of us. Sometimes you are welcomed with open arms by
nice people. But on the other hand you get sudden rebuffs. Or what
is worse, people simply avoid you as if you had some infectious
disease. They are just cold and distant.'

Sanderson filled his glass slowly. 'I know what you mean,' he
said, sipping his glass and then holding it up to the light. 'I worked
in London, too, for a few months, and I found people very cold
and distant. I often wondered whether there was something wrong
with me. People behave very strangely in cities, you know, Hughes.
They tend to be secretive and shy as a protection against the vast-
ness surrounding them. And anything stranger than usual, like a
man with a dark complexion, makes it even more so.'

Hounslow chuckled. 'By jove, you are quite the Oxford man,
Sanderson,' he said. 'You'll theorize your way to heaven and find
it hellish when you get there.' He laughed at his own words, and
then his brow swiftly darkened with heavy anger. 'You've got nothing to complain about,' he said to Hughes. 'Nor you either,' turning
to Sanderson. 'I was the disappointed one in England. I grew up
in Kenya and we thought of England as home all the time, and our
old man told us all sorts of stories of the English countryside and
our heritage. But when I went there to school nobody seemed to
bother about the things we held dear.' He stretched himself on the
chair. 'I don't suppose it was a good school,' he continued, 'but it
was a public school all right. Headmasters' Conference and all that.
It was well boosted in all the colonies, and there were special cheap
rates for the holidays for boys whose parents were overseas. My
father was a self-made man and left school early, and when he heard
about this school he thought he would make up to us educationally
for what he himself had missed.

'Did you go back to East Africa when you left school?' Sanderson
asked.

'No, I stayed on a little longer. But things were never quite the
same. I worked for a time with a big exporting firm, but didn't like
it particularly. Some of the chaps there thought I was a bit of a
Blimp. They thought I was too narrow. People seemed to have
changed so since my father's generation, whose ideas were what we
colonials had. I mean white colonials, of course,' he added hastily.

'And how did you find it changed from what you had expected?' Hughes asked conversationally.

'Oh, in all sorts of ways,' Hounslow answered after a short pause, during which he had debated whether to admit Hughes freely into the conversation and had decided that for free and easy social purposes the African could be an honorary white man for an evening. 'In all sorts of ways,' he repeated reflectively, nodding his head. 'Do you know,' he said, tapping Sanderson's knee, 'that one evening a chap tried to elbow me out of the way at the end of a show, during the National Anthem? I was standing at the end of a row, and the fellow gave me lip. Said I was to move on as he had a bus to catch, and not to block the gangway. Of course I refused to move and stood at attention. The chap leaned over and said into my ear, "Company at ease!" in a terribly common accent. I stood unflinching and he and his gang climbed over the seats and clattered out. Must have been Communists, of course. At the end of the "King" I rushed down the foyer looking for him to knock him down. But by then they had gone. Things like that made me sad,' he said, leaning back. 'No, the old country is not the same. Too much talk of freedom, equality and democracy, and not enough doing things.'

'I don't think they are as bad as that,' put in Sanderson, feeling things were rather up to him. 'You'll find things have changed in the larger cities, but curiously enough, London itself and the country-side remain always unchanged. What did you really think of London?' he said, turning to Hughes.

'Ah, London was full of wonders for me. It was the organization of everything and the clockwork efficiency which amazed me. You English are efficient. I used to go for walks at night and watch the traffic lights changing to yellow, to red, to green, to yellow again all through the night. When I was studying hard for exams I would go out at two to three in the morning to clear my brain before going to bed. Once I saw a huge motor lorry stop at a crossroad early when the lights were against it. There was no one about, not even a policeman in sight, and I was in the shadow. But he stopped just because the lights were against him. That's what I call organization and a sense of the right thing. I never shall forget that moment. Further – that moment summarized London and the English for me.' There was a pause for a few moments, and the other two looked obviously impressed. Hughes shut his eyes slightly and thought again of the Cricklewood Broadway he had so often loved but hated sometimes with a weary homesickness in the grey winter. 'To London,' he said, suddenly raising his glass.

'To London,' the others murmured. 'God bless her!'

'But mind you, I was glad to be back home,' Hughes added after a while, fearing they might think him a 'black Englishman,' which he most dreaded. 'There are things a man can do in this country which he cannot do in England.'

'For example?' Hounslow asked, with some interest.

'Well, you can start things single-handed, and finish them before your own eyes here, while you'd have to be a genius to do that in England.'

'I don't know about beginning and finishing here,' Sanderson began.

'I've built a bridge here,' Hughes interrupted. 'I came by this district last year, about four miles from here, on the Yolahun road, and there was a dry stream-bed which people used as a short cut to the big market in the dry season, but in the rains the stream was too swift for them to ford and it took them about two hours to make a detour to cross it farther up on a swinging rope bridge. In fact, that's why for generations you'd have a small famine in this district during the rains, because most people simply did not bother or could not travel properly to the large town to sell their crops and buy food. I simply couldn't understand why nobody had thought of building a bridge there before.

'Perhaps they thought of it during the rains, but forgot about it in the dry season. That often happens in this country. Or, again, people may simply have accepted it.'

'So *you* built that bridge! I wondered about it,' Sanderson said. 'I thought it was the army, but it looked too permanent for them.'

'I expect it's improved things quite a lot now, hasn't it?' Hughes asked with some triumph.

Sanderson wondered whether it was kinder to leave the truth unsaid, because in fact the bridge was seldom used by the villagers and then only by motor transport. Someone had been drowned years ago at that point, and the local legend had it there was a water-spirit there during the rains.

'Yes, I think it has improved things,' he said aloud.

'That's much sooner than I expected,' Hughes said. 'Do you know some years ago someone was drowned there? And people think there is a devil round there during the rains. In fact, I had to hire a more powerful medicine-man to sacrifice a chicken on the site and pour some rum on the ground before the labourers would begin.'

'As you know,' said Hounslow with jovial politeness, 'we prefer champagne. Break a bottle of the stuff over the prow of a ship as she slides off her slipway, just to appease the old gods. Same as you, old man; same as you.'

'Of course, I had the chicken and the rest of the rum for dinner that evening,' Hughes said, trying to show that he had treated the whole thing as a piece of whimsy to humour his workmen and had never for a moment taken it seriously. At the same time he thought Hounslow had been patronizingly polite, trying to compare it with an English custom. He had himself seen a new ship being launched at a shipyard, and had been awed by it. Of course, the ceremony bore no comparision with the blood of a white chicken and the rum poured out by a simple misguided native. In fact, in the launching on Clydeside there had been a milord about. He had had him pointed out. It bore no comparison. Anyhow, he thought, perhaps I am too sensitive.

'I envy you chaps – engineers, doctors, agriculturists and so on,' Sanderson said. 'You begin things, you finish them, and you see the result. But we never do. We never even know if we've begun. Nor when we finish. We never really know whether we are just redundant.'

Hughes was touched. 'Oh, no no,' he cried, 'you administrators, white or black, will always be needed to plan things and to manage men. When we are old and finished, then there is an end to us as engineers. Then we begin to learn your job, to administer. But I must go,' he said springing up. 'I've got to set off early tomorrow, and I know you will forgive me.' He shook hands with both, and swiftly disappeared in spite of Sanderson's protesting that he could put him up for the night. And Hounslow pressed the other man's whisky on him, to take just one more for the road.

After the African had left, Hounslow strolled up and down the room, stumbling a little. Then he stopped suddenly in front of Sanderson, who was slowly puffing a pipe. 'Do you know,' he said in a voice of such tiredness that the other glanced up swiftly – 'do you know that apropos of what you said a few minutes ago, I am beginning to feel particularly redundant in this damned country!' He sat down and rested his head on the edge of the table, with his body sprawling loosely in the chair.

'But you are not an Administrator,' Sanderson said, 'you are the senior agent of a very prosperous firm.'

'No, I'm feeling *de trop* in a different sort of way, especially when I meet educated natives like our mutual friend here this evening. They brought us up as children saying that Africa was a white man's country, and that for centuries to come we were to help and teach the black man slowly and certainly what it had taken us hundreds of years to gain. But here in my own lifetime I see these people trained to do all sorts of things, and the trouble is they sometimes do them well. Mind you, I don't say they are as good as we are. They can never be that.'

'Yes,' said Sanderson swiftly, 'just as we couldn't be them if we tried. We and they are both different, but good in our separate ways.'

'Yes, yes, I suppose you've got to say that in your poistion,' Hounslow replied. 'But whatever you say, I don't think they can do it in a generation, old man; they'll crack up when things go bad. That chap Hughes, for example, was frightened of the water-juju : I could see it in his face.' He filled his glass himself and emptied it. 'All the same, old man, they make us feel useless – damned useless. You Whitehall chaps can't see that you are trying to put us, your own kith and kin, out into the cold. You'd be surprised how hard I found it to get this job. And now Headquarters is talking about training African assistant managers. As if I didn't know what they meant ! Why are you always trying to be fair, you Johnnies? Always pushing us out into the cold?' He burst into tears. Sanderson tried first not to notice; then gave it up, went over and stood by him, putting his hand on Hounslow's shoulder. 'Don't you think the country is big enough for Hughes and you and me? Hughes has to be here because it's his country. You are here because no man can do everything in his own country. I think this idea of a man's country belonging to him is a phase we all pass through. *We* passed through it fifty years ago. Only his country-side and the profitless patches in his country belong to any man. The fat of the land is to whoever can get it, and whoever that is then tries to belong to the country even more than those whose heritage it was. It is by this eternal recruitment of the fittest alien that great nations and privileged classes survive. And that is why you'll always be here if you are good enough, Hounslow, and for no other reason.'

The other man had been listening with attention. 'I wish I'd been educated your way, Sanderson. I wish I knew what words meant and could use them. But I gather it's a case of the survival of the fittest.' The wind rose and fell, rattling the windows.

'So you think there will be room for all of us?' he said, getting up and stretching. 'I doubt it; you only have to read the local rag. But it is not a bad country, all said and done. A man can see results in it sometimes.'

'To Africa,' Sanderson toasted gravely.

'Yes, yes, to Africa; white man's country and black man's, too.' Hounslow nodded, sipping. 'A last one before I go, one for the road, so to speak,' he added, nodding all the time as if comforted but only half convinced. Sanderson picked up the bottle. But it was empty.

'Never mind,' Hounslow said thickly, 'we'll have it in soda.' He was feeling tired, sad, and then happy.

Sanderson filled the glasses. And the little pearly bubbles clung to the sides of the glasses to burst to the surface. They tickled Hounslow's nostrils, and he grimaced happily.

'Whom shall it be to this time?' Sanderson asked.

'To you, to you, old man,' Hounslow said affectionately. 'To you, old man, and me,' he chuckled.

'And Olu Hughes too?' Sanderson added.

'Yes, him too,' Hounslow agreed. 'In fact, to all good chaps everywhere. "For we are jolly good fellows," ' he hummed as he searched for his car key.

Sanderson saw him off from the small courtyard in front of his bungalow. 'Are you sure you will be able to drive yourself home?' he asked him.

'Positive, old man, I can drive home blindfolded. Give us a shove, there's a good fellow.'

Sanderson heaved and pushed for a while before the car broke into life and careered off. It headed in the opposite direction from the town, and Sanderson shouted to Hounslow to stop and turn round. But the car was soon lost to sight, although the sound could be heard in the distance. Sanderson went indoors with misgiving and wearily prepared for bed.

Hounslow put the car into gear and roared up a hill. The throb of the engine filled him with an exultant power, as did an occasional gust of wind. He knew where he was going and felt his head strangely clear. After about fifteen minutes he slowed down and stopped. He bent over his wheel and listened to the shrill call of the cicadas and the deep bass croaking of the frogs; these would stop suddenly sometimes and an eerie silence filled the heavy air. He left the head-lamps on and walked forward slowly in the broad beam of light to examine the bridge more closely. It was an ordinary one but strong, concrete and with simple, hard grace. He stood in the middle if it and jumped up and down, as if half hoping it would break. He leaned over one side and watched the growing waters between the rocks. He threw a twig in on one side and rushed over to the other side to see it appear, laughing with pleasure when it did so. Then he walked slowly back to his car. And Olu Hughes, standing by the shadows, where he had hidden when he had first heard the car, marvelled that Hounslow had not detected his presence, his heart had been beating so loudly. He had walked far out of town to come and see the bridge he had fashioned with love and care. He had come in the dark of night, defying the dark to show himself that he was not afraid of the water-spirit. He had been strangely pleased and a little puzzled at the look on the white man's face as he strode past slowly.

It leaped suddenly into the middle of the road and stood there, poised, dazzled by the light from the head-lamps. Hounslow sat quickly upright in the driver's seat to watch it. Hughes restrained a startled cry and gazed with fascination. It was a curious beast. It had the shape of an antelope but was reddish-brown on the back and white underneath, with a sharp boundary-line between the two colours as if it had been swimming and washed off its colour. It had slender curved horns on a head held proudly and supported on a delicate neck. It had black vertical stripes down each buttock and one on its back continuing to the tail. It stood there for a few long seconds. Hounslow then sounded his horn sharply and the beast bounded high into the air and forward, to be lost as suddenly as it had appeared, like a secret memory.

'Oh, it's only a red-buck,' Hounslow shouted aloud, as he thought, to himself. He started the car, reversed carefully into the side of the road, and turned round and drove back steadily to town.

It was, after all, only a red-buck, an impala, that they were afraid of, Hughes meditated, as he climbed on to the bridge. He put the small spirit-level he always carried about with him on one of the railings and shone his torch on it. He nodded with satisfaction as he watched the air-bubble oscillate and settle in the centre; and then, reluctantly, he started to walk back to the rest-house. He stopped suddenly, held out his hand a moment or so, and then broke into a steady run. For the rain had begun to fall in single heavy drops like the slow, quiet weeping of a woman proud, proud to distraction for an only son, yet vaguely afraid.

Nkem Nwankwo

from DANDA

It was the night before Danda was to cut the ici.[1] The prospects of the ordeal did not seem to have affected his spirits. He stood full-blown in the middle of the compound talking to a crowd and

[1] Tribal marks made with a sharp knife by the ogba ici, or medicine man, on a boy's cheeks.

laughing. There was a young moon and its soft light gave Danda's blue cloak a satiny hue. His bells, polished for the occasion, twinkled like fireflies.

'That's how it is, people of your land.' And Danda began to sing.

As soon as the first notes of the oja were heard outside the compound a crowd gathered – men, women, children jostled into Araba's compound to hear Danda sing his last song in Aniocha. He sang with the flute but it was easy for most people in the audience to translate the notes into words, they had heard the song many times before.

'I have been everywhere. Remember when we were at Mbaukwu which is as red as camwood. Where are you, Okoyeocha, my friend? My voice is ringing for you.

Hai. Another animal climbs with the monkey and breaks its neck. Where is Okoyeocha. Come and ring my hand or my tone will dry.

They said to me, sing. I sang of the hunter who misses the first ndulu. Let him not bite his lips for another will come, I said. And of the child who carries fire and carries a knife. If the fire does not burn him the knife will cut him. And of the spear thrown at an antheap? It will either break or bend I told them.

Kokoya! I sang to them. I said do not complain that soup has entered in your eyes when you are inside a stream. The snake climbs the top of the iroko tree. Without hand or feet but with his chi. You have your chi.

Kokoya! They said to me, sing. I sang to them. Men of the land of alulani. They threw nsi at me. I said to them, why do you throw nsi at me. If what is good is not good to you then let your wives give birth to crocodiles and let's see how you will like it.

Kokoya! Spare the flower and the ododo. The ododo is meant to be admired. It's not meant to be used for a burial. Why do you keep the wine in the pot? That which is in the pot should be in the belly. And no colour of camwood can colour night into day.

So let's get home to the land of our fathers. The day is closing in upon us. The sun is footsore and has gone to sleep. When things go hard with the poor man he calls his kindred.

So we turned to the mkpuke of our mothers. And the land broke its legs and became a ravine. And our voice became dry.'

As soon as he finished there was a chorus of cheering. Many coins were thrown at him by admirers but he ignored them. Okoli Mbe, smiling shrewdly, gathered the coins and tied them in a loop at the edge of his wrapper.

After a moment Nnoli Nwego broke out into his own song in a sepulchral voice which caused laughter and some ironic cheers.

'Go it, son of our fathers!'

'That's how it is, men of our lands.' Danda took over from him. 'The children are hungry. Let their mothers return from the market and give them food.'

'It is too late,' said Nwafo Ugo.

'They won't succeed,' Nwora Otankpa cut in.

'Why shouldn't they succeed?' said Nwokeke Idemmili rubbing his extensive stomach tenderly.

'True,' mused Okelekwu, waving his whisk. 'It is better to have the ici when one is young. But there is no harm in cutting it later. The skin of the older man is tough but he is also stronger and can bear it better.'

'I have never seen anyone of Danda's age cutting the ici,' said Nwafo. 'Whatever concerns Danda is different.'

There was laughter. Nwafo rubbed his bottom with the pride of a wit.

The morning had just awakened from sleep, throwing off its cold blue wrapper and yawning. More and more men were drifting into the Araba compound to watch the ici. Some had brought their own stools, others cowhides. Those who had neither stool nor cowhide sliced off leaves of the plantain spread them on the ground and sat on them.

They waited.

Suddenly there broke through the air the song of ngwele kwonwu. This strange bird got its name from what it seems to say : ngwele kwonwu – kwonwu – kwonwu – kwonwu (lizard there is death – death – death).

A most accurate augurer of death; whenever it whistles its mournful tale men shiver.

'Who has died?' asked Nwafo Ugo.

'I haven't heard,' sighed Okelekwu.

Nwafo made a sign round his head to ward off the evil. 'I wonder what Danda's face will look like after the ici.'

'Not very bright!' roared Nwora Otankpa. 'I remember my own days. The ici stings like pepper.'

'If Danda is lucky he will come off without shame. He has no enemies.'

The great point of the ici is that it is a test of fortitude. The ogbu ici rips off pelts of flesh in a traditional pattern that stretches from ear to ear. The operation is excruciating. But the victim is to bear the pain if not with a smile at least without any visible show of sorrow. If he winces or cries out, he breaks the magic of the ritual and lets down himself and his kindred.

The enemies of the man whose face is being cut often take advantage of this weakness. With the aid of a strong ogwu they transform themselves into scorpions or red-ants, creep under the victim, bite or sting him and make him cry out and thereby earn the worst of shames.

'No nsi can harm Danda,' said Okelekwu. 'Araba's hand is strong. He has power.'

Strong charms hung on bamboo posts at the four corners of the compound. Then four family gods stood guard by the bed on which the ici ceremony was to be performed.

Araba and Danda sat in the obi. Between them were the rest of the family gods and a pot of palm wine topped by a guard cup.

'So all our load is on your shoulder,' Araba was whispering. 'Our name is here and the world is there. What am I saying? Do you want palm wine?'

'Yes.'

Araba's hands trembled as he gave Danda the guard cup.

'When I cut my own ici, my eyelids did not flicker. And the whole of Aniocha marvelled. They say that my father, Udeji Uwadiegwu, took his own with a heart of stone. He was a strong man. I have never yet seen a stronger. You still want more palm wine?'

'Yes.'

Araba served him absent-mindedly, still observing the past.

Danda drank thirstily and stretched his hand for more.

'Quite true,' said Araba, at last waking up from his reverie. Then he said with a firm tone :

'You must do it.'

'I will do it.'

'The eyes of our fathers are open.'

Danda next went to speak to his mother.

'Are you hungry?' Outwardly she was calm.

'What have you got?'

She scooped into a wooden plate Danda's favourite food – bread-fruit mixed with maize – and passed it to him. As he ate she watched him fixedly. She would rather there were no ici. She had seen Nwaku Eke's son cut his own ici. When they finished with him he looked dead. They crammed into his unconscious mouth various delicacies. Praise singers sang and gun shots were let off. There was glory in the ici but the penalty for failure—

Danda had finished the breadfruit.

'You want more?' she asked.

'Yes.'

She filled the plate again. And Danda once again cleaned it out. Before he went she asked him :

'You will do it?'

'Yes, I will.'

'The eyes of our fathers are open.'

The ogbu ici had just come. A lean hawk of a fellow with a sharp manner and twinkling eyes. As Danda came up to him he sharpened his knife on his palm, and beamed. His manner was reassuring. It seemed to suggest : 'Come along, don't be afraid, I will kill you with only one stroke.'

The bed was the type made of raffia and standing on four legs cut out of the branches of the akpaka tree. It was covered with a flowered piece of cloth and at its head was a bundle of clothes that would serve as a pillow.

Gingerly Danda lay flat on the bed and stared at the ogbu ici's knife which glinted with the morning sun.

'Close your eyes, Danda,' said Okelekwu.

'No,' said Nwafo. 'Let him see. Ndulu the bird says that the gun he sees cannot kill him.'

This sally was greeted with laughter. The men were in high spirits.

The ogbu ici first washed Danda's face with a soft cloth soaked in sweet-smelling ointment. Then he cut two almost parallel lines near the right eye and began to remove the pelt of skin between them.

There were some of the men around who were still squeamish about blood and involuntarily closed their eyes. But even those who were attentive could not be sure what really went wrong.

There were a few who hadn't time to get out of the way. They only felt a sensation of a body leaping over their heads. Some blood had dropped on the right hand of Nwafo Ugo. He rose and went to clean it on the body of the orange tree nearby.

For a long time the ogbu isi held that sharp knife as if he wasn't quite sure what to do with it. Finally he sighed, dropped it and went out.

Araba walked firmly into his obi, sat down before the Ikenga and began to murmur something.

'Well, what are we waiting for?' asked Nwokeke, smiling at the stupefied kindred.

The tension broke and there were murmurs of small talk as the people beat dust off their cowhides and began to disperse. Okelekwu looked curiously at Araba, felt like going in to sit by him, decided against doing so and walked home alone, caressing the air with his whisk.

'The sun is awake,' said Nwokeke to Nwora Otankpa.

'Yes,' agreed the latter, looking at the great daub of colour which took up the whole of the eastern sky. 'Today will be fine. I will go to my valley farm.'

They moved out and soon arrived at a huge akpaka tree on the side of the road. They sheltered in its shade for a long time and at last walked on still talking.

A small bird with black and dirty-copper feathers had sat directly above their heads preening his wings. And as soon as they left he stretched, yawned and flew off chanting tauntingly : ngwele kwonwu – kwonwu – kwonwu.

Onuora Nzekwu

from BLADE AMONG THE BOYS

A deep silence fell on the gathering and all but he looked as if they had been hit by a terrible plague.

'One day you'll perish in your own foolishness,' Ononye said, when he recovered from the shock given him by his nephew's statement. 'Ike, Etuka and Akudo are respected leaders of the Christian community among us, but still they make charms and consult diviners. Only last year Ike bore the cost of his grandmother's traditional funeral rites and Akudo sponsored his brother for the *ozo*-title. Mark you, these men were in the Church before you were born and they've got more Christian teachings in them than you've ever had. How can you, of all people, let the Church make a senseless woman of you? Why can't you apply a bit of common sense in pursuing your own ruin?'

'I do not gauge my faith by other people's standards,' Patrick replied haughtily, 'no matter in what regard the society holds them. I did not become a Christian to impress the society in which I live.'

'Do not let Christianity make you blind to the truths of life,' said one of the elders. 'You can't say that you have failed to read any meaning into every event that has taken place around you recently.'

'You've got to mellow down,' another pleaded, 'and find a place in your heart for that which is dearest to your own kith and kin. We fail to understand how you can become so obsessed with a for-

H

eign way of life to the utter neglect of your own – your own which distinguishes you from all other peoples, which we are all proud of, which sustained your ancestors and which means life and death to us.'

'Man, the office of *okpala* is yours by right,' a young member of the delegation put in. 'You have built yourself a house. It now remains for you to marry and take the *ozo*-title to qualify for the office. You've got the means to face these responsibilities squarely. I cannot understand why you are being unnecessarily difficult.'

'Brethren,' Patrick said, wishing to end the whole interview. 'You cannot move me with your arguments. My mind is made up and you cannot make me change it no matter what you say or do.'

Patrick had originally declined to assume office on the grounds that he was a Christian. Christianity to him, as to many other people, was synonymous with education, with progressive ideas and with modern thought. He would therefore have nothing, directly or indirectly, to do with an aspect of his traditional culture so conspicuously heathenish. He didn't care whether the life of the whole society depended on his acceptance of the office or not. What he cared about most was the salvation of his own soul. Now, as he faced the delegation, he had an added reason for not wanting to take up the office, but he feared to tell them this other reason.

One after another the people spoke, trying to convince him. They pleaded with him to no avail. They threatened him without success. Then Ononye went on to cite for him examples of people who had perished because of their obstinacy in refusing to accept the inevitable. He reminded him of Lucia Ezekamba, the Christian lady who, just before he left Ado, had run amok in the market place because, as everyone said, she had refused to succeed as the priestess of her lineage on the grounds that her Christian faith forbade the holding of such 'pagan' offices. A few days after she was taken home from the market she disappeared from her house, leaving no trace whatsoever of her whereabouts. And, though the police were quickly called in, she had never been found.

Much as Patrick feared to meet with a similar fate, he was unbending in his will. He was feeling uncomfortably hot inside him when Ononye lost his temper and shouted at him to respect the wishes of his relations.

'I won't!' he shouted back, a strong desire welling up in him to send them away. 'You respect my wishes. Must I for ever be a slave to your desires so as to promote harmony within the lineage when God has endowed me with a free will? When I was young you made me do things which I shouldn't have done, simply because you were caring for your selfish ends. When I started to earn a salary you made me give a large portion of my earnings to you, under the pretext that when I am old others will look after me. What guarantee is there that they will do it, now that our economy is fast changing into a cash economy? Now you want me to share out over seven hundred pounds to you as *ozo*-title fees and, not only that, you want me to come home and spend the rest of my life spilling blood on carvings and offering pieces of food to inanimate objects. I am sick of this forced loyalty to the lineage and am going to have no more of it.'

'Who are you shouting at?' Ononye asked menacingly.

'I'm shouting at all of you who wouldn't let a man live the way he pleases; at all of you who want to ruin my life for me.'

Ononye rose to his feet and spat, with a hissing sound like a cobra's. 'Curse be upon you,' he began. 'From this day on—'

'Don't,' shouted all the elders present.

'How dare you curse your own?' one of the elders sitting beside him asked. 'Already he has condemned himself to grapple with the gods. Why waste valuable powder?'

'Leave him,' shouted Patrick, trembling with anger where he stood. 'The curses of the likes of him are never potent.'

'Stop tempting the old man,' Izualor shouted from behind him, and hit him a hammer-like blow which knocked him out. As soon as this happened the delegates began to sneak away, for much as they wanted the issue of *okpala* resolved, they hated a rough house.

When Patrick woke up Ononye alone was with him.

'How do you feel?' he asked, tenderly.

'Better,' Patrick answered.

'You were rash, talking to us the way you did. You should have been more prudent in your language.

'I'm sorry.'

'Now be warned. The people you'll serve are ready waiting for you to take your rightful place among them. Remember that one false move will land you with a crisis on your lap. The odds will be against you, for you will be only one against an angry mob of relatives.'

'Rather than do what you ask I'll hang myself,' Patrick answered, determined to carry out his threat if the need arose.

After a total of two weeks at Ado he returned to Umuahia, and remained there until it was time for him to go to the seminary. He had disposed of all his possessions and put his money in a bank, where he left standing orders as to what allowance should be made his mother every month. At last the day came when he was to report at the seminary, and after bidding his friends farewell he took a mammy waggon bound for Uchi on his way to the Seminary of the Resurrection.

It was not until two months later that his relations got to know that he was no longer working, and was no longer at Umuahia. It was another month before they knew his whereabouts. As soon as his mother got the information she travelled to Uchi without a definite plan, but intent on coming home with her son. A few inquiries at the motor park at Uchi put her on the right road to the seminary. Arrived there, she was shown the principal's office by the porter at the gate. The principal was in and she told him her problem.

'No man is ever forced to become a priest,' the principal explained, when he had listened to her. 'Your son made his own decision to come here. However, you will understand that he is mature. He knows what he wants and he is responsible for his own actions.'

'He is my son,' she insisted. 'No matter how old he claims to be, to me he is still a child and needs a mother's care and guidance. I should have been consulted on this but I was not. I want to make it clear that neither I nor his relations approve of his becoming a priest.'

'But you said you are a Catholic; baptized, confirmed and married in the church. How can you not give him to God?'

'You are a white man and cannot understand the values which we place on certain issues.'

'I think I do. I have lived here for fifteen years.'

'No. No white man ever does. Because your culture is entirely different from ours, you cannot understand the fear which right now is eating out my heart, a terrible fear that there is going to be no issue in the family. He is my only child and God made him a son so that the family will continue. He is not a eunuch as people are beginning to say in Ado, even to my face. You cannot understand what terrible anguish such statements cause a mother. If you were a woman perhaps you would understand a little of the torment it is to see your son slowly waste away under your very eyes.'

'But God gave His only Son to die for your salvation,' the priest argued.

'Yes He did. He could do it because He was God. I am only human and, what is more, a woman.'

'You seem to forget Mary. Jesus was her only son and she was a woman like you.'

'She knew beforehand that a sword was going to pierce her heart and that had prepared her for what was going to happen. Moreover, being a Jew, her culture and her sense of values were quite different from mine.'

'Did Patrick tell you about the train accident at Gerti?' the priest asked, changing his line of argument. 'Did he tell you about the robbery and the bribe incident?'

'Yes, he did.'

'And you did not see in them the finger of God guiding your son towards the role He meant him to play?'

'His uncle would have told you that the gods and ancestors were employing these incidents to warn him that he should take up the office of *okpala* of his patrilineal lineage,' she answered. 'But that is beside the point. Right now I implore you,' and she fell on her knees, 'to release him. I beg you by that which you hold most dear; by the Blessed Sacrament; in the name of God; to pity a poor widow whose only hope is in her one child.'

'Well, why not talk to Patrick first and after that you can see me again?'

This seemed a reasonable proposition and she agreed.

Gabriel Okara

from THE VOICE

'If only what?' Okolo asked his inside, but his inside said nothing. For silence had flooded it, driving away words, teaching words. So leaning on the thinking-nothing wall Okolo sat seeing only darkness, the kind of darkness you see when you close your eyes. Seeing only darkness in front like the wall, Okolo looked back at his early days when he was a small boy, a small boy going to the farm with his mother in a canoe and making earth heaps to receive the yam seedlings. How sweet his inside used to be when at the day's finishing time with the sun going down, they paddled home singing; and how at harvest time when the rain came down almost ceaselessly, they returned home with the first yam, only for small boys, like him, to eat first. How in expectation of the first yams he went through the long planting time . . . then the death of his mother and then his father. Then he remembered his father's spoken words when he was dying : 'I could have been a big rich

man be,' his father had whispered with his last voice, holding
Okolo's hand, 'if the straight thing I had not spoken, if the straight
thing I had not done. But I have a sweet inside and clean as the
eye of the sky. The world is changing and engine canoes and whiteman's houses have everybody's inside filled. But open your ears
and listen, son. Let the words I am going to speak remain in your
inside. I wanted you to know book because of the changing world.
But whiteman's book is not everything. Now listen, son, believe in
what you believe. Argue with no one about whiteman's god and
Woyengi, our goddess. What your inside tells you to believe, you
believe and, always the straight thing do and the straight thing
talk and your spoken words will have power and you will live in
this world even when you are dead. So do not anything fear if it
is the straight thing you are doing or talking.'

Okolo's running thoughts were held by the opening door. He
raised his head and coming in was an officer of the listeners and behind him, standing outside, was a group of people and in front of
the group of people stood the mother-in-law.

Thoughts knocked each other down in Okolo's inside. He looked
at the group again but the mother-in-law was there. He gathered
his thoughts together in his inside and strengthened them and
strengthened his body as one about to be thrown on the ground.
But he saw nothing to fear.

'You know them?' asked the officer.

'Only the woman,' said Okolo.

Thereupon the officer turned to the group outside. 'You say you
want to take him?' asked the officer. 'He is a madman be and if
I in this city see him, you will enter into trouble.'

The mother-in-law and the men put their heads together and
nodded their heads in agreement.

'A canoe is going tomorrow so we will send him back home,' said
one of the men.

'You will go with them?' the officer turned and asked Okolo.

Okolo's inside became sweet and immediately turned bitter when
reminded of the mother-in-law. But another voice told him that
since he did not touch her body he should fear nothing.

'Yes, I will go with them,' said Okolo with a straight voice.

'Get up then and go,' said the officer with a strong voice as if to
break even the wall.

Thereupon Okolo stood up from his seat and passed out of the
door.

'If we see you again in Sologa, you will be taken to the asylum,'
the officer said loudly as Okolo with the mother-in-law and the
group of men moved away.

Night had fallen and in one of the unpaved streets in the slum areas of Sologa the darkness was more than darkness because it had been forgotten. In the forgotten street stood a house with corrugated iron sheet walls and roof held together with nails and sticks. And in the house, sitting round an oil lamp, were the mother-in-law and her son, Ebiere, the bride, and her brother and a group of men and old women.

And sitting apart in a corner was Okolo, waiting, listening to his inside.

'Without him can't we something do?' said one impatiently.

'Let's wait small,' said another.

'Go and call him,' said the impatient one.

'He will come. He worked overtime. Let us wait small,' said the patient one.

Then silence fell and the people were as still as the fallen silence.

'A dead man's shadow has entered this house,' said one.

Everybody at once began talking and laughing as if something had their insides sweetened. Then there was a knock and everybody stopped talking and turned their eyes on the door. The questioning one who questioned Ebiere the other day entered in his work clothes.

'Have you come?' asked one.

'Yes, from the work place.'

He then, with importance in front of him, found a place in the group and sitting, looked round and saw Okolo in the corner.

'Is he the one?' he asked.

'Yes, that's him,' said one.

'If so, let's start. I have not reached house, and hunger is holding me hard. Now, Okolo, did you not this girl's body touch?' he asked pointing at Ebiere, the bride, and looking at Okolo with eyes that wanted to see his inside. Okolo got up from his seat and into the circle of light moved.

'No. I did not her body touch. You ask her. She will tell you if any part of her body I touched,' he said with a strong voice.

The questioning one smiled and said Ebiere would not have known in her sleep.

'Have you your body prepared to swear by Amadosu?' he asked.

'I know I did not her body touch, so I have my body prepared to swear by any god you say,' said Okolo as one who is saying the straight thing.

'Your inside is your box. We cannot open it and see what is inside. Only the gods can, so swear,' said the questioning one.

Okolo thereupon moved, with no fear in his inside, to the door, then to the dark dark night outside in the forgotten street and raised his right hand and began to swear :

'Hear, O Amadosu. Something has fallen on my head which I do not know how to remove. If I did the thing which they are putting on my head, show in the usual manner. Things of the ground, also, hear and the dead, also, hear !'

Okolo thus swearing entered the house and sat on his seat at the corner.

'Have you seen that my sister knows nothing?' said the bride's brother with smile smile in his mouth.

'Wait until she is about to deliver a child,' said the mother-in-law in a soft, strong voice. 'Yes, that is the time indeed when things of the ground and the dead will hold her and she will not be able to deliver unless she confesses.'

Nobody had ever been made to prove his innocence by swearing on a matter like this and Okolo sat in his corner asking his inside the bottom of it. And the answer came clear but nothing more he knew to ask or think. So he sat praying to Woyengi to put hand for him not to forget his father's voice in his inside coming from afar. It sounded louder and louder until thunder it became and drove all other voices from his inside.

Solomon T. Plaatje

from MHUDI, AN EPIC OF SOUTH AFRICAN NATIVE LIFE A HUNDRED YEARS AGO

Light and Shade of Memorable Days

At the Barolong settlement of Thaba Ncho, the day broke as if reluctantly, over a thick mist, which, mingling with the early morning smoke from the thousands of hearths in the huts and courtyards, created a light fog. But this was soon dispersed when the African sun rose over the north-eastern horizon. The top of Thaba Ncho hill, visible for scores of miles in each direction, dwarfed every hillock and kopje round about as though standing sentinel over the surrounding landscape. It had been snowing the previous night, and the picturesque brow of the hill (skirted by a thick black forest round the sides) was enhanced by a clear white cap of snow that covered its peak. But, once the sun had risen, his rays were so powerful that one could scarcely realize the wintry weather or the recent fall of snow.

On this particular morning the Chiefs Moroka and Tauana had announced a big game drive, at which it was intended to count all the guns and other weapons of war in the place. This was a part of the plan for arming the tribe against the dreaded Matabele. The day's exercises, as previously arranged, were preceded by one of the favourite national sports, viz., a long foot-race by the men. The race was made a contest between the tribes of Ra-Tshidi – the subjects of Tauana – and of Seleka – the subjects of Moroka. Chieftains of both sections, mounted on swift Basuto ponies, went out as starters, the meeting point being a kopje, nine miles distant from Thaba Ncho town. Over two hundred young men took part in the race. The prize to be given by the chief of the losing clan was a huge bullock to be slaughtered at a subsequent feast in honour of the winners. In addition, a prize of one heifer was to be awarded to the young man who should carry off the emblem of victory, the switch end of a white ox-tail, and deliver it to one of the waiting chiefs at the goal. The competitors were up and off long before the first streak of dawn, so that they were already on the return journey when the sun rose. A long black train appeared in view and thousands of people, who lined the route to the goal, were waiting to cheer and encourage the leading runners in their final effort. At that distance it could not be seen who the leaders were, only a score of them having yet climbed the ridge. The rest of the train, following the graceful curve of the road towards the top of the incline, moved like a giant serpent nearly half a mile in length.

By the side of the string of runners the starters rode, Tshabadira and Motshegare, chieftains of the respective clans, each urging on his side.

Already the ears of the fleet-footed racers caught the shrill but clear notes of the coldoo-ooldoo-oo-oo of the Barolong girls, and the runners did their very best. The silvery white switch could be seen fluttering in the morning breeze, held aloft by the leading runner who, coming nearer and nearer, was observed to be none other than Ra-Thaga. He was ten yards ahead of the next runner, and it seemed certain that he would carry the switch home; but as they came within four hundred yards of the goal, another man overhauled him and seized the white switch.

Ra-Thaga, still doing his best, was not reluctant to hand over the emblem of victory, for he found that his rival was Mapipi, his fellow clansman. He was running close behind the latter, when, after another hundred and fifty yards, Pheko of the Seleka clan ran level with him. Pheko sped along so fast that within a short time he took over the switch from Mapipi.

The imminent danger of losing the prize and the prospect of forcing his chief to pay incited Ra-Thaga to accelerate his speed and without knowing how he did it he was abreast of Mapipi, and past Pheko – who was still carrying the switch. With careful running and cool judgement he led the race, reached the goal, and received the coveted prize with the congratulations of both chiefs. Pheko, still bearing the emblem, tied for the second place with Mapipi.

The cheers of the spectators rent the air as more and still more of the runners arrived. By that time the winners had already taken up positions among the onlookers and were watching the advance of their own long trail.

In the meantime a faction fight broke out towards the rear between a number of young men of the rival teams. This arose through one of the Seleka tribe declaring that Ra-Thaga had not won the race for the Ra-Tshidi; for while reaching the winning post at the head of the competitors, he had failed to take over the switch from Pheko of the Seleka, the bell-bearer, and Mapipi of the Ra-Tshidi who carried no switch. But Pheko being abreast of him should be counted equally as a winner. In the speaker's opinion, no side had won and the race was a draw. This argument was resented by the winning side, who maintained that Ra-Thaga, their man, had outstripped the alleged winner by six paces.

'But,' shouted the other, 'the emblem was not in his hand.'

'Hang the emblem, hang the hand!' cried a chorus on the other side. 'They did not run on the emblem, nor on their hands; they ran on their feet.'

Arguments grew heated and changed into abuse, till one of the disputants, getting infuriated, picked up a stone and struck an opponent in the face, causing it to bleed. The bleeding youth was led to the presence of the chiefs, who shook their heads with indignation.

The Chief Moroka in a serious voice asked, 'What son of a menial had perpetrated this outrage?' A headman pleaded that the wound was inflicted accidentally in the excitement of the moment by some rowdy youths after the race, and moreover, added the advocate, the wound was not very serious.

'Deliver the offender to me,' commanded the great Moroka; 'let me teach him, and others through him, that an assault is a crime according to Barolong law, even though the victim did not suffer any permanent injury. See how he bleeds. We abhor human blood.

Assault not serious! Let it be known that we Barolong abominate human blood in any form. Do you people take my court for a den of beasts?'

'Mercy, O Chief!' shouted the crowd. *'A e ne modiga!'* (mercy on him).

'Now,' said the Chief, 'listen to my mercy. Fetch me two bullocks from his father's herd and slaughter them for the entertainment of the youths who ran in the race this morning. In future, anyone spoiling for human blood may go and join the Matabele, and there slake his thirst for blood. They are the only nation I know who delight in bloody accidents. Assault not serious! Let me hear no more of such bloody sports.'

'Behold, here comes a stranger. A Boer; he looks tired and frightened. Make way for him, give him a stool. Be seated, stranger. Who are you?'

'I am Schalk von Merrel, Captain Marock,' replied the newcomer, 'a messenger from Sarel Siljay who trekked through here last year, but I am dying for a drink of water.'

'Bring him a gourd of cool water,' said Chief Moroka. 'Well Schalk, I and my councillors are pleased to see you. What is Sarel's pleasure?'

The seething crowd surged forward to listen to the startling story told by the young Boer after he had quenched his thirst. Not being fluent in the Barolong tongue, he was imperfectly understood; yet his news sent a shocking thrill through the heart of every listener.

After the Boer had spoken, Chief Moroka asked dejectedly, 'You say all your oxen are captured by the Matabele! In spite of all the guns you had?'

'Yes, Captain,' replied the young Boer.

'Did not Sarel and his Boers smoke at them with those wooden poles with the spit-fire noses?' asked the second chief. 'And they rushed on all the same through the fire and captured your stock? Had the Matabele fire-arms too? Then how did they manage it?'

'I hope,' said the third chief, 'they captured none of your smoking-sticks?'

'They did seize two or three rifles but they cannot very well use them, as I understand they have neither powder nor lead,' replied Schalk.

'His news is very disturbing,' said the fourth chief.

'King Mosheushue should be told of this,' said another. 'An overwhelming force must be organized and armed against the common foe. Death seems to have no effect upon this ferocious people. Truly, their warriors, like cats, have several lives.'

'Well said,' concluded Chief Moroka. 'Dismiss the crowd. Supply the Boer with some refreshments. I will take council with my head-men immediately. Let there be rain!' And shouts of *Poolah* followed the remarks.

The people had scarcely begun to disperse when three men came forward through the throng.

Unlike the rest of the crowd massed in the Khotla,[1] these three apparently had not come from their homes as they carried bundles on their shoulders like ordinary travellers. Chief Moroka recognized the leading man and returning his salute said, 'You are Rantsau, son of Thibedi, are you not? A much travelled young man of considerable experience at home and abroad? You understand the language of the Basuto, and of the Qoranna and Hlubis, and the Boers down in Graaf Reinet, don't you, Rantsau? Of course I know you. Have you not learnt to speak the language of the Fish-eaters[2] yet? You must speak Setebele too? I would like to send you as a spy to Inzwinyani before we proceed to attack Mzilikazi. You will go? I know you will when I command you.'

'Well, Rantsau, where have you been to this time? I have not seen you for a long while. Give us your news.'

Rantsau then addressed the chiefs. 'My lord and chiefs, I have no news, except that the Boers who passed through here several moons back have befallen a catastrophe. They have been wiped out by a Matabele, and I am afraid that not one of them has survived to tell the story.'

'But,' said Chief Moroka, 'here is a Boer who says the others are still alive. He left them the day before yesterday.'

'Then,' said Rantsau amid sensation, 'he must have come from another party, not from Sarel Siljay's army. No, my lord.'

'But he is *from* Sarel Siljay's army,' said the chief. 'Sarel himself sent him here to me. Anyway, Rantsau, let us have your version.'

'The three of us were returning from Bopediland near the Vaal River,' proceeded Rantsau. 'When we reached the forest beyond the Namagadi River, we noticed two naked men emerging from the bush and looking in the opposite direction. They withdrew directly they saw us. I should explain, my lord and chiefs, that by this time we were not far from the place where on our forward journey, two moons back, we found Siljay's army encamped. After passing this bush we saw another man spying at us from a tree-top. He scrambled down from the tree directly upon observing that we were looking at him. We then hastened to put as much space as possible between us and that bush.

'Later we came across two Boers whom we warned that the

[1] Assembly place.
[2] English.

Matabele were going to ambush them. Sometime after we heard the sound of many guns some distance off. The guns rattled and never ceased for a long, long time. As a matter of fact I have never heard such a din before. Judging by the incessant noise we came to the conclusion that the Matabele must have been massacred. Later three mounted Boers came into view hurrying forward a large flock of sheep. We climbed a ridge to give the alarm to the Boers, when we saw another mounted Boer galloping towards the three, shouting at the top of his voice, "Mieklass, Mieklass![1] Come back, we are surrounded by the Kafirs! Never mind the sheep, Mieklass, return to the wagons!" At this the Boers left the sheep and rode away very fast. Late in the afternoon, a group of Matabele appeared. They rounded up the sheep and drove them off.

'Reaching the peak of the nearest hill, and looking about we saw huge clouds of dust and numbers of Matabele in the distance driving the herds and the flocks of the Boers and not a sign of the owners anywhere; no, not even the sound of a gun, so we came to the conclusion that the Boers had been surrounded and massacred, like our own people had been years ago at Kunana.'

No one listened more attentively to Rantsau's story than Ra-Thaga. He had always been nursing a bloody revenge in his heart, and the preparations for arming the tribe against the Matabele had been proceeding too slowly for his liking. He desired retribution before he died, and he was fearful lest some natural or unnatural cause should shorten his life before he greeted that glad day. But the news of this latest success of the Matabele against the well-armed Boers conveyed to his mind the staggering impression that this ferocious nation was super-human, and that nothing in this world would ever punish them. Could it be a fact, he asked himself, that there is absolutely not power to exact judgement in return for all the wrongs and cruelties of the past, and for the loss of so many of his relatives who died guiltless deaths at the hands of the Matabele? The idea was revolting. Amid such thoughts Ra-Thaga scarcely heard the Chief Moroka thanking Rantsau for his news, unpleasant as it was.

At sunset the crowd began to collect at the Chief's court to hear the Council's decision on Sarel's message. It was on the night of the full moon, and the powerful rays of the big round aerial ball, mingling with the waning light of the passing day seemed to dispel the settling dusk, and to prolong the twilight; and so it was not at all dark as old men and young men collected and sat down to hear the ominous decision. Many of the men had already taken up their places in the Khotla.

[1] Nicholas.

The chiefs were a long time coming, and little knots of debaters automatically grouped themselves here and there. Soon there was a low but insistent hubbub in the centre of the open-air court, for the discussions, carried on in low tones, were decidedly animated.

Some were for letting the Boers stew in their own juice, as the Barolongs had perforce to do years before; others were for combining with the Boers against the Matabele; some again were for letting the enemy well alone as long as he remained on the far side of the Vaal River – that river of many vicissitudes and grim histories – yet many believed that a scrap with the Matabele with the aid of the Boers would give each one an opportunity of avenging the blood of his relations before he himself joined his forefathers. Such were the conflicting views that found expression among the waiting throng. One grizzly old man with small jaws and very short teeth, touching his shins said : 'Oh, that I could infuse some youth into these old bones and raise my shield ! I would march against the vampires with spear in hand. Then Mzilikazi would know that among the Barolong there was a man named Nakedi – just as the pack of lions at Mafika-Kgocoana knew me to their cost.'

One man raised a laugh among the serious groups. 'What a truthful thing is a proverb,' he said. 'According to an old saying "Lightning fire is quenched by other fire." It seems a good idea then to fight the Matabele with the help of the women, for they always kill women in their attacks. If Sarel Siljay's women had not helped the Boers, they would not have defied Gubuza's army and Schalk would not be here to tell the tale.'

The chiefs arrived almost simultaneously and took their seats without giving any indication of what they had decided to do. There was some little delay after this. Every man bent forward expectant how the question, War, *to be or not to be*, was to be decided. This delay severely taxed the patience of the waiting crowd, but it was unavoidable. One chief, representing a powerful clan, had not yet appeared and an announcement, so momentous, could not be made before his arrival.

Not until Chief Moroka had twice asked, 'Where is Morahti?' did he arrive and take his seat to the right of the presiding chief. Morahti (for that was the name of the late-comer) was not exactly of royal blood. He owed his eminent position to a rather liberal endowment of this world's goods, as the gods are partial in their bestowal of fortune; secondly, his position was due to his marriage to a princess of the first royal house.

Morahti sat down with an air of pomp as though proud of the fact that business did not proceed without him. One of his equals, in sarcastic allusion to the lateness of his appearance, indulged in a little banter at his expense. The object of the squib, turning round to his railer, said 'How unbecoming to your dignity these frivolous remarks are on a serious occasion like this.'

'Quite so,' put in a third chief sitting just two chairs away. 'They are almost as frivolous as the flippancy of my cousin Morahti, who must needs keep the chiefs and people waiting while he stays indoors to watch how gracefully my cousin Neo – the late-comer's wife – puts on her anklets.'

'It must indeed be true,' retorted Chief Morahti, 'in the words of a Barolong proverb, that "kings sometimes beget dross" or else I could not account for a lineal descendant of the great Tau, attributing to me such weakness as that of regulating my actions by Neo's anklets.'

The chief was about to call the assembly to order when, in the waning light of the evening, a horseman was observed riding into the town. He was recognized as another Boer urging along his exhausted and hungry mare by repeatedly striking his heels against her flanks. One chief said, 'I hope that he is not coming to report that the Matabele returned to the attack and killed every Boer.'

'Nor that Gubuza is following hard on his heels,' remarked another.

They were soon set at rest, however, for the new arrival, a young Boer named Phil Jay, came in the wake of Schalk to support his appeal for relief. The Boers, said Phil, were anxious to hear that the chief would come to their rescue before the enemy returned to surround them.

The meeting was then called to order.

Chief Moroka was not as great an orator as most of the Native Chiefs but he excelled in philosophy. In that respect his witty expressions and dry humour were equal to those of Moshueshue, the Basuto King. He spoke in a staccato voice, with short sentences and a stop after each, as though composing the next sentence. His speeches abounded in allegories and proverbial sayings, some traditional and others original. His own maxims had about them the spice of originality which always provided his auditors with much food for thought.

He knew he had no right to join hostilities without the consent of the tribesmen, yet he delivered a speech which, while leaving no doubt as to his personal sympathies, left the main decision in the hands of the assembly. When he called for silence, the stillness was like unto that of a deserted place. The crowd pressed forward and eagerly hung on to every word, but it is to be regretted that much of the charm is lost in translation.

'Men of the Barolong,' he said aloud, 'Listen! Old people say that "the foolish dam suckles her young while lying down; but the wise dam suckles hers standing up and looking out for approaching hunters." This day has brought with it the most appalling news since we pitched our abode on the banks of the Sepane River. For the first time, since we experienced their depredations, the marauders of Mzilikazi have forded the Lekwa.[1] They are now prowling on our side of that deep stream.

'You all remember the visit of Sarel Sil-Jay, the Boer Chief, who called on us last year and inquired the way. You saw his mounted followers and their flowing beards; you saw his women and children in their hooded wagons, like a moving city travelling northward, where they said they were proceeding in search of God. Well, they have found the Matabele instead.

'Crossing the Kikwe and the Kikwane, they forded the Namagadi River, and then camped at a place which we must now call Battlehill. Here they remained in their wheeled houses and peacefully fed their children on the meat of the springbok, the wildebeest and other antelopes of our plains. Then, while the Boers were quietly drying their venison in the sun, Mzilikazi, without a word of warning, sent his big man Gubuza with an army which cast a thousand spears into Sarel's city. A desperate fight must have taken place, for the Boer women left their boiling meat-pots on the fires and stood at the backs of their men to reload their guns as fast as the long-beards could fire them.

'As the result of the fight the attackers were driven off; but Gubuza, on retiring, looted every beast in the possession of our white friends. Now they are anxious to remove their families but have no draft animals left to pull their wagons. These young men have come to tell us that "the ox is found".[2] Now I wish you to know from you whether help shall be forthcoming and, if so, how quickly?

'Personally I think that, if we must perish, it were better to die fighting (for then our women could flee into Basutoland) than to wait until Gubuza's impis are in our very midst.

'Those of you whose mothers and grandmothers have perished at the point of the Matabele assegai must realize the danger to which Sarel's women are exposed if they remain any longer at Battlehill, for "no jackal-skin could possibly be sewn to a Matabele pelt."

'Gubuza, fortunately, has not yet seized my cattle and I have enough bullocks to pull Sarel's own wagon and bring his wife back. Will anyone else's oxen go up with mine, or must we leave the other wives stranded on the plains? What say the Hammersmiths to the

---

[1] Vaal River.
[2] 'There is a state of war.'

Boer appeal? What say' the sons of Mokgopa-a-Mazeppa whose tribal totem is iron? What answer is forthcoming from the descendants of Moroa-Phogole? Will these young Boers return to their parents smiling, or must they go back and say, "the Barolong are afraid; their Chief alone will help us !" What say the sons of Kwena and the offspring of Mhurutshe who venerate the baboon?'

By this time the speech had stirred a feeling in the centre of the crowd. The commotion was made audible by the mention of the several sections of the tribe; and the various clansmen loudly responded : 'We are with thee, O Chief.' 'We will be there at thy command.'

A hurricane of enthusiasm arose from the throng as first one and then another of the men cried, 'My oxen will be ready by daybreak, O Chief.' 'I am going off to fetch mine from the cattle station.' 'Mine are available, they are pasturing just outside the city.' 'No woman brave enough to load a gun to kill the Matabele shall perish while I have a pack-ox.' 'The day will soon be breaking, let us wait no longer.'

The spontaneity of these offers showed that there would be more than enough oxen to go round. So the Chief said : 'I knew that the Barolong were no cowards. Our friends shall know that it is not wrought iron we venerate but that our tribal badge is a hammer made of tempered metal. Let the Boers come here and camp at the foot of the Black Mountain. Here Sarel and I will tarry.'

With the Boers at Moroka's Hoek

During the Boer's sojourns at Thaba Ncho, there sprang up a lively friendship between Phil Jay, a young Boer, and Ra-Thaga. The two were constantly together, at the Boer settlement, at Moroka's Hoek, and at the Barolong Town of Thaba Ncho proper. They made up their minds to learn each other's language, so Phil taught Ra-Thaga how to speak the Taal and Ra-Thaga taught the Boer the Barolong speech. They were both very diligent and persevering, and, having ample opportunities for practice, they both made very good progress. There was one special bond of fellow-feeling between them, namely, their mutual aversion to the Matabele.

Ra-Thaga could never forgive the sacking of Kunana, nor Phil Jay the loss of his cattle and those of his relatives. His Boer pride was repeatedly hurt when he recollected how badly they had been worsted by the wild folk whom his people called 'nude kafirs'. He thought likewise of his particular cow, Driekol, which yielded abundant supplies of milk. When he remembered that enemy children were being fed on the milk of his cows, while his own brothers and sisters lived partly on Barolong charity, the soothing words of his mother could scarcely allay his wrath. Sometimes he would burst out in her presence saying : 'Oh that our cattle were captured by friendly Hottentots, or reasonable Natives such as the Barolong, instead of those wild savages !'

Whenever he confided his grief to Ra-Thaga the effect was only to fan the glowing embers of revenge that were burning in his breast.

Then Ra-Thaga would exclaim : 'Whenever I visit the homes of other men and see the beautiful dishes that their mothers-in-law prepare and send over to them, and find no one near my dwelling to mind the babies when Mhudi goes a-faggoting, I think of her and say : "This faithful child of my mother, so lonely and forlorn, is without help, because without a mother's advice !" Shall I ever forgive the Matabele ! But for them, my mother-in-law would be alive and active. And when I see a sheep-master select the fattest wether in his sheep kraal and proudly send it to his mother-in-law, I grieve and wish that she were alive, for then my cattle-fold would hold no kine, my sheep-pen no fat-tailed mutton and my hunting snares would catch no venison too good for her. The plains would feed no game, the silver jackals grow no furs and no eland falling to my musket would have fore-quarters so fat and tasty but would be all hers.

'Yesterday again I was looking at my poor wife at work, and there was that everlasting gap which only a mother-in-law can fill; and it was poignantly brought home to me that I have married an orphan, and am therefore orphaned also.'

At times they fell into a discussion and schemed and plotted for means of avenging these wrongs. If their secret maledictions did not affect the Matabele far away, they always seemed to increase their liking for each other.

By this time Ra-Thaga's admiration for the Boers embraced not only Phil Jay's family, but other members of the Boer settlement. Almost every time he went up to the Hoek he returned to his house with tales of fresh virtues he had discovered among the Boers. Their unerring shooting, their splendid horsemanship, the dexterity of Boer women with the needle; the beautiful aroma of the food they cooked (possibly due to the fact that their iron pots were always systematically scrubbed and cleaned), and the lustre of their eating utensils.

Ra-Thaga's intense love of the Boers, however, was not shared by his wife, for Mhudi could not understand why they were so hairy, and why they were so pale. But her husband always said : 'Wait until you taste the beautiful food they cook, and you will fall head over heels in love with them all.' She wished she could believe her husband, but somehow she could not master an inexplicable dread that lingered in her mind.

One day Ra-Thaga induced her to accompany him to the Boer settlement at the Hoek. He succeeded in getting Phil Jay to speak to his wife the few Rolong words he had taught him in exchange for his own Boer vocabulary. This had a reassuring effect on Mhudi who met at least one Boer who could talk her language. Phil and her husband visited other parts of the Boer camp and left her with Phil's mother, but they could not understand each other's language. The Boer lady gave her some cookies which were exceedingly tasty, and she made a parcel of them to take to her children; she began to reflect that after all her husband had not exaggerated the virtues of the Boers. It was fortunate for these feelings that she could not understand their language, for some of the Boers who eyed her curiously, exchanged among themselves several remarks about her that were not too complimentary. Phil and Ra-Thaga were away rather long, and Mhudi, as her husband had predicted, began to 'fall in love with every Boer'. How wrong she had been in her first dislike of her husband's friends! She already began to reproach herself for having doubted the wisdom of her resourceful husband, when something occurred that shook to its foundations her newly found faith in the character of the Boers.

Outside one of the huts close by she observed a grizzly old Boer who started to give a Hottentot maid some thunder and lightning with his tongue. Of course Mhudi could not understand a word; but the harangue sounded positively terrible and its effect upon the maid was unmistakable. She felt that the Hottentot's position was unenviable, but more was to come. An old lady sitting near a fire behind the wagon took sides against the maid. The episode which began rather humorously developed quickly into a tragedy. The old lady pulled a poker out of the fire and beat the half naked girl with the hot iron. The unfortunate maid screamed, jumped away and writhed with the pain as she tried to escape. A stalwart young Boer caught hold of the screaming girl and brought her back to the old dame, who had now left the fireplace and stood beside a vice near the wagon. The young man pressed the head of the Hottentot girl against the vice; the old lady pulled her left ear between the two irons, then screwed the jaws of the vice tightly upon the poor girl's ear. Mhudi looked at Phil's mother, but, so far from showing any concern on behalf of the sufferer, she went about her own domestic business as though nothing at all unusual was taking place. The screams of the girl attracted several Dutch men and women who looked as though they enjoyed the sickly sight.

Mhudi's first impulse was to rush to the rescue, but, suddenly, remembering that every Boer had a gun, she feared that such cruel people might as easily riddle her with a score of bullets, for she was revolted by their callous indifference to the anguish of the unfortunate girl.

At last Ra-Thaga and Phil came back and Mhudi appealed to her husband to help the girl. Ra-Thaga explained to Phil, and the latter immediately went up to unscrew the vice and the grateful maid, still screaming very loudly, fell at his feet and thanked him.

Mhudi, whose love for the Boers was thus shattered as quickly as it had been formed, retained a strong confidence in the sagacity of her husband who apparently had the sense to make friends with the one humane Boer that there was among the wild men of his tribe. And when they left, she shook the dust of Moroka's Hoek off her feet and vowed never to go there again.

That night Ra-Thaga could scarcely go to sleep. Mhudi pestered him with questions about the Boers and her interrogations continued almost to the small hours of the morning. 'What sort of people are these friends of yours?' she would ask. 'Have not the Boers got a saying like ours : *a e ne modiga?*'[1]

Queen Umnandi's Flight

Hardly knowing where he was going Umpitimpiti walked through the courtyard into the open space where the assemblies were held and cases were tried. There he found himself in the midst of a large crowd of men. Two of them cowering in front of the King, were closely guarded by four stalwart young soldiers. Umpitimpiti pressed his way into the thick of the crowd until he could hear what was being said. He understood that one was a doctor, who, on being commanded to divine the whereabouts of Umnandi, had prophesied something which proved hopelessly inaccurate. The second man was Dlhadhlu who had failed to report the disappearance of his missing Rolong maid; he was shaking with fear like a reed at the mercy of the wind. Umpitimpiti also trembled when he remembered how hopelessly implicated he himself was in the same case; presently he heard the angry King raise an imperious voice, saying, 'Their ears have heard my anxious inquiries but paid no heed to them. Cut off their ears!' This order was promptly obeyed by the four warders in charge of the unfortunate men.

'Their feet walked out of my way so that useful information might not reach me until too late,' proceeded King Mzilikazi. 'Chop off their feet!'

---

[1] A plea on behalf of someone who is chastised.

'Their tongues lied to me in my distress. Cut our their tongues !'
'Their eyes have seen the cause of my anguish. Pluck out their
eyes !'
All these drastic commands were obeyed as soon as they were
uttered, for any hesitation on the part of an unwilling attendant
might have increased by one the number of victims.

Efua Theodora Sutherland

NEW LIFE AT KYEREFASO

Shall we say
Shall we put it this way
Shall we say that the maid of Kyerefaso, Foruwa, daughter of the
Queen Mother, was as a young deer, graceful in limb? Such was she,
with head held high, eyes soft and wide with wonder. And she was
light of foot, light in all her moving.
Stepping springily along the water path like a deer that had
strayed from the thicket, springily stepping along the water path,
she was a picture to give the eye a feast. And nobody passed her
by but turned to look at her again.
Those of her village said that her voice in speech was like the
murmur of a river quietly flowing beneath shadows of bamboo leaves.
They said her smile would sometimes blossom like a lily on her lips
and sometimes rise like sunrise.
The butterflies do not fly away from the flowers, they draw near.
Foruwa was the flower of her village.
So shall we say,
Shall we put it this way, that all the village butterflies, the men,
tried to draw near her at every turn, crossed and crossed her path?
Men said of her, 'She shall be my wife, and mine, and mine and
mine.'
But suns rose and set, moons silvered and died and as the days
passed Foruwa grew more lovesome, yet she became no one's wife.
She smiled at the butterflies and waved her hand lightly to greet
them as she went swiftly about her daily work :

'Morning, Kweku
Morning, Kwesi
Morning, Kodwo'
but that was all.
And so they said, even while their hearts thumped for her :
'Proud!
Foruwa is proud . . . and very strange'
And so the men when they gathered would say :
'There goes a strange girl. She is not just stiff-in-the-neck proud, not just breasts-stuck-out I-am-the-only-girl-in-the-village proud. What kind of pride is hers?'

The end of the year came round again, bringing the season of festivals. For the gathering in of corn, yams and cocoa there were harvest celebrations. There were bride-meetings too. And it came to the time when the Asafo companies should hold their festival. The village was full of manly sounds, loud musketry and swelling choruses.

The pathfinding, path-clearing ceremony came to an end. The Asafo marched on towards the Queen Mother's house, the women fussing round them, prancing round them, spreading their cloths in their way.

'Osee!' rang the cry. 'Osee!' to the manly men of old. They crouched like leopards upon the branches.
Before the drums beat
Before the danger drums beat, beware!
Before the horns moaned
Before the wailing horns moaned, beware!

They were upright, they sprang. They sprang. They sprang upon the enemy. But now, blood no more! No more thundershot on thundershot.

But still we are the leopards on the branches. We are those who roar and cannot be answered back. Beware, we are they who cannot be answered back.

There was excitement outside the Queen Mother's courtyard gate.
'Gently, gently,' warned the Asafo leader. 'Here comes the Queen Mother.
Spread skins of the gentle sheep in her way.
Lightly, lightly walks our Mother Queen.
Shower her with silver,
Shower her with silver for she is peace.'

And the Queen Mother stood there, tall, beautiful, before the men and there was silence.
'What news, what news do you bring?' she quietly asked.
'We come with dusty brows from our pathfinding, Mother. We

come with tired, thorn-pricked feet. We come to bathe in the coolness of your peaceful stream. We come to offer our manliness to new
life.'

The Queen Mother stood there, tall and beautiful and quiet.
Her fanbearers stood by her and all the women clustered near. One
by one the men laid their guns at her feet and then she said :

'It is well. The gun is laid aside. The gun's rage is silenced in the
stream. Let your weapons from now on be your minds and your
hands' toil.

'Come maidens, women all, join the men in dance for they offer
themselves to new life.'

There was one girl who did not dance.

'What, Foruwa!' urged the Queen Mother, 'Will you not dance?
The men are tired of parading in the ashes of their grandfathers'
glorious deeds. That should make you smile. They are tired of the
empty croak : "We are men, we are men."

'They are tired of sitting like vultures upon the rubbish heaps
they have piled upon the half-built walls of their grandfathers. Smile
then, Foruwa, smile.

'Their brows shall now indeed be dusty, their feet thorn-picked,
and "I love my land" shall cease to be the empty croaking of a
vulture upon the rubbish heap. Dance, Foruwa, dance!'

Foruwa opened her lips and this was all she said : 'Mother, I do
not find him here.'

'Who? Who do you not find here?'

'He with whom this new life shall be built. He is not here, Mother.
These men's faces are empty; there is nothing in them, nothing at
all.'

'Alas, Foruwa, alas, alas! What will become of you, my
daughter?'

'The day I find him, Mother, the day I find the man, I shall
come running to you, and your worries will come to an end.'

But, Foruwa, Foruwa,' argued the Queen Mother, although in
her heart she understood her daughter, 'five years ago your rites
were fulfilled. Where is the child of your womb? Your friend
Maanan married. Your friend Esi married. Both had their rites
with you.'

'Yes, Mother, they married and see how their steps once lively
now drag in the dust. The sparkle has died out of their eyes. Their
husbands drink palm wine the day long under the mango trees,
drink palm wine and push counters across the draughtboards all
the day, and are they not already looking for other wives? Mother,
the man I say is not here.'

This conversation had been overheard by one of the men and soon others heard what Foruwa had said. That evening there was heard a new song in the village.

'There was a woman long ago,
Tell that maid, tell that maid,
There was a woman long ago,
She would not marry Kwesi,
She would not marry Kwaw,
She would not, would not, would not.
One day she came home with hurrying feet,
I've found the man, the man, the man,
Tell that maid, tell that maid,
Her man looked like a chief,
Tell that maid, tell that maid,
Her man looked like a chief,
Most splendid to see,
But he turned into a python,
He turned into a python
And swallowed her up.'

From that time onward there were some in the village who turned their backs on Foruwa when she passed.

Shall we say
Shall we put it this way
Shall we say that a day came when Foruwa with hurrying feet came running to her mother? She burst through the courtyard gate; and there she stood in the courtyard, joy all over. And a stranger walked in after her and stood in the courtyard beside her, stood tall and strong as a pillar. Foruwa said to the astonished Queen Mother :

'Here he is, Mother, here is the man.'

The Queen Mother took a slow look at the stranger standing there strong as a forest tree, and she said :

'You carry the light of wisdom on your face, my son. Greetings, you are welcome. But who are you, my son?'

'Greetings Mother,' replied the stranger quietly, 'I am a worker. My hands are all I have to offer your daughter, for they are all my riches. I have travelled to see how men work in other lands. I have that knowledge and my strength. That is all my story.'

Shall we say,
Shall we put it this way,
strange as the story is, that Foruwa was given in marriage to the stranger?

There was a rage in the village and many openly mocked saying, 'Now the proud ones eat the dust.'

Yet shall we say,
Shall we put it this way
that soon, quite soon, the people of Kyerefaso began to take notice
of the stranger in quite a different way.

'Who,' some said, 'is this who has come among us? He who
mingles sweat and song, he for whom toil is joy and life is full and
abundant?'

'See,' said others, 'what a harvest the land yields under his cease-
less care.'

'He has taken the earth and molded it into bricks. See what a home
he has built, how it graces the village where it stands.'

'Look at the craft of his fingers, baskets of kente, stool or mat,
the man makes them all.'

'And our children swarm about him, gazing at him with wonder
and delight.'

Then it did not satisfy them any more to sit all day at their
draughtboards under the mango trees.

'See what Foruwa's husband has done,' they declared; 'shall the
sons of the land not do the same?'

And soon they began to seek out the stranger to talk with him.
Soon they too were toiling, their fields began to yield as never before,
and the women laboured joyfully to bring in the harvest. A new spirit
stirred the village. As the carelessly built houses disappeared one by
one, and new homes built after the fashion of the stranger's grew up,
it seemed as if the village of Kyerefaso had been born afresh.

The people themselves became more alive and a new pride
possessed them. They were no longer just grabbing from the land
what they desired for their stomachs' present hunger and for their
present comfort. They were looking at the land with new eyes, feeling
in it their blood, and thoughtfully building a permanent and beautiful place for themselves and their children.

'Osee!' It was festival-time again. 'Osee!' Blood no more. Our
fathers found for us the paths. We are the roadmakers. They bought
for us the land with their blood. We shall build it with our strength.
We shall create it with our minds.

Following the men were the women and children. On their heads
they carried every kind of produce that the land had yielded and
crafts that their fingers had created. Green plantains and yellow
bananas were carried by the bunch in large white wooden trays.
Garden eggs, tomatoes, red oil-palm nuts warmed by the sun were
piled high in black earthen vessels. Oranges, yams, maize filled shining brass trays and golden calabashes. Here and there were children
proudly carrying colourful mats, baskets and toys which they themselves had made.

The Queen Mother watched the procession gathering on the new village playground now richly green from recent rains. She watched the people palpitating in a massive dance towards her where she stood with her fanbearers outside the royal house. She caught sight of Foruwa. Her load of charcoal in a large brass tray which she had adorned with red hibiscus danced with her body. Happiness filled the Queen Mother when she saw her daughter thus.

Then she caught sight of Foruwa's husband. He was carrying a white lamb in his arms, and he was singing happily with the men. She looked on him with pride. The procession had approached the royal house.

'See!' rang the cry of the Asafo leader. 'See how the best in all the land stands. See how she stands waiting, our Queen Mother. Waiting to wash the dust from our brow in the coolness of her peaceful stream. Spread skins of the gentle sheep in her way, gently, gently. Spread the yield of the land before her. Spread the craft of your hands before her, gently, gently.

'Lightly, lightly walks our Queen Mother, for she is peace.'

Amos Tutuola

from THE PALM-WINE DRINKARD

On the Way to an Unknown Place

The same day that the father of my wife told me the place that my tapster was, I told my wife to pack all our belongings and she did so, then we woke up early in the morning and started to travel to an unknown place, but when we had travelled about two miles away to that town which we left, my wife said that she forgot her gold trinket inside the house which I had burnt into ashes, she said that she had forgotten to take it away before the house was burnt into ashes. She said that she would go back and take it, but I told her that it would burn into ashes together with the house. She said that it was a metal and it could not burn into ashes and she said that she was going back to take it, and I begged her not to go back, but she refused totally, so when I saw her going back to take it, then I followed her. When we reached there, she picked a stick and began to scratch the ashes with it, and there I saw that the middle of the ashes rose up suddenly and at the same time there appeared a half-bodied baby, he was talking with a lower voice like a telephone.

At the same time that we saw the ashes rise up and change into half-bodied baby, and he was also talking with a lower voice, then we started to go. Then he was telling my wife to take him along with us, to wait and take him, but as we did not stop and take him with us, he then commanded that our eyes should be blinded and we became blinded at the same moment as he said it; still we did not come back and take him, but we were going on, when he saw that we did not come back and take him, he commanded again that we should stop breathing, truly speaking we could not breathe. When we could not breathe in or out, we came back and took him along with us. As we were going on the road, he told my wife to carry him by head, and as he was on my wife's head, he was whistling as if he was forty persons. When we reached a village we stopped and bought food from a food-seller to eat as we were very hungry before reaching there, but when we were about to eat the food, the half-bodied baby did not allow us to eat it, instead of that he took the food and swallowed it as a man swallows a pill, so when the food-seller saw him do so, she ran away and left her food there, but when our half-bodied baby saw that the food-seller had left her food, he crept to the food and swallowed it as well.

So this half-bodied baby did not allow us to eat the food, and we did not taste it at all. When the people of that village saw the half-bodied baby with us, they drove us away from the village. Then we started our journey again and when we had travelled about seven miles away from that village, there we reached another town; we stopped there also, and we bought other food there, but this half-bodied baby did not allow us to eat that again. But by that time we were annoyed and we wanted to eat it by force, but he commanded as before and at the same time we became as he commanded, then we left him to swallow it.

When the people of that town saw him there with us again, they drove us away with juju and they said that we were carrying a spirit about and they said that they did not want a spirit in their town. So if we entered any town or village to eat or sleep, they would drive us away at once and our news had been carried to all towns and villages. Now we could not travel the roads unless from bush to bush, because everybody had heard the information that a man and a woman were carrying a half-bodied baby or spirit about and they were looking for a place to put him and run away.

So by this time we were very hungry and then when we were travelling inside the bush, we tried all our efforts to put him down

somewhere and run, away, but he did not allow us to do that. After
we had failed to put him down, we thought that he would sleep
at night, but he did not sleep at night at all, and the worst part of it,
he did not let my wife put him down once since she had put him
on her head; we were longing to sleep heavily, but he did not allow
us to do anything except carry him along. All the time that he was
on my wife's head, his belly swelled out like a very large tube, because he had eaten too much food and yet he did not satisfy at any
time for he could eat the whole food in this world without satisfaction. As we were travelling about in the bush on that night, my
wife was feeling overloading of this baby and if we put him on a
scale by that time, he would weight at least 28 lbs; when I saw
that my wife had tired of carrying him and she could not carry
him any longer, then I took over to carry him along, but before I
could carry him to a distance of about one quarter of a mile. I
was unable to move again and I was sweating as if I bath in water
for overloading, yet this half-bodied baby did not allow us to put
him down and rest.

Ah! how could we escape from this half-bodied baby? But God
is so good and as we were carrying him to and fro in the bush on
that night, we heard as if they were playing music somewhere in
that bush and he told us to carry him to the place that we were
hearing the music. Before an hour had passed we reached there.

Three Good Creatures Took Over Our Trouble – They Were – Drum, Song and Dance

When we carried him to the place, there we saw the creatures that
we called 'Drum, Song and Dance' personally and these three
creatures were living creatures as ours. At the same time that we
reached there the half-bodied baby came down from my head, then
we thanked God. But as he came down from my head he joined the
three creatures at once. When 'Drum' started to beat himself it was
just as if he was beaten by fifty men, when 'Song' started to sing,
it was just as if a hundred people were singing together and when
'Dance' started to dance the half-bodied baby started too, my wife,
myself and spirits etc., were dancing with 'Dance' and nobody who
heard or saw these three fellows would not follow them to wherever
they were going. Then the whole of us were following the three fellows and dancing along with them. So we followed the three fellows
and were dancing for a good five days without eating or stopping
once, before we reached a place which was built in the form of a
premises by these creatures with mud.

There were two soldiers stood at the front of the premises, but when we reached there with these three fellows, my wife and myself etc., stopped at the entrance of the premises, only the three fellows and our half-bodied baby entered the premises, after that, we, saw them no more. N.B. We did not want to follow them up to that place, but we could not control ourselves as we were dancing along with them.

So nobody in this world could beat drum as Drum himself could beat, nobody could dance as Dance himself could dance and nobody could sing as Song himself could sing. We left these three wonderful creatures by two o'clock in the mid-night. Then after we had left these creatures and our half-bodied baby, we started a fresh journey, but we travelled for two days before we reached a town and stopped there and rested for two days. But we were penniless before reaching there, then I thought within myself how could we get money for our food etc. After a while I remembered my name which was 'Father of gods who could do anything in this world'. As there was a large river which crossed the main road to that town, then I told my wife to follow me to the river; when reaching there, I cut a tree and carved it into a paddle, then I gave it to my wife and I told her to enter the river with me; when we entered the river, I commanded one juju which was given me by a kind spirit who was a friend of mine and at once the juju changed me to a big canoe. Then my wife went inside the canoe with the paddle and paddling it, she used the canoe as 'ferry' to carry passengers across the river, the fare for adults was 3d. (three pence) and half fare for children. In the evening time, then I changed to a man as before and when we checked the money that my wife had collected for that day, it was £7 5s. 3d. After that we went back to the town, we bought all our needs.

Next morning we went there by 4 o'clock as well before the people of that town woke up, so that they might not know the secret and when we reached there, I did as I did yesterday and my wife continued her work as usual, on that day we came back to home by 7 o'clock in the evening. So we stayed in that town for one month and doing the same work throughout that month, when we checked the money that we collected for that month, it was £56 11s. 9d.

Then we left that town with gladness, we started our journey again, but after we had travelled about eighty miles away to that town, then we began to meet gangs of the 'highway-men' on the road, and they were troubling us too much. But when I thought over that the danger of the road might result to the loss of our money or both money and our lives, then we entered into bush, but to travel in this bush was very dangerous too, because of the wild animals, and the boa constrictors were uncountable as sand.

John Pepper Clark

from SONG OF A GOAT

Final Movement

ZIFA : Do not run, oh do not run away you
People. I said the wretch has gone and
Hanged himself on the loft. But it is I
Indeed have killed the boy – my brother,
Poor, poor brother, do you hang aloft
There smiling in my face? I sought to kill
You but in that office you have again
Performed my part.
You veer away from me, why should you
Not avoid me as one with small-pox when
I have taken my brother's life? For though
You see me bloodless it is this arm
Did this deed and this cutlass you see dry
Is flowing even now with the red blood
Of my brother, the brother, the boy born after me
To look after but who now has twice taught me
My duty. Here I break my matchet upon
My head and may everything fly apart
Even as I throw these iron bits asunder.
The poor, brave boy has truly done for me.
Good people, I hope you understand. It
Is not that I desired to drink out
Of his scalp which is unnatural, but that boy,
He went in to my wife, my wife who
Although under my roof for five years
I could not possess, for you see
I am powerless between my thighs. Was
That not a brotherly act? He sought to keep
What his brother was powerless to keep
In the house. My house, it has collapsed
In season that is calm to others. My fathers
Built it before my time that my children
And theirs to come may find a roof above
Their heads. And now what have I done

254

With it? In my hands it falls into a state
Of disrepair and now is fallen,
Fallen. Nothing stands; I will go
And find a new place of rest.

3RD NEIGHBOUR : Where is the man going has brought this ruin
On his head?

2ND NEIGHBOUR : There follow him quick,
He is making for the beach as one in sleep.

1ST NEIGHBOUR : And what is to happen to this poor woman
Now a bundle of rags on the ground?

ORUKORERE : Let me be, oh, do not try to lift me
Up but let me lie in the ruins they have
Wrought between them.

2ND NEIGHBOUR : Let us follow the man.

1ST NEIGHBOUR : Shut the door, keep it shut. There comes his son.

3RD NEIGHBOUR : Indeed, that is no sight for women or
Children to see.

DODE : Mother, where is Ebiere?
I heard my father's voice – who is he
Angry with? Not with Tonye or Ebiere?

ORUKORERE : Cast your catch aside there and come over
Here and sit between my knees.

DODE : I'll put them in first. Isn't there a lamp
In this house?

ORUKORERE : There will never be light again in this
House, child, this is the night of our race,
The fall of all that ever reared up head
Or crest.

DODE : Mother, what are you saying?

ORUKORERE : How should I know, son? I looked for a staff
Long enough to kill a serpent I knew
Was strangling my goat. In my search is my defeat.

Wole Soyinka

from THE LION AND THE JEWEL

Morning

A clearing on the edge of the market, dominated by an immense 'odan' tree. It is the village centre. The wall of the bush school flanks the stage on the right, and a rude window opens on to the stage from the wall. There is a chant of the 'Arithmetic Times' issuing from this window. It begins a short while before the action begins. Sidi enters from left, carrying a small pail of water on her head. She is a slim girl with plaited hair. A true village belle. She balances the pail on her head with accustomed ease. Around her is wrapped the familiar broad cloth which is folded just above her breasts, leaving the shoulders bare.

Almost as soon as she appears on the stage, the schoolmaster's face also appears at the window. (The chanting continues – 'Three times two are six', 'Three times three are nine', etc.) The teacher Lakunle, disappears. He is replaced by two of his pupils, aged roughly eleven, who make a buzzing noise at Sidi, repeatedly clapping their hands across the mouth. Lakunle now re-appears below the window and makes for Sidi, stopping only to give the boys admonitory whacks on the head before they can duck. They vanish with a howl and he shuts the window on them. The chanting dies away. The schoolmaster is nearly twenty-three. He is dressed in an old-style English suit, threadbare but not ragged, clean but not ironed, obviously a size or two too small. His tie is done in a very small knot, disappearing beneath a shiny black waist-coat. He wears twenty-three-inch-bottom trousers, and blanco-white tennis shoes.

LAKUNLE : Let me take it.

SIDI : No.

LAKUNLE : Let me. (*Seizes the pail. Some water spills on him.*)

SIDI : (*delighted.*)
          There. Wet for your pains.
          Have you no shame?

LAKUNLE : That is what the stewpot said to the fire.
Have you no shame – at your age
Licking my bottom? But she was tickled
Just the same.

SIDI : The schoolteacher is full of stories
This morning. And now, if the lesson
Is over, may I have the pail?

LAKUNLE : No. I have told you not to carry loads
On your head. But you are as stubborn
As an illiterate goat. It is bad for the spine.
And it shortens your neck, so that very soon
You will have no neck at all. Do you wish to look
Squashed like my pupils' drawings?

SIDI : Why should that worry me? Haven't you sworn
That my looks do not affect your love?
Yesterday, dragging your knees in the dust
You said, Sidi, if you were crooked or fat,
And your skin was scaly like a. . . .

LAKUNLE : Stop!

SIDI : I only repeat what you said.

LAKUNLE : Yes, and I will stand by every word I spoke.
But must you throw away your neck on that account?
Sidi, it is so unwomanly. Only spiders
Carry loads the way you do.

SIDI : (*huffily, exposing the neck to advantage.*)
Well, it is my neck, not your spider.

LAKUNLE : (*looks, and gets suddenly agitated.*)
And look at that! Look, look at that!
(*Makes a general sweep in the direction of her breasts.*)
Who was it talked of shame just now?
How often must I tell you, Sidi, that
A grown-up girl must cover up her. . . .
Her . . . shoulders? I can see quite . . . quite
A good portion of – that! And so I imagine
Can every man in the village. Idlers
All of them, good-for-nothing shameless men
Casting their lustful eyes where
They have no business. . . .

SIDI : Are you at that again? Why, I've done the fold
So high and so tight, I can hardly breathe.
And all because you keep at me so much.
I have to leave my arms so I can use them. . . .
Or don't you know that?

I

LAKUNLE : You could wear something.
   Most modest women do. But you, no.
   You must run about naked in the streets.
   Does it not worry you . . . the bad names,
   The lewd jokes, the tongue-licking noises
   Which girls, uncovered like you,
   Draw after them?
SIDI : This is too much. Is it you, Lakunle,
   Telling me that I make myself common talk?
   When the whole world knows of the madman
   of Ilujinle, who calls himself a teacher!
   Is it Sidi who makes the men choke
   In their cups, or you, with your big loud words
   And no meaning? You and your ragged books
   Dragging your feet to every threshold
   And rushing them out again as curses
   Greet you instead of welcome. Is it Sidi
   They call a fool – even the children –
   Or you with your fine airs and little sense!
LAKUNLE : (*first indignant, then recovers composure.*)
   For that, what is a jewel to pigs?
   If now I am misunderstood by you
   And your race of savages, I rise above taunts
   And remain unruffled.
SIDI : (*furious, shakes both fists at him.*)
   O . . . oh, you make me want to pulp your brain.
LAKUNLE : (*retreats a little, but puts her aside with a very lofty
   gesture.*)
   A natural feeling, arising out of envy;
   For, as a woman, you have a smaller brain
   Than mine.
SIDI : (*madder still.*)
   Again! I'd like to know
   Just what gives you these thoughts
   Of manly conceit.
LAKUNLE : (*very very, patronizing.*)
   No, no. I have fallen for that trick before.
   You can no longer draw me into arguments
   Which go above your head.
SIDI : (*can't find the right words, chokes back.*)
   Give me the pail now. And if you ever dare
   To stop me in the streets again. . . .
LAKUNLE : Now, now, Sidi. . . .
SIDI : Give it or I'll. . . .

LAKUNLE : (*holds on to her.*)
    Please, don't be angry with me.
    I didn't mean you in particular.
    And anyway, it isn't what I say.
    The scientists have proved it. It's in my books.
    Women have a smaller brain than men
    That's why they are called the weaker sex.

SIDI : (*throws him off.*)
    The weaker sex, is it?
    Is it a weaker breed who pounds the yam
    Or bends all day to plant the millet
    With a child strapped to her back?

LAKUNLE : That is all part of what I say.
    But don't you worry. In a year or two
    You will have machines which will do
    Your pounding, which will grind your pepper
    Without it getting in your eyes.

SIDI : O-oh. You really mean to turn
    The whole world upside down.

LAKUNLE : The world? Oh, that. Well, maybe later.
    Charity, they say, begins at home.
    For now, it is this village I shall turn
    Inside out. Beginning with that crafty rogue,
    Your past master of self-indulgence – Baroka.

SIDI : Are you still on about the Bale?
    What has he done to you?

LAKUNLE : He'll find out. Soon enough, I'll let him know.

SIDI : These thoughts of future wonders – do you buy them
    Or merely go mad and dream of them?

LAKUNLE : A prophet has honour except
    In his own home. Wise men have been called mad
    Before me and after, many more shall be
    So abused. But to answer you, the measure
    Is not entirely of my own coinage.
    What I boast is known in Lagos, that city
    Of magic, in Badagry where Saro women bathe
    In gold, even in smaller towns less than
    Twelve miles from here. . . .

SIDI : Well go there. Go to these places where
    Women would understand you
    If you told them of your plans with which
    You oppress me daily. Do you not know
    What name they give you here?

Have you lost shame completely that jeers
Pass you over.

LAKUNLE : No. I have told you no. Shame belongs
Only to the ignorant.

SIDI : Well, I am going.
Shall I take the pail or not?

LAKUNLE : Not till you swear to marry me.
(*Takes her hand, instantly soulful.*)
Sidi, a man must prepare to fight alone.
But it helps if he has a woman
To stand by him, a woman who . . .
Can understand . . . like you.

SIDI : I do?

LAKUNLE : Sidi, my love will open your mind
Like the chaste leaf in the morning, when
The sun first touches it.

SIDI : If you start that I will run away.
I had enough of that nonsense yesterday.

LAKUNLE : Nonsense? Nonsense? Do you hear?
Does anybody listen? Can the stones
Bear to listen to this? Do you call it
Nonsense that I poured the waters of my soul
To wash your feet?

SIDI : You did what?

LAKUNLE : Wasted! Wasted! Sidi, my heart
Bursts into flowers with my love.
But you, you and the dead of this village
Trample it with feet of ignorance.

SIDI : (*shakes her head in bafflement.*)
If the snail finds splinters in his shell
He changes house. Why do you stay?

LAKUNLE : Faith. Because I have faith.
Oh Sidi, vow to me your own undying love
And I will scorn the jibes of these bush minds
Who know no better. Swear, Sidi,
Swear you will be my wife and I will
Stand against earth, heaven, and the nine
Hells. . . .

SIDI : Now there you go again.
One little thing
And you must chirrup like a cockatoo.
You talk and talk and deafen me
With words which always sound the same
And make no meaning.

I've told you, and I say it again
I shall marry you today, next week
Or any day you name.
But my bride-price must first be paid.
Aha, now you turn away.
But I tell you, Lakunle, I must have
The full bride-price. Will you make me
A laughing-stock? Well, do as you please.
But Sidi will not make herself
A cheap bowl for the village spit.

LAKUNLE : On my head let fall their scorn.

SIDI : They will say I was no virgin
That I was forced to sell my shame
And marry you without a price.

LAKUNLE : A savage custom, barbaric, out-dated,
Rejected, denounced, accursed,
Excommunicated, archaic, degrading,
Humiliating, unspeakable, redundant.
Retrogressive, remarkable, unpalatable.

SIDI : Is the bag empty? Why did you stop?

LAKUNLE : I own only the Shorter Companion
Dictionary, but I have ordered
The Longer One – you wait!

SIDI : Just pay the price.

LAKUNLE : (*with a sudden shout.*)
An ignoble custom, infamous, ignominious
Shaming our heritage before the world.
Sidi, I do not seek a wife
To fetch and carry,
To cook and scrub,
To bring forth children by the gross. . . .

SIDI : Heaven forgive you! Do you now scorn
Child-bearing in a wife?

LAKUNLE : Of course I do not. I only mean. . .
Oh, Sidi, I want to wed
Because I love,
I seek a life-companion. . . .
(*pulpit-declamatory.*)
'And the man shall take the woman
And the two shall be together
As one flesh.'
Sidi, I seek a friend in need.
An equal partner in my race of life.

SIDI : (*attentive no more. Deeply engrossed in counting the beads on her neck.*)
Then pay the price.

LAKUNLE : Ignorant girl, can you not understand?
To pay the price would be
To buy a heifer off the market stall.
You'd be my chattel, my mere property.
No, Sidi ! (*very tenderly.*)
When we are wed, you shall not walk or sit
Tethered, as it were, to my dirtied heels.
Together we shall sit at table
– Not on the floor – and eat,
Not with fingers, but with knives
And forks, and breakable plates
Like civilized beings.
I will not have you wait on me
Till I have dined my fill.
No wife of mine, no lawful wedded wife
Shall eat the leavings off my plate –
That is for the children.
I want to walk beside you in the street,
Side by side and arm in arm
Just like the Lagos couples I have seen
High-heeled shoes for the lady, red paint
On her lips. And her hair is stretched
Like a magazine photo. I will teach you
The waltz and we'll both learn the foxtrot
And we'll spend the week-end in night-clubs at Ibadan.
Oh I must show you the grandeur of towns
We'll live there if you like or merely pay visits.
So choose. Be a modern wife, look me in the eye
And give me a little kiss – like this.
(*Kisses her.*)

SIDI : (*backs away.*)
No, don't ! I tell you I dislike
This strange unhealthy mouthing you perform.
Every time, your action deceives me
Making me think that you merely wish
To whisper something in my ear.
Then comes this licking of my lips with yours.
It's so unclean. And then,
The sound you make – 'Pyout !'
Are you being rude to me?

LAKUNLE : (*wearily*.) It's never any use.
    Bush-girl you are, bush-girl you'll always be;
    Uncivilized and primitive – bush-girl!
    I kissed you as all educated men –
    And Christians – kiss their wives.
    It is the way of civilized romance.
SIDI : (*lightly*.) A way you mean, to avoid
    Payment of lawful bride-price
    A cheating way, mean and miserly.
LAKUNLE : (*violently*.) It is not.

George Awoonor-Williams

THE SEA EATS THE LAND AT HOME

At home the sea is in the town,
Running in and out of the cooking places,
Collecting the firewood from the hearths
And sending it back at night;
The sea eats the land at home.
It came one day at the dead of night,
Destroying the cement walls,
And carried away the fowls,
The cooking-pots and the ladles,
The sea eats the land at home;
It is a sad thing to hear the wails,
And the mourning shouts of the women,
Calling on all the gods they worship,
To protect them from the angry sea.
Aku stood outside where her cooking-pot stood,
With her two children shivering from the cold,
Her hands on her breast,
Weeping mournfully.
Her ancestors have neglected her,
Her gods have deserted her,
It was a cold Sunday morning,
The storm was raging,
Goats and fowls were struggling in the water,
The angry water of the cruel sea;
The lap-lapping of the bark water at the shore,
And above the sobs and the deep and low moans
Was the eternal hum of the living sea.
It has taken away their belongings,
Adena has lost the trinkets which
Were her dowry and her joy
In the sea that eats the land at home,
Eats the whole land at home.

WE HAVE FOUND A NEW LAND

The smart professionals in three piece
Sweating away their humanity in dribblets
And wiping the blood from their brow
    We have found a new land
    This side of eternity
    Where our blackness does not matter
    And our songs are dying on our lips.
Standing at hellgate you watch those who seek admission
Still familiar faces that watched and gave you up
As the one who had let the side down
'Come on, old boy, you cannot dress like that'
And tears well in my eyes for them
These who want to be seen in the best company
Have adjured the magic of being themselves
And in the new land we have found
The water is drying from the towel
Our songs are dead and we sell them dead to the other side
Reaching for the Stars we stop at the house of Moon
And pause to relearn the wisdom of our fathers.

Kwesi Brew

THE SEARCH

    The past
    Is but the cinders
    Of the present;
    The future
    The smoke
    That escaped
    Into the cloud-bound sky.

Be gentle, be kind my beloved
For words become memories,
And memories tools
In the hands of jesters.
When wise men become silent,
It is because they have read
The palms of Christ
In the face of the Buddha.

So look not for wisdom
And guidance
In their speech, my beloved.
Let the same fire
Which chastened their tongues
Into silence,
Teach us – teach us!

The rain came down,
When you and I slept away
The night's burden of our passions;
Their new-found wisdom
In quick lightning flashes
Revealed the truth
That they had been
The slaves of fools.

Dennis Brutus

SABOTAGE, 1962

Here, thunderheads rear in the night,
dominating the awed quiet sky;

on the quiet-breathing plains
fractured metals shriek abandoned wails;

my country, an ignorantly timid bride
winces, tenses for the shattering releasing tide.

SOMEHOW WE SURVIVE

Somehow we survive
and tenderness, frustrated, does not wither.

Investigating searchlights rake
our naked unprotected contours;

over our heads the monolithic decalogue
of fascist prohibition glowers
and teeters for a catastrophic fall;

boots club on the peeling door.

But somehow we survive
severance, deprivation, loss.

Patrols uncoil along the asphalt dark
hissing their menace to our lives,

most cruel, all our land is scarred with terror,
rendered unlovely and unlovable;
sundered are we and all our passionate surrender

but somehow tenderness survives.

Léon Damas

WE THE AMAZONS

Let us tear out refuse and reject our hearts
Let the men go and harvest the maize
Let us tear out refuse and reject our hearts
Let the men go and harvest the maize
We the amazons
Let us tear out and rend and reject our hearts

Let the men go and harvest the maize
Until our mouths open and swallow the calabash
And the path of blood leads into a path of blood
Let us tear out and rend and reject our hearts
Let the men in our stead
Go and harvest the maize.

DEAD-BORN LOVE

Haven't you seen the woman who looks for Aouagbe
Who makes Aouagbe run away as soon as she comes
A torn loincloth which cannot cover the body
Does not even resemble a loincloth
I Aouagbe say
I'm fed up having you always at my heels
I don't like your smell
And I avoid it.
Woman
You are like a butterfly, now here now there
And everywhere
The whole country knows you
We, your people know you well enough
You and your false promises of love
Like a trap missing its prey she did not get me
And
Taking up my song again to end it
I say
Haven't you seen that woman who runs after Aouagbe's love
Who makes Aouagbe run away as soon as she comes
A torn loincloth is not a loincloth
The shrew mouse who never washes herself always leaves a strong
    smell
When she passes.

Birago Diop

DIPTYCH

The Sun hung by a thread
In the depths of the Calabash dyed indigo
Boils the great Pot of Day
Fearful of the approach of the Daughters of fire
The Shadow squats at the feet of the faithful.
The savannah is bright and harsh
All is sharp, forms and colours.
But in the anguished Silences made by Rumours
Of tiny sounds, neither hollow nor shrill,
Rises a ponderous Mystery,
A Mystery muffled and formless
Which surrounds and terrifies us.

The dark Loincloth pierced with nails of fire
Spread out on the Earth covers the bed of Night.
Fearful at the approach of the Daughters of shadow
The dog howls, the horse neighs
The Man crouches deep in his house.
The savannah is dark,
All is black, forms and colours
And in the anguished Silences made by Rumours
Of tiny sounds infinite or hollow or sharp
The tangled Paths of the Mystery
Slowly reveal themselves
For those who set out
And for those who return.

David Diop

AFRICA

Africa my Africa
Africa of proud warriors in ancestral savannahs
Africa of whom my grandmother sings
On the banks of the distant river
I have never known you
But your blood flows in my veins
Your beautiful black blood that irrigates the fields
The blood of your sweat
The sweat of your work
The work of your slavery
The slavery of your children
Africa tell me Africa

Is this you this back that is bent
This back that breaks under the weight of humiliation
This back trembling with red scars
And saying yes to the whip under the midday sun
But a grave voice answers me
Impetuous son that tree young and strong
That tree there
In splendid loneliness amidst white and faded flowers
That is Africa your Africa
The grows again patiently obstinately
And its fruit gradually acquire
The bitter taste of liberty.

Michael Echeruo

MELTING POT

It is dark, now, and grave

This bowl of a world
That rings me round and round
And will not let me marvel enough
At this dull sky

At the ignorance of these men
Who cannot know what chance can do

I shudder
Before this bowl of a world,
At this dull sky.

Will they not, all of them,
Call me names when they hear
Their blind man of this city
Stumbled on an udara underfoot
And lost it in the search for more?

Wish they could see half
What my eyes see, or know
Half what I know!
The Century's blind man!

Ellis Ayitey Komey

THE CHANGE

Your infancy now a wall of memory
In Harmattan the locusts filled the sky
Destroying the sweat put into the field
And restless seas shattered canoes
The fisher-folk put to sail by noon.
The impatience in your teens
Yet silent were your dreams
With the fires in your heart
Breaking the mask of innocence.
The evasive solitude in your womb
And the determination of your limbs
With eyes like the soaring eagle
Shattering the glass of ignorance.
Your infancy now a wall of memory
Before this you, like the worms,
Leaning on for vain indecorous dreams
And the cobras with venomous tongues
Licking the tepid blooms of hibiscus.

Valente Malangatana

TO THE ANXIOUS MOTHER

Into your arms I came
when you bore me, very anxious
you, who were so alarmed
at that monstrous moment
fearing that God might take me.
Everyone watched in silence
to see if the birth was going well
everyone washed their hands
to be able to receive the one who came from Heaven
and all the women were still and afraid.
But when I emerged
from the place where you sheltered me so long
at once I drew my first breath
at once you cried out with joy
the first kiss was my grandmother's.
And she took me at once to the place
where they kept me, hidden away
everyone was forbidden to enter my room
because everyone smelt bad
and I all fresh, fresh
breathed gently, wrapped in my napkins.
But grandmother, who seemed like a madwoman,
always looking and looking again
because the flies came at me
and the mosquitoes harried me
God who also watched over me
was my old granny's friend.

Joe G. Mutiga

TO THE CEREMONIAL MUGUMO (FIG TREE)

Holy huge tree, you tax my memory :
Over you, boys awaiting circumcision,
Proudly threw 'ndorothi'¹ to show ability
To shoulder social responsibility,
While all danced in heartful joy,
Bearing proudly the tribal decorum :

With proud ostrich feathers
Blowing in the dancing air,
And the rattles rattling in tune,
While all throats sang hoarse;
You are a memory of beauty,
Of annual tribal festivity;

A memory of olden days
When the Agikuyu were a tribe,
Though now but part of a nation,
A nation that is soon to be :
It is happier thus in all,
But the beauty of old is gone;

Around you was the life,
The loyalty and spirit of the tribe;
But now the ground,
On which the dancers once trod,
Is laden with the green of crops,
The holy ground no more holy;

¹ 'Ndorothi' is a type of perennial plant which grows thin and straight
and up to about six feet. The 'ndorothi' stalks were used like javelins to be
thrown over the fig tree. This part of the circumcision ceremony was done
on the afternoon of the day before the circumcision took place. The area
around the ceremonial tree was planted with grass and, although cattle
could graze there, nobody could cultivate any part of it.

No decorum but hoe and soil,
No dancing on the ground,
The lonely digger sweats alone;
Sweats as he destroys
The preserve of many an age :—
It is sad :

Our customs are dug up,
And put aside, like the grass
On which the dancer trod,
And foreign crops implanted;
And we pass by, eyes on the ground,
submitting to the foreign as ours.

Gabriel Okara

THE SNOWFLAKES SAIL
GENTLY DOWN

The snowflakes sail gently
down from the misty eye of the sky
and fall lightly lightly on the
winter-weary elms. And the branches
winter-stripped and nude, slowly
with the weight of the weightless snow
bow like grief-stricken mourners
as white funeral cloth is slowly
unrolled over deathless earth.
And dead sleep stealthily from the
heater rose and closed my eyes with
the touch of silk cotton on water falling.

Then I dreamed a dream
in my dead sleep. But I dreamed
not of earth dying and elms a vigil
keeping. I dreamed of birds, black

birds flying in my inside, nesting
and hatching on oil palms bearing suns
for fruits and with roots denting the
uprooters' spades. And I dreamed the
uprooters tired and limp, leaning on my roots –
their abandoned roots
and the oil palms gave them each a sun.

But on their palms
they balanced the blinding orbs
and frowned with schisms on their
brows – for the suns reached not
the brightness of gold !

Then I awoke. I awoke
to the silently falling snow
and bent-backed elms bowing and
swaying to the winter wind like
white-robed Moslems salaaming at evening
prayer, and the earth lying inscrutable
like the face of a god in a shrine.

PIANO AND DRUMS

When at break of day at a riverside
I hear jungle drums telegraphing
the mystic rhythm, urgent, raw
like bleeding flesh, speaking of
primal youth and the beginning,
I see the panther ready to pounce,
the leopard snarling about to leap
and the hunters crouch with spears poised;

And my blood ripples, turns torrent,
topples the years and at once I'm
in my mother's lap a suckling;
at once I'm walking simple
paths with no innovations,
rugged, fashioned with the naked
warmth of hurrying feet and groping hearts
in green leaves and wild flowers pulsing.

Then I hear a wailing piano
solo speaking of complex ways
in tear-furrowed concerto;
of far-away lands
and new horizons with
coaxing diminuendo, counterpoint,
crescendo. But lost in the labyrinth
of its complexities, it ends in the middle
of a phrase at a daggerpoint.

And I lost in the morning mist
of an age at a riverside keep
wandering in the mystic rhythm
of jungle drums and the concerto.

WERE I TO CHOOSE

When Adam broke the stone
and red streams raged down to
gather in the womb,
an angel calmed the storm;

And I, the breath mewed
in Cain, unblinking gaze
at the world without
from the brink of an age

That draws from the groping lips
a breast-muted cry
to thread the years.
(O were I to choose)

And now the close of one
and thirty turns, the world
of bones is Babel, and
the different tongues within
are flames the head
continually burning.

And O of this dark halo
were the tired head free.

And when the harmattan
of days has parched the throat
and skin, and sucked the fever
of the head away,

Then the massive dark
descends, and flesh and bone
are razed. And (O were I
to choose) I'd cheat the worms
and silence seek in stone.

ONE NIGHT AT VICTORIA BEACH

The wind comes rushing from the sea,
the waves curling like mambas strike
the sands and recoiling hiss in rage
washing the Aladuras' feet pressing hard
on the sand and with eyes fixed hard
on what only hearts can see, they shouting
pray, the Aladuras pray; and coming
from booths behind, compelling highlife
forces ears; and car lights startle pairs
arm in arm passing washer-words back
and forth like haggling sellers and buyers –

Still they pray, the Aladuras pray
with hands pressed against their hearts
and their white robes pressed against
their bodies by the wind; and drinking
palm-wine and beer, the people boast
at bars at the beach. Still they pray.

They pray, the Aladuras pray
to what only hearts can see while dead
fishermen long dead with bones rolling
nibbled clean by nibbling fishes, follow
four dead cowries shining like stars
into deep sea where fishes sit in judgement;
and living fishermen in dark huts
sit round dim lights with Babalawo
throwing their souls in four cowries
on sand, trying to see tomorrow.

Still, they pray, the Aladuras pray
to what only hearts can see behind
the curling waves and the sea, the stars
and the subduing unanimity of the sky
and their white bones beneath the sand.

And standing dead on dead sands,
I felt my knees touch living sands –
but the rushing wind killed the budding words.

Christopher Okigbo

from PRELUDE TO THE LIMITS

An image insists
   from the flag-pole of the heart,
The image distracts
   with the cruelty of the rose. . . .

   My lioness,
(No shield is lead-plate against you)
Wound me with your sea-weed face,
   Blinded like a strong room.
Distances of your
   armpit-fragrance
Turn chloroform,
   enough for my patience –
When you have finished,
& done up my stitches,
Wake me near the altar,

   & this poem will be finished.

Lenrie Peters

WE HAVE COME HOME

We have come home
From the bloodless war
With sunken hearts
Our boots full of pride –
From the true massacre of the soul
When we have asked
'What does it cost
To be loved and left alone?'

We have come home,
Bringing the pledge
Which is written in rainbow colours
Across the sky – for burial
But it is not the time
To lay wreaths
For yesterday's crimes
Night threatens
Time dissolves
And there is no acquaintance
With tomorrow
The gurgling drums
Echo the star
The forest howls –
And between the trees
The dark sun appears.

We have come home
When the dawn falters
Singing songs of other lands
The Death March
Violating our ears
Knowing all our lore and tears
Determined by the spinning coin.

We have come home
To the green foothills
To drink from the cry
Of warm and mellow birdsong.
To the hot beaches
Where boats go out to sea
Threshing the ocean's harvest
And the harassing, plunging
gliding gulls shower kisses on the waves.

We have come home
Where through the lightning flash
And thundering rain
The Pestilence, the drought
The sodden spirit
Lingers on the sandy road
Supporting the tortured remnants
Of the flesh
That spirit which asks no favour
Of the world
But to have dignity.

IF I WAS ASKED

If I was asked
How I would face the task
Of camping out in space
        I would reply
With infinite distaste
That I would rather die
Because to meddle
        In this confounded puzzle
Would only represent
        My innate discontent.
That if it was my face
        Men seemed to hate
Then it would be in place
        To offer an estate
On some deserted piece of earth
Where suited to my girth
And my most earthly temperament
        I would be proud to represent
The non-progressive element.

If I was offered more –
    An offer just as poor.
Perhaps the earth
    As a reward
For traffic up in heaven
    I would present
The quite unconvincing argument
    That far from being competent
The Maker of the instrument
    Should show me how it went.
Thus in the end
    Those minds gone round the bend
Would have all to themselves
    The Lunar firmament
And we could laugh
    At what appears daft.
Cows that have jumped over the moon.

Jean-Joseph Rabéarivelo

THE WHITE BULL

This cross shaped constellation, is it the Southern Star?
I prefer to call it the White Bull like the Arabs.
He comes from a garden stretching to the limits of the evening
and stands guard between two milky ways.
The river of light has not quenched his thirst
and he drinks eagerly in the cloudy bay.
In the realms of day he was like a blind youth
who could not caress anything with his horns,
But now the rivers are born in the prairies of night
and the moon grazes on the waters and leaps like a heifer
now the white bull regains his sight, and he appears stronger than
    the blue bulls
and the wild bulls that sleep in the desert.

BIRTH OF DAY (II)

One hardly knows
whether the first call
has come from East or West.
But now
the cocks
in their coops pierced by stars
and the other spears of darkness
they summon each other
they breathe into sea shells
they respond from all sides.
And he returns
he who went to sleep in the ocean,
the skylark ascends
and goes to meet him with songs
imbibed with dew.

BIRTH OF DAY (III)

All the stars melted together
in the crucible of time
then chilled in the sea
have become a crystallized stone.
Dying rock, the night puts her heart into it
and her yearning for millstones
that dissolve, dissolve
like ashes touched by the wind.
Lovingly she cuts the prism.

But it is a luminous stone
which the artist will have erected
on his invisible tomb.

Flavien Ranaivo

SONG OF A YOUNG GIRL

Oaf
the young man who lives down there
beside the threshing floor for rice;
like two banana-roots
on either side the village ditch,
we gaze on each other,
we are lovers,
but he won't marry me.
Jealous
his mistress I saw two days since at the wash house
coming down the path against the wind.
She was proud;
was it because she wore a lamba thick
and studded with coral
or because they are newly bedded?
However it isn't the storm
that will flatten the delicate reed,
nor the great sudden shower
at the passage of a cloud
that will startle out of his wits
the blue bull.
I am amazed;
the big sterile rock
survived the rain of the flood
and it's the fire that crackles
the bad grains of maize.
Such this famous smoker
who took tobacco
when there was no more hemp to burn.
A foot of hemp?
– Sprung in Andringitra,
spent in Ankaratra,
no more than cinders to us.

False flattery
stimulates love a little
but the blade has two edges;
why change what is natural?
– If I have made you sad
look at yourself in the water of repentance,
you will decipher there a word I have left.
Good-bye, whirling puzzle,
I give you my blessing :
wrestle with the crocodile,
here are your victuals and three water-lily flowers
for the way is long.

LOVE SONG

(translated by Miriam Koshland)

Do not love me, my friend,
like your shadow –
shadows fade in the evening
and I will hold you
until the cock crows –
Do not love me like pepper,
it makes my belly too hot,
I cannot eat pepper
when I am hungry.
Do not love me like a pillow –
we would meet in sleep
and not see each other during the day.
Do love me like a dream –
for dreams are your life in the night
and my hope in the day.

Shaaban Robert

OUR FRAME

(*translated by Shaaban Robert and Gerald Moore*)

Our frame is poor even when we are in security
    Of our existence
Of the world's grace and majesty and vanity,
    In this age of ours
So full of delusiveness and pomp and artifice.

In the defective form of this creation
    That holds our humanity
A state of perfection is to us like a vision
    Which passes a man
And disappears beyond a call of his memory.

To continue in weakness is habitual to us,
    Because our life
Has no better changes to give than these ones
    in our Steps,
Which are short or long in every field of life.

And at this time of death when life fails
    A grave keeps us
To cover rottenness – our bad smells.
    It is not man's habit
To abide in purity whatever his state may be !

Léopold Sédar Senghor

IN WHAT TEMPESTUOUS NIGHT

What dark tempestuous night has been hiding your face?
And what claps of thunder frighten you from the bed
When the fragile walls of my breast tremble?
I shudder with cold, trapped in the dew of the clearing.
O, I am lost in the treacherous paths of the forest.
Are these creepers or snakes that entangle my feet?
I slip into the mudhole of fear and my cry is suffocated in a watery rattle.
But when shall I hear your voice again, happy luminous morn?
When shall I recognize myself again in the laughing mirror of eyes, that are large like windows?
And what sacrifice will pacify the white mask of the goddess?
Perhaps the blood of chickens or goats, or the worthless blood in my veins?
Or the prelude of my song, the ablution of my pride?

Give me propitious words.

NEW YORK

New York! At first I was confused by your beauty, by those great golden long-legged girls.
So shy at first before your blue metallic eyes, your frosted smile
So shy. And the anguish in the depths of skyscraper streets
Lifting eyes hawkhooded to the sun's eclipse.
Sulphurous your light and livid the towers with heads that thunderbolt the sky
The skyscrapers which defy the storms with muscles of steel and stone-glazed hide.
But two weeks on the bare sidewalks of Manhattan

–At the end of the third week the fever seizes you with the pounce
of a leopard
Two weeks without rivers or fields, all the birds of the air
Falling sudden and dead on the high ashes of flat rooftops.
No smile of a child blooms, his hand refreshed in my hand,
No mother's breast, but only nylon legs. Legs and breasts that have
no sweat nor smell.
No tender word for there are no lips, only artificial hearts paid for
in hard cash
And no book where wisdom may be read. The painter's palette
blossoms with crystal of coral.
Nights of insomnia oh nights of Manhattan! So agitated by flickering
lights, while motor-horns howl of empty hours
And while dark waters carry away hygienic loves, like rivers flooded
with the corpses of children.

Noemia de Sousa

APPEAL

Who has strangled the tired voice
of my forest sister?
On a sudden, her call to action
was lost in the endless flow of night and day.
No more it reaches me every morning,
wearied with long journeying,
mile after mile drowned
in the everlasting cry : Macala!

No, it comes no more, still damp with dew,
leashed with children and submission. . . .
One child on her back, another in her womb
– always, always, always!
And a face all compassed in a gentle look,
whenever I recall that look I feel
my flesh and blood swell tremulous,

throbbing to revelations and affinities. . . .
– But who has stopped her immeasurable look
from feeding my deep hunger after comradeship
that my poor table never will serve to satisfy?

Io mamane, who can have shot the noble voice
of my forest sister?
What mean and brutal rhino-whip
has lashed until it killed her?

– In my garden the seringa blooms.
But with an evil omen in its purple flower,
in its intense inhuman scent;
and the wrap of tenderness spread by the sun
over the light mat of petals
has waited since summer for my sister's child
to rest himself upon it. . . .
In vain, in vain,
a chirico sings and sings perched among the garden reeds,
for the little boy of my missing sister,
the victim of the forest's vaporous dawns.
Ah, I know, I know : at the last there was a glitter
of farewell in those gentle eyes,
and her voice came like a murmur hoarse,
tragic and despairing. . . .

O Africa, my motherland, answer me :
What was done to my forest sister,
that she comes no more to the city with her eternal little
    ones
(one on her back, one in her womb),
with her eternal charcoal-vendor's cry?
O Africa, my motherland,
you at least will not forsake my heroic sister,
she shall live in the proud memorial of your arms !

Wole Soyinka

TELEPHONE CONVERSATION

The price seemed reasonable, location
indifferent. The landlady swore she lived
Off premises. Nothing remained
But self-confession. 'Madam,' I warned,
'I hate a wasted journey – I am African.'
Silence. Silenced transmission of
Pressurized good-breeding. Voice, when it came,
Lipstick-coated, long gold-rolled
Cigarette-holder pipped. Caught I was, foully.
'HOW DARK?' . . . I had not misheard. . . . 'ARE YOU LIGHT
OR VERY DARK?' Button B. Button A. Stench
Of rancid breath of public hide-and-speak.
Red booth. Red pillar-box. Red double-tiered
Omnibus squelching tar. It *was* real! Shamed
By ill-mannered silence, surrender
Pushed dumbfounded to beg simplification.
Considerate she was, varying the emphasis –
'ARE YOU DARK? OR VERY LIGHT?' Revelation came.
'You mean – like plain or milk chocolate?'
Her assent was clinical, crushing in its light
Impersonality. Rapidly, wave-length adjusted,
I chose. 'West African sepia' – and as afterthought,
'Down in my passport.' Silence for spectroscopic
Flight of fancy, till truthfulness clanged her accent
Hard on the mouthpiece. 'WHAT'S THAT?' conceding
'DON'T KNOW WHAT THAT IS.' 'Like brunette.'
'THAT'S DARK, ISN'T IT?' 'Not altogether.
Facially, I am brunette, but madam, you should see
The rest of me. Palm of my hand, soles of my feet
Are a peroxide blonde. Friction, caused –
Foolishly madam – by sitting down, has turned
My bottom raven black – One moment madam!' – sensing
Her receiver rearing on the thunderclap
About my ears – 'Madam,' I pleaded, 'wouldn't you rather
See for yourself?'

DEATH IN THE DAWN

Traveller, you must set out
at dawn. And wipe your feet upon
The dog-nose wetness of the earth.

Let sunrise quench your lamps. And watch
Faint brush pricklings in the sky light
Cottoned feet to break the early earthworm
On the hoe. Now shadows stretch with sap
Not twilight's death and sad prostration.
This soft kindling, soft receding breeds
Racing joys and apprehensions for
A naked day. Burdened hulks retract,
Stoop to the mist in faceless throng
To wake the silent markets – swift, mute
Processions on grey byways. . . . On this
Counterpane, it was –
Sudden winter at the death
Of dawn's lone trumpeter. Cascades
Of white feather-flakes . . . but it proved
A futile rite. Propitiation sped
Grimly on, before.
> The right foot for joy, the left, dread
> And the mother prayed, Child
> May you never walk
> When the road waits, famished.

Traveller, you must set forth
At dawn.
I promise marvels of the holy hour
Presages as the white cock's flapped
Perverse impalement – as who would dare
the wrathful wings of man's Progression. . . .

But such another wraith! Brother,
Silenced in the startled hug of
Your invention – is this mocked grimace
This closed contortion – I?

Bibliography

(White South-African and British writing is included here, but no West Indian or Negro American or African French, except where these are either on Africa or have English translations.)

ABRAHAMS, PETER, (South Africa, b. *c.* 1919)
The Path of Thunder, novel, Harper, New York, 1948
Wild Conquest, novel, Faber and Faber, London, 1951
Return to Goli, novel, Faber and Faber, 1953
Tell Freedom, autobiography, Faber and Faber, 1954
Mine Boy, novel, Faber and Faber, 1954
A Wreath for Udomo, novel, Faber and Faber, 1956

ACHEBE, CHINUA, (Nigeria, b. 1930)
Things Fall Apart, novel, Heinemann, London, 1958
No Longer at Ease, novel, Heinemann, 1960
Arrow of God, novel, Heinemann, 1964

ADALI-MORTTI, GEORMBEEYI, (Togoland, b. 1916 [?])
poems in *Voices of Ghana*, Ministry of Information, Accra, 1958

AIDOO, CHRISTIANA A., (Ghana)
'Cut Me A Drink', short story, *Modern African Stories*, Faber and Faber, London, 1964

AIG-IMOUKHUEDE, FRANK, (Western Nigeria, b. 1935)
poems in *Black Orpheus* and in *Modern Poetry from Africa*, Penguin African Library, 1963

ALUKO, T. M., (Nigeria, b. 1918)
One Man, One Wife, novel, Nigerian Publishing Co., Lagos, 1959
One Man, One Matchet, novel, Heinemann, 1964

ATIYAH, EDWARD, (Lebanon, b. *c.* 1900)
Black Vanguard, novel, Peter Davies, London, 1952

AWOLOWO, OBAFEMI, (Western Nigeria, b. 1909)
Awo, autobiography, Cambridge University Press, 1960

AWOONOR-WILLIAMS, GEORGE (Ghana, b. 1935)
ed. *Okyeame* (literary review); poems in *Modern Poetry from Africa*
Rediscovery, poems, Mbari Publications, Ibadan, Nigeria, 1964

BEDWEI, ATO, (Ghana)
'Me and the Fish God', short story, *Modern African Stories*, Faber and Faber, 1964

BELLOW, SAUL, (United States, b. 1915)
Henderson the Rain King, Weidenfeld and Nicolson, 1959

BETI, MONGO, (Alexandre Biyidi) (Cameroun Republic, b. 1932)
Mission to Kala, novel, (tr. Peter Green) Muller, London, 1958
King Lazarus, novel, (tr. Peter Green) Muller, 1960

BREW, KWESI, (Ghana, b. 1928)
poems in *Black Orpheus, Transition*, etc.

BRUTUS, DENNIS, (South Africa. Proscribed by the South African Government)
Poems, Mbari Publications, Ibadan, 1963
Sirens, Knuckles, Boots, Mbari Publications, 1964

BUAHIN, PETER KWAME, (Ghana)
'This is Experience Speaking', short story, *Modern African Stories*, Faber and Faber, 1964

CARY, JOYCE, (Britain, b. 1888, d. 1957)
Aissa Saved, novel of Nigeria, Michael Joseph, London, 1932
Mister Johnson, novel of Nigeria, Michael Joseph, 1939

CASELY-HAYFORD, ADELAIDE, (Ghana)
'Mista Courifer', short story, *Modern African Stories*, Faber and Faber, 1964

CLARK, JOHN PEPPER, (Nigeria, b. 1935)
Poems, Mbari Publications, Ibadan, 1962
Song of a Goat, play, Mbari, 1962
Three Plays, Oxford University Press, 1964
America, their America, André Deutsch, 1964

CONTON, WILLIAM, (Sierra Leone, b. 1925)
The African, novel, Heinemann, London, 1960
'The Blood in the Washbasin', short story, *Modern African Stories*, Faber and Faber, 1964

COPE, JACK, (South Africa, b. 1913)
The Golden Oriole, novel, Heinemann, London, 1958
The Tame Ox, Heinemann, London, 1960

DIOP, BIRAGO, (Senegal, b. 1906)
poems in *Modern Poetry from Africa*, (see Anthologies)
Samba of the Night', *African Written Prose*, Oxford University Press, 1964

DIOP, DAVID, (Senegal, b. Bordeaux 1927, d. 1960)
poems in *Modern Poetry from Africa, Black Orpheus*, No 5 (tr. Ulli Beier)
Coups de Pilon, poems, Présence Africaine, 1956

DHLOMO, H. I. E., (South Africa, d. 1957)
Valley of a Thousand Hills, poem, Knox Publishing Press, Durban, 1941, (3rd edition 1944)

DHLOMO, R. R. R., (South Africa)
An African Tragedy, novel, Lovedale Press, 1928

EASMON, R. SARIF, (Sierra Leone)
Koya, short story, *Modern African Stories*, Faber and Faber, 1964

ECHERUO, MICHAEL J. C., (Nigeria, b. 1937)
poems in *Modern Poetry from Africa*

EGBUNA, OBI B., (Nigeria)
Wind Versus Poligamy, novel, Faber and Faber, 1964

EKWENSI, CYPRIAN, (Nigeria, b. 1921)
People of the City, novel, Dakars, London, 1953
Jagua Nana, novel, Hutchinson, London, 1961
The Drummer Boy, boys' story, Cambridge University Press, 1960
The Passport of Mallam Ilia, boys' story, O.U.P., 1960
An African Night's Entertainment, fable, African University Press, Lagos, 1962
Burning Grass, novel, Heinemann, 1962
Beautiful Feathers, novel, Hutchinson, 1963

EKWERE, JOHN, (Eastern Nigeria)
poems in *Reflections* (see Anthologies)

EQUIANO, OLAUDAH, (Sierra Leone, b. 1745)
The earliest book by an African. *The Interesting Narrative of The Life of Olaudah Equiano or Gustavus Vassa, the African, written by himself*, London, 1790

FAGUNWA, D. O., (Nigeria, b. *c.* 1900)
four novels in Yoruba awaiting translation
'The Forest of the Lord', *A Selection of African Prose (2)*, Oxford University Press, 1964

FITZPATRICK, J. PERCY, (South Africa, b. 1862, d. 1931)
The Outspan, short stories, Heinemann, London, 1898
Jock of the Bushveld, Longmans, Green, 1907

GATHERU, R. MUGO, (Kenya b. 1921)
Child of Two Worlds, autobiography, Routledge & Kegan Paul, London, 1964

GORDIMER, NADINE, (South Africa, b. 1923)
Soft Voice of the Serpent, novel, Gollancz, London, 1953
Six Feet of the Country, novel, Gollancz, 1956
A World of Strangers, novel, Gollancz, 1958

GORDON, GERALD,
Four People, novel, Macdonald, London, 1964

GRAFT, J. C. DE, (Ghana b. 1930)
Sons and Daughters, play, Oxford University Press, 1964

HONWANA, LUIS BERNARDO, (Mozambique, b. 1937)
'Papa, the Snake and I', short story, *Modern African Prose,* Heinemann, 1965

HUSSEIN, TAHA, (Egypt, b. 1889)
The Stream of Days, tr. autobiography, Longmans, London, 1943

HUTCHINSON, ALFRED, (South Africa, b. c. 1932)
Road to Ghana, autobiography, Gollancz, 1960

HUXLEY, ELSPETH, (Kenya, b. 1907, London)
Red Strangers, stories, Chatto and Windus, London, 1955
The Flame Trees of Thika, autobiography, Morrow & Co. New York, 1959

JACOBSON, DAN, (South Africa, b. 1929)
The Evidence of Love, novel, Weidenfeld and Nicolson, London, 1959
Beggar My Neighbour, short stories, Weidenfeld and Nicolson, 1964

IKE, VINCENT CHUKWUEMEKA, (Nigeria, b. 1937?)
Toads for Supper, novel, Harvill Press, London, 1965

JABAVU, NONI, (South Africa-Xhosa)
Drawn in Colour, novel, Murray, London, 1960
The Ochre People, novel, Murray, 1963

JONES, HORATIO EDWARD BABATUNDE, (Nigeria, b. c. 1935)
The Mockers, novel, Artemis Verlag, Switzerland, 1963

JORDAN, A. C., (South Africa-Bantu, Xhosa, b. c. 1912)
Ingqumbo Yeminyanya (The Wrath of the Ancestors), novel, Moriji Press, Basutoland

KARIARA, JONATHAN, (Kenya, b. 1935)
'Her Warrior', short story from *Modern African Prose,* Heinemann, 1965

KARIM, AHMED AWAD, (Sudan, b. c. 1900)
Shukria Shepherds' poems, published for the first time in this survey.

KARIUKI, JOSIAH, (Kenya, b. 1929)
Poem in *Modern Poetry from Africa*
Mau Mau Detainee, autobiography, Oxford University Press, 1963

KOMEY, ELLIS AYITEY, (Ghana, b. 1927)
Poems in *Black Orpheus,* No. 9
ed. (with Ezekiel Mphahlele) *Modern African Stories,* Faber and Faber, 1964
ed. *Flamingo* (Magazine)

KRIGE, UYS, (South Africa-Afrikaans, b. 1910)
The Dream and the Desert, short stories, Collins, 1953
The Way Out, novel, Collins, 1955

KUNENE, MAZIZI, (South Africa, b. 1930), poet and journalist
Short stories in *Drum* magazine

LA GUMA, ALEX, (South Africa, b. *c.* 1925)
A Walk in the Night, novel, Mbari, Ibadan, 1962
'Out of Darkness', short story in *Africa South* magazine
'Coffee for the Road', short story in *Modern African Stories*, 1964
And a Threefold Cord, novel, Seven Seas Books, East Berlin, 1965

LAYE, CAMARA, (Upper Guinea, b. 1924)
The Dark Child, tr. James Kirkup, autobiography, Collins, London, 1955 (as *The African Child* in Fontana Books, 1959)
The Radiance of the King, tr. James Kirkup, novel, Collins, London, 1956
'The Eyes of the Statue', tr. Una MacLean, *Black Orpheus*, No 5

LESSING, DORIS, (Southern Rhodesia, b. 1919)
The Grass is Singing, Michael Joseph, London, 1950
This was the Old Chief's Country, Michael Joseph, 1952
etc.

LUTFI, ALI, (Sudan, b. 1930)
Translations from Arabic of Shukria Shepherd's poems and modern Shukria poems (see Karim, A. A. and Rabu, W. H.) Printed for the first time in this Survey.

LEWIS, ETHELREDA, (South Africa)
'Blind Justice', short story, (see Parnwell, E. C. under Anthologies)
The Flying Emerald, novel, Hodder and Stoughton, 1925
The Harp, novel, Hodder and Stoughton, 1925
Mantis, novel, Hodder and Stoughton, 1926

MAIMANE, ARTHUR, (South Africa, b. *c.* 1930)
'Just a Tsotsi', short story

MALANGATANA, VALENTE, (Mozambique, b. 1936)
poems in *Modern Poetry from Africa*

MATTHEWS, JAMES, (South Africa)
'The Second Coming', short story, *Modern African Stories*. Faber and Faber, 1964

MATSHIKIZA, TODD, (South Africa, b. *c.* 1935)
Short story in *African Treasury* (see Anthologies)
Music of *King Kong*

MBITI, JOHN S., (Kenya, b. 1931)
poems in *Transition*, etc.

MILLIN, SARAH GERTRUDE, (South Africa, b. 1889)
God's Stepchildren, novel, Central News Agency, Johannesburg, 1924
The Herr Witchdoctor, novel, Heinemann, London, 1941
etc.

MODISANE, BLOKE (WILLIAM), (South Africa, b. *c.* 1930) now living in London
poems in *Modern Poetry from Africa*
Blame Me on History, autobiography, Thames and Hudson, 1963
'The Dignity of Begging', short story, *Drum* magazine

MODUPE, PRINCE, (West Africa, b. *c.* 1900)
I Was a Savage, autobiography, Museum Press, London, 1958

MOFOLO, THOMAS, (South Africa-Basutoland, b. 1877? d. 1948)
The Pilgrim of the East, novel, S.P.C.K. Press, 1920
Chaka, novel, (tr. Rev. F. H. Dutton). O.U.P. for International African Institute, 1931, English Reader's Library, 1963

MOTSISI, CASEY, (South Africa)
'On the Beat – Sketches of South African Life', short story, *Modern African Stories*, Faber and Faber, 1964

MPHAHLELE, EZEKIEL, (South Africa, b. 1919)
Man Must Live, short stories, African Bookman, Cape Town, 1946
Down Second Avenue, autobiography, Faber and Faber, London, 1959
The African Image, criticism, Faber and Faber, London, 1962
The Living and the Dead, short stories,
ed. (with Ellis Ayitey Komey) *Modern African Stories*, Faber and Faber, 1964

MPHAHLELE, MOSES, (South Africa), poet of the 1920's

MUTIGA, J. G., poem in *Transition 3*

NGUGI, JAMES, T., (Kenya, b. 1938)
Short stories, in *Transition*
Weep not, Child, novel, Heinemann, London, 1964
The Black Hermit, play, Makerere University Press, 1963
The River Between, novel, Heinemann, 1965

NJAU, REBECCA, (Kenya)
Short stories in *Transition*
'The Scar', play, *Transition*, No 8

NJAU, ELIMO, (Kenya)
Stories and poems in *Transition*

NKOSI, LEWIS, (South Africa, 1935)
The Rhythm of Violence, play, Oxford University Press, 1964

NICOL, ABIOSEH, (Sierra Leone, b. 1920)
'The Devil at Yolahun Bridge', short story, *Darkness and Light*,
ed. Peggy Rutherford (see Anthologies etc.)
'The Continent that lies within us', short story, *Anthology of West
African Verse*
'As the Night, the Day', short story, *An African Treasury*, ed.
Langston Hughes

NKETIA, KWABENA, (Ghana) writer and scholar
'Akan Poetry', article, *Black Orpheus*, No 3, May, 1958, etc.

NTARA, SAMUEL YOSIA, (South Africa, b. *c*. 1900)
Headman's Enterprise, novel, 1930

NWANKWO, NKEM, (Nigeria, b. 1936)
Danda, novel, André Deutsch, London, 1964

NZEKWU, ONUORA, (Eastern Nigeria, b. *c*. 1930)
Wand of Noble Wood, novel, Hutchinson, London, 1961
Blade Among the Boys, novel, Hutchinson, 1962

OGOT, GRACE, (Kenya)
'The Rain Came', short story, *Modern African Stories*, Faber and
Faber, 1964

OKARA, GABRIEL, (Southern Nigeria, b. 1921)
poems in *Black Orpheus, Modern Poetry from Africa*, etc.
The Voice, novel, André Deutsch, London, 1964

OKIGBO, CHRISTOPHER, (Eastern Nigeria, b. 1932)
Heavensgate, poems, Mbari, Ibadan, 1962
The Limits and Other Poems, Mbari, 1964

OWOYELE, DAVID, (Nigeria)
'The Will of Allah', short story, *Modern African Stories*, Faber
and Faber, 1964

PATON, ALAN, (White South Africa, b. 1903)
Cry, the Beloved Country, Cape, London, 1950
etc.

PETERS, LENRIE, (Gambia, b. 1932)
Poems in *Modern Poetry from Africa*
Poems, Mbari, 1964
The Second Round, novel, Heinemann, 1965

PLAATJE, SOLOMON T., (South Africa-Bechuanaland, b. *c*. 1900, d. *c*.
1940)
Mhudi, novel, Lovedale Press, South Africa, 1930

PLOMER, WILLIAM, (South Africa, b. 1903)
Turbott Wolfe, novel, Hogarth Press, London, 1926
etc.

PRINGLE, THOMAS, (South Africa, b. 1789, d. 1834)
African Sketches, stories, Edward Moxon, London, 1934
Afar in the Desert and Other South African Poems, 1881

RABÉARIVELO, JEAN JOSEPH, (Madagascar, b. 1901, d. 1939)
24 Poems, Mbari, Ibadan, 1962

RABU, WAD HASAB, (Sudan, b. *c.* 1920)
Shukria Shepherds' poems published for the first time in this Survey

RANAIVO, FLAVIEN, (Malagasy Republic, b. 1914)
L'ombre et le vent, poems in French and English, 1947

RIVE, RICHARD, (South Africa, b. 1931)
African Songs, Seven Seas Books, Berlin, 1963
Emergency, novel, Faber and Faber, 1964

ROBERT, SHAABAN, (Tanganyika, 1909-62)
Leading Swahili poet, who wrote also in English.
Maisha Yangu, Nelson, London, 1949
Rusadikika, Nelson, 1951
Adili na Ndugaze, Macmillan, London, 1952

RUBADIRI, DAVID, (Malawi Republic, b. 1930)
poems in *Modern Poetry from Africa*, 1963

SALEH, TALIB, (Sudan, b. *c.* 1935)
'The Doum Tree', short story, *Encounter*, November, 1962

SCHREINER, OLIVE, (South Africa, b. 1855, d. 1920)
The Story of an African Farm, novel, Benn, London, 1951 etc.

SCULLY, WILLIAM CHARLES, (South Africa, b. 1855, d. 1943)
Kaffir Stories, Fisher Unwin, London, 1895
A Tale of an African Desert, novel, Methuen, 1898
Voices of Africa, Knox Publishing Co., Durban, 1943

SENGHOR, LÉOPOLD SÉDAR, (Senegal, b. 1906)
leading French-African poet of *Négritude* movement
Selected Poems, tr. John Reed and Clive Wake, Oxford University Press, 1964

SEGUN, MABEL, (Nigeria)
poems in anthologies

SENTSO, DYKE, (South Africa, b. *c.* 1935)
Short stories in *Drum* Magazine, etc.

SOUSA, NOEMIA DE, (Mozambique, b. 1927)
Poems in anthologies

SOYINKA, WOLE, (Nigeria, b. 1935)
ed. *Black Orpheus*,
The Lion and the Jewel, play, Oxford University Press, London, 1963

The Dance of the Forests, play, Oxford University Press, 1963
Three Plays, Mbari, Ibadan, 1962
The Interpreters, novel, André Deutsch, London, 1965

STEIN, SYLVESTER, (South Africa, b. 1920)
Second Class Taxi, novel, Faber and Faber, London, 1958

SUTHERLAND, EFUA THEODORA, (Ghana)
'It Happened', poem in _Anthology of West African Verse_
Poems in other anthologies
'New Life at Kyerefaso', _African Treasury_, ed. Langston Hughes,
(see Anthologies)

THEMBA, CAN, (South Africa, b. 1922)
Ed. _Golden City Post_
'The Dube Train', short story, _Modern African Stories_, Faber
and Faber, 1964

TUTUOLA, AMOS, (Nigeria, b. 1920)
The Palm-Wine Drinkard, story, Faber and Faber, 1952
My Life in the Bush of Ghosts, story, Faber and Faber, 1954
Simbi and the Satyr of the Dark Jungle, story, Faber and Faber,
1955
The Brave African Huntress, story, Faber and Faber, 1958
Feather Woman of the Jungle, story, Faber and Faber, 1961

U TAM'SI, FELIX TCHICAYA, (Congo, b. 1931)
Poems in _Modern Poetry from Africa_ and in _Transition_

VAN DER POST, LAURENS, (South Africa, b. 1906, d. 1964)
In a Province, Cape, London, 1950
The Lost World of the Kalahari, a study of the Bushmen,
Hogarth, 1958

VENTER, FRANS, (South Africa-Afrikaans)
Dark Pilgrim, novel, tr. G. and W. Gordon, Collins, London, 1959

VILAKAZI,[1] B. W., (South Africa-Natal, d. 1947) tr. A. C. Jordan
'In the Gold Mines', poem, in _African South_

WILLIAMS, GRENFELL, and MAY, HENRY JOHN (Naturalized British)
I am Black, novel, Cassell, London, 1936

Anthologies and Selections

ADEMOLA, FRANCES (ed.) _Reflections_ (Nigerian Prose and Verse)
African Universities Press, Lagos, 1962

BASSIR, OLUMBE (ed.) _An Anthology of West African Verse_, Ibadan
University Press, 1957

[1] Spelt as in Ezekiel Mphahlele's _The African Image_

BEIER, ULLI, (ed.) *Black Orpheus*, Longmans, 1965

BUTLER, GUY, (ed.) *A Book of South African Verse*, Oxford University Press, 1959

GILLMAN, Q. (ed.) *Following the Sun*, (Anthology of Australian, Indian and African Tales) Mills and Boon

HUGHES, LANGSTON (ed.) *African Treasury*, Crown Publishers, New York, 1960, and Gollancz, London

MOORE, GERALD, and BEIER, ULLI (eds.) *Modern Poetry from Africa*, Penguin, 1963

PARNWELL, E. C. (ed.) *Stories of Africa*, Oxford University Press, 1930

RIVE, RICHARD (ed.) *Modern African Prose*, Heinemann, 1965

RUTHERFORD, PEGGY (ed.) *Darkness and Light*, Drum and Faith Press, 1959

SEARY, E. R. (ed.) *South African Short Stories*, Oxford University Press, Cape Town, 1947

SLATER, F. C. (ed.) *The New Centenary Book of South African Verse*, Longmans, 1951

SMITH, PRUDENCE (ed.) *Africa in Transition*, Max Reinhardt, London, 1958

SWANZY, HENRY (ed.) *Voices of Ghana*, Ministry of Information, Accra, 1958

WHITELEY, W. H. (comp.) *A Selection of African Prose*, Oxford Library of African Literature, London, 1964
Vol. I : *Traditional Oral Texts*. Vol. II : *Written Prose*

YOUNG, CALLEN (ed) *African New Writing*, Lutterworth Press, 1947

General References

EVANS-PRITCHARD, E. E., *Witchcraft, Oracles and Magic among the Azande*, Clarendon Press, Oxford, 1932
An Historical Introduction to a Study of Zande Society, Oxford African Studies, Vol. 17. 1950

FAGE, J. D., *An Introduction to the History of West Africa*, Cambridge University Press, 1955

HAILEY, MALCOLM, *An African Survey*, first published 1938 (revised ed.) Oxford University Press, 1957

HALLETT, ROBIN (ed.), *Records of the African Association*, 1788-1831, Nelson, 1964

HERSKOVITS, MELVILLE J., *The Human Factor in Changing Africa*, Knopf, New York, 1962

JANHEINZ, JAHN, *Muntu*, Faber and Faber, London, 1960.

JANHEINZ, JAHN and RAMSARA, JOHN, *Approaches to African Literature*, Ibadan, 1959

MARSH, ZOE, *East Africa Through Contemporary Records*, Cambridge University Press, 1961

MOORE, GERALD, *Seven African Writers*, Oxford University Press, 1962

MORRIS, HENRY F., *Heroic Recitations of the Bahima of Ankole*, Oxford Library of African Literature, 1964

MURDOCK, GEORGE P., *Africa, Its Peoples and their Cultural History*, McGraw, New York, 1959

NKRUMAH, KWAME, *I Speak of Freedom: a statement of African ideology*, Heinemann, 1961
Consciencism, Heinemann, 1964

PERHAM, MARGERY and SIMMONS, J., *African Discovery*, Faber and Faber, 1942

RITTER, E. A., *Shaka Zulu*, Panther Books, 1958; first published, Longmans, Green, 1955

SELIGMAN, G. G., *Races of Africa* (3rd ed.) Oxford University Press, 1961

SITHOLE, NADBANINGI, *African Nationalism*, Oxford University Press, 1959

TALMADGE, M., 'Themes in the West African Novel', *West African Review* Vol. 30. Nos. 383-5, 1959

Incidental References

Atlantic   April, 1957
The Guardian   8 August, 1962
London Magazine   February, 1957
Odu   (A Journal of Yoruba, Edu, and related studies) (passim)
Sudan Notes and Records   (passim)
The Times Literary Supplement   March, 1959; 10 August, 1962
Twentieth Century   April, 1959

Index